ACADEMIC ETHICS

Academic Ethics

Problems and Materials on Professional Conduct and Shared Governance

Neil W. Hamilton

AMERICAN COUNCIL ON EDUCATION
PRAEGER
Series on Higher Education

Library of Congress Cataloging-in-Publication Data

Hamilton, Neil W.
   Academic ethics : problems and materials on professional conduct and shared
governance / Neil W. Hamilton.
      p.   cm.—(American Council on Education/Praeger series on higher education)
   Includes bibliographical references and index.
   ISBN 1–57356–372–2 (alk. paper)
      1. College teachers—Professional ethics—United States.   2. College teaching—
Moral and ethical aspects—United States.   3. Academic freedom—Moral and
ethical aspects—United States.   I. Title.
LB1779.H37 2002
174'.9372—dc21   2002067836

Formerly ACE/Oryx Press Series on Higher Education

British Library Cataloguing in Publication Data is available.

Library of Congress Catalog Card Number: 2002067836
ISBN: 1–57356–372–2

First published in 2002

Praeger Publishers, 88 Post Road West, Westport, CT 06881
An imprint of Greenwood Publishing Group, Inc.
www.praeger.com

Printed in the United States of America

The paper used in this book complies with the Permanent Paper Standard issued by the
National Information Standards Organization (Z39.48–1984).

10 9 8 7 6 5 4 3 2 1

Copyright Acknowledgments

The author and publisher gratefully acknowledge permission for use of the following
material:

Excerpts reprinted from American Association of University Professors (AAUP),
Policy Documents and Reports, 9th edition, 2001. Washington, DC: AAUP.

"Indian Girls," reprinted by permission of Linda McCarriston.

"1998 Association of Governing Boards' Statement on Governance" by Association of
Governing Boards of Universities and Colleges (1998).

Excerpts from *Zealotry and Academic Freedom: A Legal and Historical Perspective.* New
Brunswick, NJ: Transaction Publishers, 1995.

Contents

Preface

In the tradition of the learned professions, society and the members of the profession form an unwritten social compact whereby the members of the profession agree to restrain self-interest, to promote ideals of public service and professional excellence, and to maintain minimum standards of performance within the peer group. In return, society grants the profession both substantial power over a critical area essential for society's well-being and substantial autonomy to regulate itself through peer review.

The American Association of University Professors' (AAUP) 1915 Declaration, the foundational theoretical justification for our tradition of academic freedom, recognizes this social compact for the academic profession.

> It is conceivable that our profession may prove unworthy of its high calling and unfit to exercise the duties that belong to it.... [T]he existence of this association [the AAUP] must be construed as a pledge not only that the profession will earnestly guard those liberties without which it cannot rightly render its distinctive and indispensable service to society, but also that it will with equal earnestness seek to maintain such standards of professional character and of scientific integrity and competence as shall make it a fit instrument for that service.[1]

This social compact between society and the members of a learned profession must be renewed in each generation through education of both the members of the profession and the public about the traditions and ethics of the profession. The education must emphasize the transcendental purpose the profession serves and how the profession fulfills its duties to serve the common good in its area of responsibility. If, in a market economy, a profession does not renew the social compact through continuing education, money and economic efficiency will eventually sweep the field to define all professional relationships as simply economic transactions between consumers and service providers for profit.

Continuing education also should mitigate the tendency of a peer collegium to abdicate the role of effective peer review, permitting all but gross and obvious deviance in performance in order to protect maximum individual autonomy in work performance. Professor John Bennett emphasizes the risk this abdication poses for the academic profession.

> Those who argue against external regulation of the academy must rest their case squarely upon the appropriateness and efficacy of faculty and institutional self-regulation by peers. This self-regulation is not easy and the fragility of the peer review mechanism is the Achilles' heel of [professional] and institutional independence. If peer review fails, other agencies will take its place.[2]

Continuing education should lead academics to see differences between espoused values and actual practice in both their own personal conduct and the conduct of the peer collegium. Cognitive dissonance can lead to changed behaviors over time. Education also provides the professorate the knowledge necessary to educate the public about the social compact, academic tradition and ethics, and how the public's interests are served.[3]

This book is designed to provide materials and problems to assist in the ongoing project of renewing the social compact for both those entering and those currently in the academic profession. It provides a history of the American tradition of academic freedom, peer review, and shared governance. This background should assist the reader to understand and internalize both the ethics of duty, which is the floor below which conduct merits sanctions, and the ethics of aspiration, which represents the highest ideals of the academic profession. The Appendix summarizes the principles of professional conduct in a quickly accessible form.

The book also provides a spectrum of ethical problems in academic life for peer discussion. Peer discussion of ethical dilemmas provides a vehicle to create shared understandings of both minimum standards and aspirational ideals in a community of professionals. It is through peer review that we define for each other the lower bound of acceptable professional conduct, and it is through peer review that we create cultures committed to the highest professional ideals. In a learned profession, informal norms and culture are far more important in shaping conduct than rules, regulatory schemes, and sanctions. Peer discussion of ethical dilemmas can help create and shape both a healthy peer culture and a robust collective conscience. If readers of this book have suggestions to improve the problems or develop their own discussion problems and are willing to share them, please share them with me at nwhamilton@stthomas.edu.

Our profession, and the university that we serve, are among humankind's most remarkable achievements. The reductive pressure of the market, in this period of history, is a great threat to both the profession and the university. There is also always the threat of episodic waves of zealotry from both inside and outside the walls that threaten academic freedom by suppressing opposing ideas. Understanding and defending our tradition and the principles on which our profession stands are among the greatest contributions a professor can make.

NOTES

1. American Association of University Professors, "The 1915 Declaration of Principles," reprinted in *Academic Freedom and Tenure* (Louis Joughin ed. 1969): app. A, 155,170.

2. John B. Bennett, *Collegial Professionalism: The Academy, Individualism and the Common Good* (1998):16.

3. Professor Richard De George emphasizes, "The greatest danger to both academic freedom and tenure is that those within the university seem too often to forget what they are and what they are for. Those who forget, or who never knew, are unlikely to know the responsibilities that go with [academic freedom and tenure]. And not knowing, they are unlikely to fulfill those responsibilities. Not knowing, they are also unable to articulate the rationale and defenses of academic freedom and tenure to those outside the university, and to their family and constituents." Richard T. De George, *Academic Freedom and Tenure: Ethical Issues* (1997):112.

Acknowledgments

This book was possible only through the support of many people. I
owe them the deepest debt of gratitude.

The work of the American Association of University Professors
and its committees over the past century in defining and developing our
tradition of academic freedom, peer review, shared governance, and academic ethics is the foundation on which I build. It is a living tradition;
while we may disagree with the AAUP on some matters, we stand on the
shoulders of those who have drafted the AAUP Statements.

My initial work on professional academic freedom appeared in Chapter
4 of *Zealotry and Academic Freedom* (Transaction Publishers, 1995). I expanded that chapter and then made revisions based on the comments of
the scholars listed in the next paragraph, culminating in what appears in
this book in Chapter 2. For the history of the seven waves of zealotry attacking academic freedom in the United States since the formation of the
university following the Civil War, an analysis of the First Amendment
protection for academic freedom, and proposals on how to defend academic
freedom, I recommend *Zealotry and Academic Freedom*. I thank Transaction Publishers and its chairman, Irving Louis Horowitz, for permission to
use material from Chapter 4 of the earlier book.

I also owe a debt of gratitude to the scholars who commented on earlier
drafts of parts of the book, especially Chapter 2: Prof. John Bailar III; Prof.
Robert Bellah; Prof. Clark Byse; Prof. Richard Chait; Pres. George Den-
nison; Prof. Douglas Feig; Prof. Tom Fish; Dr. Mark Frankel; Prof. Paul

Gross; Prof. Martin Gunderson; Prof. Oscar Handlin; Prof. Thomas Haskell; Pres. Nils Hasselmo; Prof. and former Pres. Donald Kennedy; Prof. Nelson Yuan-skeng Kiang; Prof. Mary Lefkowitz; Prof. Michael Olivas; Prof. Robert O'Neil; Prof. Russell Pannier; Dean Dennis Pendleton; Dean David Rabban; Dr. Judith Swazey; Dr. Cathy Trower; Prof. William Van Alstyne; and Prof. Bernard Waxman. I made a number of revisions based on their comments; all remaining errors are my own.

I also wish to thank William Mitchell College of Law for both its sabbatical support in the spring of 2000 and summer research grants in 1999 and 2000, the University of St. Thomas for summer research support in 2001, and the Earhart Foundation for its research support in the spring and summer of 2000. I am not speaking for any of these organizations in this book.

I could not have finished the book without the untiring and gracious help of Linda Thorstad in word processing at William Mitchell College of Law. She is a consummate professional. My research assistant at William Mitchell, Sally Silk, lent me her many years of experience as a French professor in discussing a number of the problems and putting her hand to a first draft. Both Sally and my daughter, Maya, gave me valuable editing help. My research assistant, Ruth Rivard, helped design the diagrams. My wife, Uve, gave me the emotional support needed for several years to see this project to completion.

Essentially, we as professors are about trying to help the next generation do better than we have done. I dedicate this book to those three of the next generation who are closest to me, my children, Shaan, Maya, and Kyra.

This book also borrows ideas from and builds on my other earlier published works: "Are We Speaking the Same Language? Comparing AAUP & AGB," *Liberal Education*, 24 (Fall 1999); "The Academic Profession's Leadership Role in Shared Governance," *Liberal Education*, 12 (Summer 2000); "Academic Tradition and the Principles of Professional Conduct," 27 *Journal of College and University Law* 609 (2001); and "The Ethics of Peer Review in the Academic and Legal Professions," 42 *South Texas Law Review*, (2001): 227.

CHAPTER 1

Introduction

WHY TEACH ACADEMIC ETHICS?

The autonomy and traditions of the academic profession and its sister professions, law and medicine, are under assault. Essentially the challenge for all three professions boils down to the relentless reductive pressure of the market to define all professional relationships as nothing more than consumer/service provider or employer/employee relationships. Professor Eliot Krause, having studied the professions of law, medicine, the professorate, and engineering in the United States, Britain, France, Germany, and Italy concludes as follows:

> Both the professions of medicine and law—especially their elites—have increasingly bought the capitalist model itself and have imposed capitalist rationalization upon those lower in the professional pecking order. Engineering has always accepted capitalist values and has therefore never been a profession acting in its own interest in competition with the values and aims of capitalism. The university itself, the source of the professional training, has increasingly been made over in the image of capitalist interests.... Perhaps this process is a final example of what Weber would have called *"die Entzauberung der Welt"* [translated as disenchantment of the world], the loss of any non-capitalist values within the professions, both because of external pressures we have considered here and because of the surrender of positive guild values—of collegiality, of concern for the group, of a higher professional ethic beyond mere profit—that has eroded the distinction between professions and any other occupation and thus left them together as the middle-level employees of capitalism.[1]

Even if the professions have not completely lost "any noncapitalist values," Professor Krause forces consideration of the degree to which we are renewing and defending academic tradition and principles in the face of market pressures. With the academic profession, legislators, governing boards, and administrations emphasize a number of market realities: (1) costs of higher education have been rising much more rapidly than the costs of other goods and services for many years, and tuition and revenue growth cannot continue to keep pace; (2) legislators and governors want public higher education to focus more on current economic development and workforce needs; (3) students increasingly view themselves as consumers and demand responsiveness to their needs at various stages in their lives; (4) corporate for-profit and on-line enterprises in the higher education market are effectively competing for students; and (5) enrollment patterns are changing more rapidly.[2] In response, many governing boards and administrations propose, and in some cases carry out, a dramatic increase in the use of part-time and adjunct faculty, post-tenure review. A handful of institutions have moved to abolish tenure altogether. The 1998 Association of Governing Boards' (AGB) *Statement on Institutional Governance* emphasizes managing higher education similarly to other nonprofit enterprises, with reduced power for the voting faculty.[3] University of California President Emeritus Clark Kerr predicts a trend toward more external investigation of academic conduct, more laws subjecting higher education to public enforcement procedures and more decision-making by the courts.[4]

Similarly emphasizing the ascendance of market values, corporations are providing growing financial support for academic research, creating potential conflicts of interests and drawing research activity toward corporate agendas. Some scholars take a financial interest or even a management role in these corporate funders of research. Market-focused individual faculty members who achieve celebrity status or whose knowledge has high profit potential increasingly emphasize personal gain outside the walls in the allocation of their time and productive energy.

Is it inevitable that the market will eventually eliminate associations and traditions that do not worship solely at the altar of economic efficiency? In analyzing economic inevitability arguments in the context of the tradition of the learned professions, consider that we live in the period of the greatest wealth creation in our society's history. During such a period, human nature exaggerates the importance of the market and economic efficiency in relation to other societal values. The traditions and ethics of the learned professions will appear "inefficient" when the market dominates our thinking. In the face of the reductive pressure of the market, the professions must publicly defend the economic and *noneconomic* benefits that their social compact provides society. To build the public's trust and its willingness to grant the profession autonomy, a learned profession must, in each generation, renew its social compact for both the public and those within the profession, thus reassuring the public that their interests are being served and that the profession may be trusted with high public purposes.

What is the social compact and what does it require? The academic profession is one of the four great learned professions for which the medieval university provided education. Professor Stephen Barker points out that the two central features of the late-medieval conception of a profession remain with us today: (1) a profession requires mastery of an extensive body of knowledge and skills achieved by years of university study; and (2) entrants into a profession are required to commit themselves to a distinctive ideal of public service that imposes ethical demands, to which ordinary citizens are not subject, to restrain self-interest and to use the special knowledge and skills gained for the common good.[5] Professor Barker lists six possible definitions of "profession," but focuses on a seventh approach that emphasizes the etymology of the term as it came to be used to describe the original learned professions coming out of the late medieval universities. This essay examines the continuing development in the United States of the tradition that Professor Barker references, focusing upon the academic profession.[6]

Society and members of a profession form an unwritten social compact whereby the members of a profession agree to restrain self-interest, to promote ideals of public service, and to maintain high standards of performance, while society in return allows the profession substantial autonomy to regulate itself through peer review. The ethics of each profession are descriptive of the profession's duties under the social compact.[7] To maintain the social compact and its autonomy, a profession must create peer collegia of *both* high aspirations in terms of professional ideals *and* effective peer review to maintain minimum standards of competence and ethical conduct. To create a culture of both high aspiration and effective maintenance of minimum standards, a profession must have: (1) a clear, comprehensive, and accessible code of ethics, including a statement of professional ideals; (2) an effective means of socialization for both new entrants and veterans in the profession concerning the tradition of the profession, the profession's social compact, its ideals, its minimum standards, and the duties of peer review; and (3) ethical leadership from within the peer collegium itself that fosters a culture of high aspiration and effective peer review.

A Code of Ethics

In the academic profession, the only organization attempting to define a code of ethics that cuts across the disciplines is the American Association of University Professors (AAUP). The AAUP's 1940 Statement of Principles on Academic Freedom and Tenure mentions only broad correlative duties of competence and ethical conduct. The AAUP goes further in its 1966 Statement on Professional Ethics, but unlike the American Bar Association's (ABA) Model Code of Professional Conduct, adopted three years later in 1969, the 1966 AAUP statement is not comprehensive. It covers only partially the relevant topics. The 1966 statement's structure makes it difficult to draw out the applicable principles, and some of the principles suffer from vagueness.[8] It is similar in these regards to the ABA's earlier 1908 Canons of Professional Ethics. The AAUP's dominant focus is to protect the rights of academic freedom, not to articulate clearly its corresponding duties. The AAUP does not investigate or prosecute individual cases for the violation of the corresponding duties of academic freedom.

Almost thirty years ago, the Commission on Academic Tenure in Higher Education created by the AAUP and college administrators in the American Association of Colleges (AAC)[9] urged faculties to consider and discuss the adoption of a faculty statement on professional conduct. The Commission recommended that "The faculty of the institution ... must be the source for the definition and clarification of standards of professional conduct and must take the lead in ensuring that these standards are enforced."[10]

The Commission further specified that

> The Commission believes that faculties should be authorized and encouraged to develop codes of professional conduct for the guidance of their members and as a basis for sanctions against those whose conduct falls below professional norms. Such codes should reflect the broad precepts embodied in such existing formulations as the 1940 Statement of Principles and the 1966 Statement on Professional Ethics and should attempt to articulate the traditional sentiments of academic persons as to the demands of their calling....
> The very effort to provide a statement of professional standards will serve to dramatize the faculty's own responsibility for its integrity and that of the institution.
> The Commission recommends that the faculty of each institution assume responsibility for developing a code of faculty conduct and procedures and sanctions for faculty self-discipline, for recommending adoption of the code by the institution's governing board, and for making effective use of the code when it has been approved.[11]

Both University of California President Emeritus Clark Kerr and Professor Eric Ashby urge faculties to adopt a "declared professional code of practice" to address the problem of a disintegrating profession.[12] Professors John Braxton and Alan Bayer urge adoption of a formal code of teaching conduct.[13] A professional code of practice should include a statement of professional ideals, the principles of professional conduct, and the procedures to be followed for a violation of the principles.

There has been a growing interest in some of the sciences and social sciences in disciplinary codes of ethics. A September 2000 report by the American Association for the Advancement of Science (AAAS) and the U.S. Office of Research Integrity notes that

> in 1992, the National Academy of Sciences, the National Academy of Engineering, and the Institute of Medicine undertook a study to review factors affecting the integrity of scientific research processes.... Their report, Responsible Science, found that ethics were still marginal in most scientific societies, and recommended far more systematic efforts to foster responsible research practices.[14]

In the fall of 1999, the AAAS surveyed 126 societies to determine what societies are doing to promote research integrity and to assess the effectiveness of their efforts. Forty-six societies (37%) responded. The sample itself was based on identification by AAAS staff as societies that were likely to have developed ethics activities relating to the conduct of research. It seems probable that those societies with ethics statements and activities were more likely to respond to such a survey than those without such a statement or activities. The AAAS cautions against extrapolation of the data as representative of the population of disciplinary associations. Thirty-four of the 46 responding societies (75%) had ethics statements of some sort.[15] Professor Braxton and Professor Bayer found in a 1995 study of 62 professional academic associations, 36 (58%) had written ethics policies.[16] My own survey in 2000 of the ethics statements for twelve of the major professional academic associations found substantial variation among the statements. Five of the associations had comprehensive, clear, and accessible codes of ethics, three had ethics statements that covered some of the relevant topics, and three had ethics statements limited to one or two issues like harassment and discrimination, conflicts of interest, or graduate students' rights. One had no statement on ethics.

A fair summary is that presently, some of the disciplinary associations, perhaps a quarter to a third, have adopted codes of ethics that are comprehensive, clear, and accessible. Some of that group has chosen also to adopt enforcement mechanisms. The significant majority of disciplinary associations have neither comprehensive, clear, and accessible codes of ethics, nor the capability to enforce those codes of ethics.

Of those disciplinary associations that do have codes of ethics, few know if the codes are working. Mark S. Frankel, director of AAAS's Scientific Freedom, Responsibility and Law Program, found the lack of knowledge about the impact of codes of ethics to be "one of the most striking aspects" of the AAAS's 1999-2000 survey of disciplinary societies' codes of ethics.[17] Substantial research is needed in this area.

The disciplinary focus of these codes of ethics contributes to the fragmentation of the academic profession and the loss of a sense of academic citizenship across the disciplines at individual colleges and universities. The history and structure of the academic profession makes the peer collegium of faculty *at the employing institution* the critical focal point for effective peer review. Unfortunately, faculty members are increasingly professionalized within the disciplines, damaging effective faculty governance and peer review at the employing institution. In addition, only a small minority of disciplinary associations have chosen to adopt enforcement mechanisms. It would be healthier for the academic profession and for individual colleges and universities to heed the 1973 AAUP/AAC Commission on Academic Tenure in Higher Education and to focus on efforts to develop a code of ethics for the academic profession that cuts across the disciplines. Each discipline can then adopt supplementary codes to cover its own unique disciplinary issues.

Umbrella academic organizations like the American Council on Education or the American Association of Colleges and Universities (the successor to the American Association of Colleges) should step forward to draft such a model code for the profession. A code of ethics that cuts across the disciplines could then be adopted by reference in employment contracts for professors. Supplementary codes to cover issues unique to a discipline could also be part of employment contracts in the relevant disciplines.

Chapter 2 analyzes academic tradition concerning the rights and corresponding duties of the academic profession. This analysis leads to an articulation of the principles of professional conduct that flow from academic tradition. Appendix A provides a restatement of these principles in a more accessible form.

Socialization in Professional Ethics

In the academic profession, few graduate programs require a course on the ethics of the profession. Some disciplinary associations are taking a greater interest in efforts to promote professional ethics. The September 2000 AAAS report noted earlier finds that 57 percent of the responding scientific societies currently engage in, or plan to engage in activities to promote research integrity.[18] Forty-one percent of those engaging in activities to promote research integrity use educational programs at meetings, and 17 percent use workshops.[19] Few departments or faculties require new entrants into the academic profession to take education on the ethics of the profession.

It is critical that individual faculty members and the peer collegium itself in each department or faculty understand the policies and codes governing ethical conduct. This is not presently the case. Based on a 1993 Acadia Institute survey of 2000 faculty and a similar number of graduate students in chemistry, civil engineering, microbiology, and sociology, Professor Melissa Anderson found that about one-half of the faculty respondents reported familiarity with the university's and the discipline's policies on research misconduct.[20] Professors Judith Swazey, Karen Louis, and Melissa Anderson found that in principle, 74 percent of the faculty respondents believed that they and their colleagues should, to a great extent, exercise collective responsibility for the conduct of their graduate students, "but only 27 percent judge that they and their departmental colleagues actually manifest to a great extent their shared responsibility for their students' professional ethical conduct."[21] Only 55 percent of the faculty respondents believed that they should, to a great extent, exercise responsibility for the conduct of their colleagues, but "just 13 percent judge that faculty in their department exercise a great deal of shared responsibility for their colleagues' conduct, whereas 30 percent hold that there is very little or no manifestation of collegial responsibility."[22] The authors conclude, "[o]ur survey data, and statements by faculty and graduate students whom we have interviewed, challenge the idea that faculty actually practice an ethic of collective governance."[23] In the same study, only 35 percent of the graduate students reported that they received significant instruction on the details of good research practice from someone in their department.[24] Mentoring of graduate students on the ethics of the profession is inadequate.

Based on the same study of 2000 faculty members, Professor Anderson finds that the most critical correlates of misconduct are likely to be at the department level.[25] Professor Anderson finds a correlation indicating that "[d]epartments whose faculty are, on the whole, knowledgeable about policies tend also to be departments whose faculty as a group feel a collective responsibility for peer and student behavior [and] … [d]epartments that exhibit strong commitment to the traditional norms and a strong sense of community are significantly less likely to expose faculty and students to misconduct or to engender expectations of retaliation.[26] She adds that, "[f]inally, there is a positive relationship between how familiar a department's faculty members are with relevant institutional and disciplinary policies and their sense of responsibility for colleagues' and peers' conduct."[27]

Based on 4,110 responses in a 1999 study of graduate students in 11 arts and science disciplines from 27 universities (a 42.3% response rate), Professors Chris Golde and Timothy Dore present findings similar to those of Swazey, Louis, and Anderson. Professors Golde and Dore conclude, "The data indicate that the ethical dimension of faculty and professional life—how to act responsibly and in the best interest of the profession, is not, as often assumed, part of graduate training."[28] The authors conclude that "… [T]he health of the academic profession, with norms of self regulation and peer review, depends on shared values and practices. Students told us that they are unclear about many of the customary practices that rely on a shared understanding of ethical behavior. Those responsible for doctoral education cannot assume that norms and practices are routinely and informally handed down."[29]

From their extensive study of faculty members in chemistry, civil engineering, microbiology, and sociology, Swazey, Louis, and Anderson found that the culture of the academic profession everywhere emphasizes personal autonomy.[30] Professors John Braxton and Alan Bayer also hypothesize that faculty who place a high value on autonomy believe that collegial and administrative interventions for teaching misconduct should be avoided.[31] Swazey, Louis, and Anderson conclude that personal autonomy takes strong precedence over a norm of collegial self-governance.[32] Professor William Tierney urges the professorate to reorient its thinking. Many in the profession currently think of evaluation as something imposed by eternal groups. Evaluation and creation of a culture of high aspiration must become core activities of what a faculty means when it says, "we are an academic community."[33]

The most effective corrective for the academic profession is to design educational programs on professional conduct and shared governance for all professors within each faculty. Many faculty members have not had any significant grounding in the tradition of academic freedom and its corresponding obligations. They are socialized into a discipline, not into the academic profession. As a result, their understanding of the traditions of the profession is poor.[34] Professor Keetji Ramo concludes that "[t]he professorate has yet to find an effective, universal means through which to systematically imbue in the future and neophyte members a sense of academic culture that cuts across disciplinary lines. Individual professors fail to identify with the professorate as a professional culture."[35] The objective of educational programs on professional conduct and shared governance is to help develop both an inner-directed ethic within each faculty member, as well as a peer culture of high aspiration regarding professional ideals and informal but direct collegial pressure concerning compliance with minimum standards.

Formal charges, adjudication, judicial severity, and litigation should rarely be necessary. Fostering such educational programs is a strong preventive law approach to governing board and administrative frustration with faculty members who present competence or ethical conduct problems. A common understanding of proper roles in shared governance should also contribute greatly to timely and effective decision making.

It is clear in the AAUP tradition that the professorate must educate itself and the public about the unwritten social compact, the benefits of academic freedom, and its corresponding obligations. The 1966 Statement on Professional Ethics concludes by emphasizing that, "[a]s citizens engaged in a profession that depends upon freedom for its health and integrity, professors have a particular obligation to promote conditions of free inquiry and to further public understanding of academic freedom."[36] This education must renew the social compact in each generation.

Ethical Leadership from within the Peer Collegium

A code of ethics and socialization for new entrants and veteran professionals are necessary but not sufficient conditions for a strong peer collegium. The premise here is that the culture or house norms of the department or faculty play the dominant roles in the way a faculty member practices the profession. Culture, in many respects, is more important than rules. Professional communities form a collective conscience where the competing pressures of professional life are worked out and the ideals of the profession reach some realization.

Amy and Leon Kass observe that,

"Ethics" and "morality" have their source in "ethos" and "mores," words that refer to the ways and attitudes, manners and habits, sensibilities and customs that shape and define a community. Communities are built upon shared understandings, usually tacitly conveyed, not only of what is right and wrong or good and bad, but also of who we are, how we stand, what things means. These matters are not well taught by ethics codes.[37]

Similarly, Michael Katz notes that the ideal university or college,

> Should be a community of persons united by collective understandings, by
> common and communal goals, by bonds of reciprocal obligation, and by a
> flow of sentiment which makes the preservation of community an object of
> desire, not merely a matter of prudence or a command of duty. Community
> implies a form of social obligation governed by principles different from
> those operative in the marketplace and the state.[38]

Commentary on leadership in the academic profession borrows from the
management literature on for profit or nonprofit corporations and typically
focuses on hierarchical leadership or management, not on the peer collegium's role in maintaining professional tradition and defining peer culture. Such emphasis is a consequence of the market's reductive pressure to
frame all relationships in purely economic terms of employer/employee or
service provider/customer.

We know little about how the collective conscience of a peer collegium
is formed and maintained. We also know very little about how ethical leadership from within a peer collegium works. This is an area where substantial research is needed.

Professor Robert Gordon, commenting on the legal profession, concludes that in order to reinvigorate professional ideals in a peer collegium,
we must focus on the "shared understandings and informal sanctions of
communities. Externally imposed rules and sanctions of regulatory regimes
can reinforce, but cannot substitute for, such informal norms and sanctions."[39] He believes these communities must take shape at the local level.

The data available from the academic profession support Professor Gordon's hypothesis that a sense of local community has a marked impact on
a peer collegium's professional ideals. Professor Francis Oakley notes that
personal observation, in-depth field studies, and survey data reveal the liberal arts college sector of higher education has

> the highest degree of agreement on the standards of good scholarship, and
> the highest degree of commitment to the importance of institutional ser-
> vice, student advising, and the delivery, evaluation, and rewarding of effec-
> tive teaching. Not surprisingly, faculty who teach in this sector are promi-
> nent among those who are at the highest end of the institutional loyalty and
> commitment scale, who feel least "trapped in a profession with limited op-
> portunity for advancement," and who accordingly evince the greatest en-
> thusiasm about their work.[40]

Common sense suggests that to invigorate professional ideals and to
maintain minimum professional standards, the professorate must focus on
the constitution or reconstitution of strong professional communities at

the departmental, faculty, and university-wide levels (this time without the ethnic, gender, and class exclusions that defined the old communities). These local communities must be much more intentional about building institutional culture.

ORGANIZATION OF THE BOOK

Chapter 2 presents an analysis of academic tradition, academic freedom, and the principles of professional conduct and shared governance. The Appendices contain both a proposed code of ethics that cuts across the disciplines and the major AAUP and Association of Governing Boards (AGB) Statements on the subject. Chapters 3–7 present typical problems in academic life to which these principles apply.

Chapter 2 and Appendix A, summarizing the principles of professional conduct, are sufficient background to inform peer discussion of the problems. If the discussion group consists of members of a single discipline, the code of ethics (if any) from the relevant disciplinary society would be also useful. If the discussion group is from one institution, the relevant institutional policies on academic freedom, discrimination, harassment, conflicts of interest, and other matters should be included. For those with a deeper interest, the other Appendices provide major resource documents.

Each discussion problem is designed for a fifty-minute discussion of a seminar-sized group of either graduate students or new and veteran faculty members. The discussion group can consist of students or faculty in just one discipline, but inclusion of a variety of disciplines will build a sense of wider academic community and culture. The "peer collegium" in our tradition of academic freedom is in fact the faculty of an institution as a whole (a faculty senate), informed by the special expertise of the peers in a department or discipline. As the disciplines have continued to proliferate in the multiversity, the senate has essentially sub-delegated many decisions to individual faculties or departments. The problems can also be used in groups larger than seminars, but the larger the class size, the greater the focus on the instructor, and the more difficult it is for each participant to contribute. Peer discussion of ethical dilemmas facilitates growth in moral reasoning. It fosters the habit and skill of reflective practice for a professional. Peer discussion is also critical to develop the skills and culture necessary for a healthy peer-review collegium. The discussion leader should seek to become one of the peers discussing the problem.

The book can be used for a weekly discussion, for example, a regular brown-bag lunch, over the course of a semester. Ideally the discussion group meets at least six times to cover selected topics of highest interest. It takes at least that long to develop trust among the discussion group participants.

The discussion problems do not catalogue the entire range of potential issues. Actual problems, reported for example in the *Chronicle of Higher Education*, or occurring on a particular campus, may also provide an excellent basis for discussion. The critical factor is for the discussion leader to select topics for discussion that fit the institutional context and interest of the group.

The most successful strategy to teaching research ethics in the sciences and professional ethics in law schools has been a problem-oriented approach. Teaching methodology and subject matter are closely related in professional ethics. The method of instruction should build the skills that academic ethics, a peer review system, and shared governance require. The participants discussing a problem should see themselves as the peer collegium trying to solve the problem. The discussion should develop the following skills of academic ethics and shared governance:

1. Recognizing ethical and shared governance issues in professional contexts;
2. Analyzing a problem based on the traditions and ethics of the profession; and
3. Questioning, disagreeing, and exploring issues, as a peer group engaged in civil discussion.

Discussion of academic ethics and shared governance problems should focus both on the ethics of duty and the ethics of aspiration. The ethics of duty define the floor below which conduct merits discipline. On these issues, there is a trend in the profession to look just to the law to define the floor rather than to focus also on the traditions and ethics of the profession, the role of peer review, and peer culture. Culture is far more critical than rules in defining a professor's ethics and quality of work life.

The sanctions available to the peer group include: (1) the informal sanctions of private expressions of peer disapproval; (2) public discussion of the individual professor's conduct at a faculty meeting; (3) public formal sanctions by a faculty vote on admonition or censure; and (4) a recommendation to the administration for the commencement of a formal proceeding leading toward suspension or dismissal. Of course, an untenured professor could not receive a contract renewal. Other sanctions available to the administration include sanctions involving salary or other benefits like sabbaticals or travel funds.

The ethics of aspiration focus on the question, "In this situation, to what do we aspire as individual academics and as an academic community?" Discussion helps both to articulate the group's professional idea's and to form a supportive peer culture of high aspiration. In the discussion of each problem, in order to experience how a peer review system works, the participants should take votes on whether particular conduct violates any ethical principles and what courses of action are most appropriate both to address the problem and to build a productive culture.

The appropriate goal in teaching a basic course on academic ethics is simply to accomplish as much as possible with the limited time and resources available. Move the discussion group as far as possible down the continuum toward becoming professors both conversant with academic tradition, academic freedom, and academic ethics, and skilled in recognizing ethical dilemmas and addressing them in the context of a peer collegium. In the legal profession, many states require continuing ethics education for experienced lawyers. The academic profession should follow this model for tenured professors.

NOTES

1. Eliot Krause, *Death of the Guilds* 281 (1996).

2. See Neil Hamilton, "Are We Speaking the Same Language? Comparing AAUP & AGB," *Liberal Education* (Fall 1999): 24.

3. See Association of Governing Board of Universities and Colleges, "AGB Statement on Institutional Governance" (Nov. 8, 1998), http://www.agb.org/governance.cfm.

4. See Clark Kerr, *Higher Education Cannot Escape History: Issues for the Twenty-first Century*, (1999): 135, 149.

5. Stephen F. Barker, "What is a Profession?" 1 *Professional Ethics* (1992): 73. There are other definitions of a profession. Professor Herbert Kritzer notes that there are at least three definitions. See Herbert Kritzer, "The Professions Are Dead, Long Live the Professions," 33 *Law and Society Review* (1999): 713, 716–718. The "lay definition" is essentially synonymous with "occupation" and is distinguished primarily by means of its antonym, "amateur." Thus in lay parlance a profession includes firefighting, plumbing, management, and medicine insofar as the professional performs a particular line of work to make a living and is committed to a set of standards. Ibid. The "historical definition" of a profession involves the creation and recognition of trained expertise and recognition of merit made not by the open market but by the judgment of similarly educated experts. See ibid. 716–717. The "sociological definition" of a profession goes beyond the historical definition by limiting recognition to those occupations that *combine* both exclu-

sivity (for example, through licensing) and the application of abstract knowledge. See ibid. 717–718. Kritzer adds that "[p]rofessions in the sociological sense have further distinguished themselves by adding notions of altruism, regulatory autonomy, thorough peer review processes, and autonomy vis-à-vis the service recipient." Ibid. 717.

6. See Barker, 84–87.

7. See ibid. There exists an unwritten social compact among the public, the university, and the professorate. In exchange for new knowledge, the education of students to become informed leaders and citizens, and the contribution of expert and professional skills and training to community issues, the public supports the university and the professorate, contributes to their finance, accepts their professional judgment and scholarly certification, and grants a unique degree of institutional autonomy and scholarly freedom. In fulfilling the compact, the university and the professorate have reciprocal obligations for the cultivation of advanced knowledge, impartial scholarship, the highest professional competence and integrity, love of learning among their students, and a sensitivity toward the need for their services in the society at large. See "The Glion Colloquium, The Glion Declaration: The University at the Millennium," (1998): 4–5.

8. See Neil Hamilton, "Academic Tradition and the Principles of Professional Conduct," 27 *Journal of College and University Law*, (2001): 609–668.

9. The AAC is now the American Association of Colleges and Universities.

10. "Commission on Academic Tenure in Higher Education, Faculty Tenure," (1973): 42.

11. Ibid. 44–45.

12. Eric Ashby, "A Hippocratic Oath for the Academic Profession," *Minerva*, 7 (Autumn–Winter 1968) 64–66; Clark Kerr, "Knowledge of Ethics and the New Academic Culture," *Change*, (January–February 1994), 12. A panel of the National Academy of Sciences recommends that research institutions urge faculty to develop formal guidelines for the conduct of research. Panel on Scientific Responsibility and the Conduct of Research, Committee on Science, Engineering and Public Policy, National Academy of Sciences, National Academy of Engineering, Institute of Medicine, "Responsible Science: Ensuring the Integrity of the Research Process," (1992): 13. The process of formulating guidelines itself may be extremely valuable for those who participate. Ibid. 137.

13. John Braxton and Alan Bayer, *Faculty Misconduct in Collegiate Teaching*, (1999): 177 [hereinafter Braxton and Bayer, *Faculty Misconduct*].

14. AAAS and U.S. Office of Research Integrity, "The Role and Activities of Scientific Societies in Promoting Research Integrity," (Sept. 2000): 1–2 [hereinafter AAAS].

15. Ibid. 3.

16. Braxton and Bayer, *Faculty Misconduct*, 140–146.

17. "Washington Update," *Chronicle of Higher Education* (Apr. 21, 2000): A38.

18. AAAS, 6.

19. Ibid.

20. Melissa Anderson, "Misconduct and Departmental Context," *Journal of Information Ethics* (1996): 15, 22. There were disciplinary differences. Sixty-five percent of sociologists and civil engineers reported familiarity with the disciplinary code of conduct, but only 40 percent or fewer of chemists and microbiologists were similarly informed. Ibid.

21. Judith Swazey, et al., "Ethical Problems in Academic Research," 81 *American Scientist* (November–December 1993): 542, 549.

22. Ibid. 2,600 of the 4,000 faculty and students surveyed returned the questionnaire with a response rate at 72 percent and 59 percent for the students and faculty, respectively. The proportions of faculty respondents agreeing strongly that faculty have a collective responsibility for their peers' conduct varied by discipline: 61 percent of the civil engineers and only 46 percent of the chemists strongly affirm collective responsibility for colleagues' behavior. Anderson, 24–25.

23. Swazey et al., 550.

24. Anderson, 23. In another recent study of faculty members at Purdue University, 82 percent of faculty respondents thought their departments should take an active role in educating faculty to deal with ethical issues in science, but only 16 percent thought the department did so. Ravisha Mathur and Stuart Offenbech, "Preliminary Observations on Faculty and Graduate Student Perceptions of Questionable Research Conduct," Proceedings: Investigating Research Integrity: Proceedings of the First Research Conference on Research Integrity (Nicholas Staneck and Mary Scheetz, eds., at http://www.personel.umich.edu).

25. Anderson, 20.

26. Ibid. at 27.

27. Ibid. at 29. In a study of faculty ethical activism in response to collegial misconduct, the respondent's degree of familiarity in the institution's policies on professional ethics mattered. For example, 63 percent of those who described themselves as very familiar with ethics policies approached a faculty member accused of misconduct and discussed the complaint with that faculty member as compared to 42 percent of those who described themselves as not familiar with such policies. Jonathan Knight and Carol Auster, "Faculty Conduct: An Empirical Study of Ethical Activism" 7 *Journal of Higher Education* (2000): 188-210.

28. C.M. Golde, and T.M. Dore, (2001): 13–14. *At Cross Purposes: What the Experiences of Doctoral Students Reveal about Doctoral Education* (www.phdsurvey.org). Philadelphia, PA: A report prepared for the Pew Charitable Trusts.

29. Ibid. 15.

30. Swazey et al., 550.

31. Braxton and Bayer, *Faculty Misconduct,* 167–168. Professor William Brown hypothesizes that the faculty collegium will not exercise sanctions because academics work independently with a focus on creativity. He or she requires stability for the exercise of creativity. It is better to ignore misconduct by a colleague

than to impose sanctions that will threaten stability. William Brown, *Academic Politics*, (1982): 17–19, 62–64.

Professors Braxton and Bayer also find supporting empirical evidence that professional solidarity shapes attitudes toward research misconduct in general and toward taking action against wrongdoing in a particular case. Professional solidarity protects the academic profession from lay interference as well as allows each individual professor a maximum degree of autonomy. John Braxton and Alan Bayer, "Perceptions of Research Misconduct and an Analysis of Their Correlates," 65, *Journal of Higher Education*, (1994): 351, 355, 364–366.

32. Judith R. Swazey et al., "The Ethical Training of Graduate Students Requires Serious Continuing Attention," *Chronicle of Higher Education*, (March 9, 1994) B1.

33. William Tierney, ed., "Tenure is Dead. Long Live Tenure," in *The Responsive University*, (1998): 58–59.

34. Reflecting on fifty years of teaching at Harvard, Professor Oscar Handlin observes a major change in the university: "In the vast playing field that the multiversity has become, numerous people scurry about, all doing their jobs, with only a few unifying links inherited from the past. Inertia, vague sentimental traditions, and catch phrases whose origins few recall trickle through among the players." Oscar Handlin, "A Career at Harvard," *American Scholar*, (Winter 1996): 58.

35. Keetjie Ramo, *Assessing the Faculty's Role in Shared Governance* 8 (1998).

36. American Association of University Professors, "Statement on Professional Ethics," reprinted in *AAUP, Policy Documents and Reports* (8th ed. 1995): 105 [hereinafter *AAUP, Professional Ethics*].

37. Amy Kass and Leon Kass, *Wing to Wing; Oar to Oar*, (1999): viii.

38. Michael Katz, quoted in William Tierney, "Academic Community and Post-Tenure Review," *Academe*, (May–June 1997): 25.

39. Robert Gordon, "The Ethical Worlds of Large-Firm Litigators: Preliminary Observations," 67 *Fordham Law Review* 67 (1998): 709, 737.

40. Francis Oakley, "The Elusive Academic Profession: Complexity and Change," *Daedalus* (Fall, 1997): 43, 56.

CHAPTER 2

The American Academic Profession: The Tradition of Academic Freedom and Shared Governance

THE ACADEMIC PROFESSION'S ROLE IN A LIBERAL INTELLECTUAL SYSTEM

The story of the profession's purpose and the American traditions of academic freedom and shared governance are rooted in the intellectual system that grew out of Western tradition, particularly the Enlightenment's conviction that reason, if left free, could discover useful knowledge. This intellectual system is liberal in the sense that it favors individual freedom, open-mindedness, and the use of reason to foster human progress.

The liberal intellectual system is understood as a social community with indefinite possibilities created by human intellectual diversity. For philosopher Karl Popper, the key insight on which the community is based is the recognition of the inherent fallibility of human thought.[1] The bedrock idea is that any and all of us might, at any time, be wrong. Knowledge is always seen to be tentative and subject to correction. If no person is immune from error, it follows implicitly in the liberal intellectual system that no belief, no matter how strongly held, is above critical scrutiny for possible correction. No person can claim to be above being checked by others.[2]

Philosopher John Searle describes the development of the liberal intellectual system along lines related to Popper's construct. For Searle, a decisive step in this tradition was the Greek creation of a "theory": "[T]he introduction of the idea of a theory allowed the western tradition to produce something unique, namely systematic intellectual constructions that were designed to describe and to explain large areas of reality in a way that was logically and mathematically accessible."[3] However, Searle posits, one essential concept the Greeks lacked, which Europe discovered in the Renaissance, was the idea of systematic experimentation. "The Greeks had logic, mathematics, rationality, systematicity, and the notion of a theoretical construct. But the idea of matching theoretical constructs against an independently existing reality through systematic experimentation really did not come until much later."[4]

A third feature of this tradition, in Searle's analysis, is its self-critical quality. Elements within it have always been under challenge; it was never a unified tradition. The idea of critique was always to subject any belief to the most rigorous standards of rationality, evidence, and logic.[5] The Enlightenment's emphasis on the use of reason and freedom of thought and speech fostered the idea of critique.

In this system, knowledge is the evolving critical consensus of a decentralized community of inquirers who adhere to the principle that knowledge claims must be capable of being checked and have withstood checking, regardless of the source of the claim or the identity of the inquirer.[6] The system must protect freedom of speech for the decentralized community of inquirers to produce knowledge, but it does not grant freedom to make knowledge claims. Only the consensus of critical inquirers has the status of a knowledge claim.[7] The liberal intellectual system, Jonathan Rauch points out in *Kindly Inquisitors*,

> absolutely protects freedom of belief and speech, but it absolutely denies freedom of knowledge: ... there is positively no right to have one's opinions, however heartfelt, taken seriously as knowledge.... A liberal intellectual regime says that if you want to believe the moon is made of green cheese, fine. But if you want your belief recognized [and acted upon] as knowledge, there are things you must do. You must run your belief through the [system] for checking.[8]

The university in a liberal intellectual system plays a critical role as the one community whose mission is specifically to seek, discover, and disseminate knowledge through public criticism.[9] Accordingly, the academic profession in universities constitutes a significant proportion of the decentralized community of inquirers on which knowledge production depends.

The major threat to the decentralized community of inquirers in general, and to the profession in particular, has been and will be from political, economic, ethnic, religious, or other groups who wish to prevent the anguish and pain that results when their beliefs are subjected to checking and criticism.[10] This is the context in which the profession has sought to gain autonomy to perform its role in the community of inquirers.

The profession saw a unique role for itself to contribute to the progress of knowledge as a community of inquirers with specialized training, information, and skills. In virtue of a professor's special competence as an inquirer in some area of study, including knowledge of the existing scholarship and mastery of the techniques of investigation and validation in some academic discipline, the professorate claimed special rights of investigation and dissemination of knowledge.[11] These unique roles ultimately justified special employment protection for a professor's right to offend in the pursuit of knowledge. As Professor Peter Byrne observes:

> Scholars work within a discipline, primarily addressing other scholars and students. Their audience understands and evaluates their speech within a tradition of knowledge, shared assumptions and arguments about methodology and criteria, and common objectives of exploration or discovery.... The ordinary criterion of success is whether, through mastery of the discipline's discourse, the scholar improves the account of some worthy subject that the discipline has previously accepted.[12]

The persons who may engage in this speech in the university are rigorously screened. The scholar must have completed the necessary undergraduate and graduate degrees to be certified by his or her peers as competent to engage in the scholarly discourse of a discipline.[13] Within the constraints of the disciplinary discourse and the criteria for certification of professional competence, the scholar is free to reach conclusions that contradict previous belief, whether within the academy or the larger society.[14]

Thus, the essential requirement for this progressive conception of knowledge within a university setting is free discourse among academic professionals within the ethical and competency constraints of a discipline.[15] During the late 1800s and early 1900s, when the disciplines formed and overall professionalization occurred, the principal threat to the realization of free discourse among competent professionals was interference by lay administrators, and boards of trustees and regents who governed higher education in the United States ("lay" is used here to refer to persons not belonging to the academic profession).

EXCEPTIONAL VOCATIONAL FREEDOM OF SPEECH AND PEER REVIEW

For several hundred years after the founding of institutions of higher education in the United States in the mid-1600s, professors labored under employment law doctrine holding that private and public employees had no right to object to conditions placed upon the terms of employment, including restrictions on free expression.[16] As the modern university and its research mission developed in the late 1800s and professors increasingly questioned and challenged the cherished beliefs of the time, the lack of employment or constitutional protection for academic speech became a critical problem.[17] No clear standard for First Amendment protection for those professors employed in public universities developed until 1968.[18]

Interference by university employers took one of two forms. First, because of financial, political, moral, or religious concerns, lay boards and administrators tended to distort intellectual inquiry by imposing constraints on offering new hypotheses or criticizing accepted ones. Second, the free exchange envisioned was to occur among *competent* academic professionals. The exchange could tolerate error but not incompetence, and only academic professionals, not lay administrators and boards, could evaluate professional qualifications and performance to determine whether error was within the range of competent and ethical inquiry.[19] The professorate sought a system that distinguishes and tolerates "honest" error, arising from the responsible and best practice of a discipline, from incompetence that is outside the range of reasonable disagreement among peers, negligence, recklessness, or intentional error. For example, the determination whether a professor's advocacy of a "flat earth" hypothesis is an error within the range of competent inquiry rests with the peer collegium.

As social scientists began a critical analysis of the economic order at the turn of the last century, some industrialists on the governing boards sought to control professorial speech.[20] This led academics in 1915 to organize a professional association, the American Association of University Professors (AAUP).[21] The AAUP pressed university employers to grant professors rights of free inquiry and speech in scholarship and teaching without interference by lay boards of trustees and administrators.[22]

With the founding of the AAUP, the professorate sought a mutual understanding and agreement on principles with employers. The term "professional academic freedom" describes this mutual understanding or tradition. University employers, serving the university's unique mission of creating and disseminating knowledge, have agreed to grant rights of exceptional vocational freedom of speech to professors in teaching, research, and extramural utterance without lay interference on the condition that individual professors meet correlative duties of professional competence and ethical conduct.[23] The faculty as a collegial body also has correlative duties both to enforce the obligations of individual professors and to defend the academic freedom of colleagues. Because of the unique history of the academic profession in the United States, governing boards act as surrogates for the public in a social compact with the profession that grants rights of academic freedom, peer review, and shared governance in return for the performance of the corresponding duties.

It is this tradition of faculty self-governance in peer review of professional competence and ethics that makes professional academic freedom unique, not the tenure system that has many parallels in other employment settings. Peer review is the linchpin of professional academic freedom and tenure.[24] This tradition has been incorporated into employment contracts with individual professors. It is also protected by professional academic organizations like the AAUP, disciplinary associations, and by accrediting authorities.

The concept of "professional academic freedom" explored here is part of a family of concepts that protect freedom of speech in the university. Diagram 1 shows all the players, how the concepts apply to the players, and the overlap among the concepts. Diagram 2 depicts "Professional Academic Freedom"—a concept developed particularly by the AAUP since

Diagram 1
The Players and the Overlapping Doctrines Relating to Academic Freedom

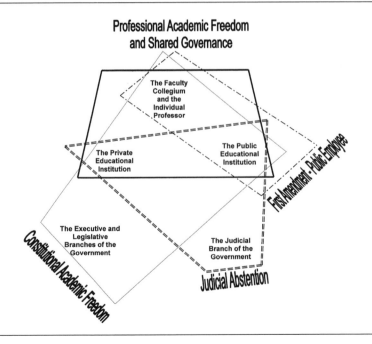

Diagram 2
Professional Academic Freedom and Shared Governance

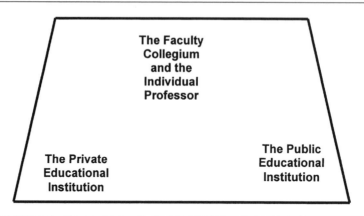

The Faculty
Collegium
and the
Individual
Professor

The Private
Educational
Institution

The Public
Educational
Institution

1915. It focuses on the employment relationship between an individual professor and his or her employing institution, whether public or private. Shared governance is a corollary of professional academic freedom where peer review defines what is professionally competent and ethical. Shared governance defines peer review.

Diagram 3 outlines "Constitutional Academic Freedom." Starting with the *Sweezy v. New Hampshire* decision in 1957,[25] the United States Supreme Court turned to the First Amendment to develop "constitutional academic freedom." The First Amendment grants both universities and professors freedom from direct governmental restrictions—by the executive or legislative branches—on either the content of speech or the right of the university to determine who may teach. This constitutional academic freedom, as it applies to the university itself, is sometimes referred to as "institutional academic freedom."

Diagram 4 sets forth the players in the public employee speech cases. In a 1968 decision, *Pickering v. Board of Education*,[26] the United States Supreme Court, again turning to the First Amendment, first articulated a clear test for protecting the freedom of speech of people as employees of public employers.[27] A subset of these public employee speech cases involves faculty speech in the public university context. Note that the *Pickering* line of cases does not apply to professors at private colleges and universities.

Diagram 5 outlines the focus of the doctrine of academic abstention where courts as a branch of government give significant deference to faculty academic judgments. The First Amendment jurisprudence explored

Diagram 3
The First Amendment and Constitutional Academic Freedom

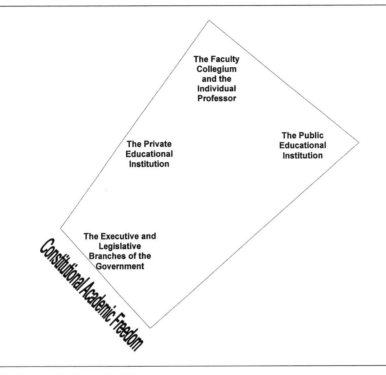

in Diagrams 3 and 4 influences the judicial doctrine of academic abstention.

Both the constitutional academic freedom cases and the First Amendment cases involving professors at public universities borrow from the earlier tradition of "professional academic freedom." The greatest confusion
in the literature concerning academic freedom has arisen over the failure
to distinguish the First Amendment doctrines of both constitutional academic freedom and public employee free speech (a subset of public employee cases deal with professors at public universities) from the earlier and
more inclusive doctrines of professional academic freedom and shared governance.[28] The doctrines address similar goals about the importance of free
inquiry and speech in higher education, but each has different legal roots.
Constitutional academic freedom is rooted in the First Amendment and
prohibits government attempts to control or direct the university or those
affiliated with it regarding either the content of their speech or discourse

Diagram 4
The First Amendment—Public Employee

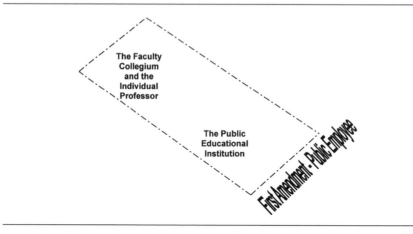

or the determination of who may teach. Professional academic freedom is an employment law concept developed by the AAUP rooted in concern over lay interference by boards of trustees and administrators in professors' research, teaching, and intramural and extramural speech. It grants rights to professors to be free from lay interference by employers in research, teaching, and intramural and extramural utterance. It also imposes correlative duties of professional competence and ethical conduct on individual professors and enforcement of these individual duties by the faculty as a collegial body through shared governance.

Professional academic freedom and the First Amendment cases providing constitutional protection for freedom of speech in the public workplace also differ substantially. First, the public employee speech constitutional cases do not apply to private universities, whereas the tradition of professional academic freedom applies to all higher education. Second, the public employee free speech cases call for a court initially to determine whether the speech is of public concern, and then, if the speech is of public concern, to balance the employee's interest in speaking out on public matters with the employer's interest in promoting the efficiency of the public service it performs. The constitutional free speech cases tend not to emphasize the truth or falsity of the speech. The more that speech is disruptive, the more likely it will be penalized. Professional academic freedom focuses on whether the speech meets the competence and ethical standards of a discipline as defined by peers. If it does, the amount of disruption it causes

Diagram 5
Academic Abstention and the Judiciary

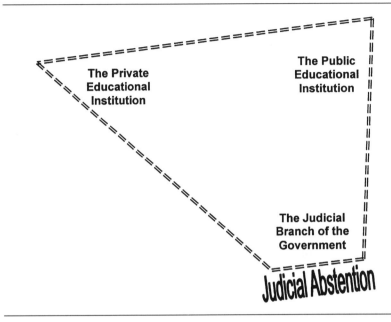

is irrelevant. The truth or falsity of the speech as measured by professional standards is critical to the protection of the speech. It is not that the speech may ultimately be shown to be in error, the question is whether the speech reflects the scholarly standards of the discipline.

This book focuses on the tradition of professional academic freedom and shared governance that are the responsibility of the professorate. The First Amendment doctrines are the province of the courts.

THE NEGOTIATED MECHANICS OF PEER REVIEW

The mechanics of this tradition of peer review have been a subject of continuing negotiation between university employers and the professorate. The essential requirement of progress in the discovery of knowledge in a university setting is free discourse among academic professionals, within the ethical and competency constraints of a discipline as defined by peers. It follows that the essential elements of a peer review system are a strong presumption in favor of a professor's free discourse and evaluation and hearing procedures to permit peers to exercise judgment. In practical terms, the negotiated mechanics of peer review have come to require some probationary period where a professor seeking continued employment carries the burden of demonstrating excellence in teaching, research, and service in an evaluation process relying principally on peer assessment. Successful candidates receive tenure, subsequent to which the burden shifts to the administration to demonstrate to a peer committee through academic due process that a professor has failed to meet correlative obligations of competence or ethics and thus merits employment sanctions. The administration generally must demonstrate a violation of duty by clear and convincing evidence. The principal purpose of academic due process is to maximize protection of the rights of academic freedom while providing the means for peers to enforce its correlative obligations. The peer review system tolerates "honest" error that peers consider within the range of competent and ethical inquiry.

The peer review process during the probationary period has been largely successful in requiring candidates to excel in meeting the correlative obligations of academic freedom. The public challenge today is directed at the failure of peer review to adequately enforce the correlative duties of professional competence and ethical conduct following the grant of tenure.

Historically, once tenure is achieved, the intensity of peer review diminishes dramatically. Administrators conduct annual evaluations of an individual professor's work and assess sabbatical or additional resource requests, but these decisions generally do not involve peer review. Administrators very rarely initiate peer-review proceedings to terminate tenure.

In the last fifteen years, as a result of growing public pressure for increased accountability, there has been significant movement toward some form of post-tenure review at a number of colleges and universities. Professor Christine Licata finds that,

> in most settings, post-tenure review is distinguished from the traditional annual merit review because it is usually a peer review-driven process and is designed specifically to systematically assess performance, nurture professional growth, promote improvement, if necessary, through a required plan (usually of one to three years), and in some situations, impose sanctions when improvement is not forthcoming.[29]

Post-tenure review policies are of two basic types: (1) "comprehensive periodic review of all tenured faculty, usually at 5–7 year intervals" or (2) selective review of some faculty triggered by poor performance apparent in some other review (usually annual review).[30]

Professor Licata reports that "[t]hirty-seven states either have adopted system-wide post-tenure policies, implemented them in selected state institutions or are considering such policies, and several regional accrediting bodies now require institutions to implement post-tenure review policies."[31] In a recent study of 217 institutions by the Harvard Project on Faculty Appointments, Professor Cheryl Sternman Rule finds that 46 percent of the 192 institutions in the study that grant tenure have post-tenure review.[32] Included in the overall proportion of 46 percent were both public institutions, where 55 percent had post-tenure review, and private institutions, where 45 percent had post-tenure review.[33]

Professor Licata observes some confusion "whether these reviews are intended primarily to promote senior faculty vitality or to reprimand underperformers."[34] Academic tradition would support both purposes, since the faculty peer collegium has correlative duties both to create a culture of high aspiration in terms of professional ideals and to hold individual faculty members accountable for meeting minimum standards of competence and ethical conduct. She concludes that because post-tenure review programs are less than seven years old, "little is known about their long-term effectiveness and their resource requirements."[35]

Prior to the movement toward post-tenure review, the peer review system in higher education historically has involved accepting some degree of misbehavior or incompetence among a subset of tenured professors because the degree of vigilance necessary to prevent it would generate greater costs than benefits. Competent review is itself time-consuming and takes tenured faculty away from research, teaching, and other public service. In addition, the university's mission of the creation and dissemination of knowledge is better served by a system that is somewhat more forgiving of error than one that is too restrictive, thus chilling some inquiry that would in fact serve the mission.

It is one thing for the academic profession de facto to recognize that close peer review of tenured colleagues on minor matters may entail more costs than benefits, but it is another matter entirely not to acknowledge the duty of peer review for tenured professors at all, or to ignore the duty except for the most egregious matters of unprofessional conduct. The evidence points toward widespread misunderstanding of professional responsibility for peer review within the academic profession. As noted earlier, only 55 percent of faculty respondents in a 1993 Acadia Institute survey of 2,000 professors in chemistry, civil engineering, microbiology, and sociology believed that they should, to a great extent, exercise responsibility for the conduct of their colleagues, and a mere 13 percent judged that faculty in their department actually exercised a great deal of shared responsibility for their colleagues' conduct.[36] Swazey, Lewis, and Anderson found differences among the disciplines; in chemistry for example, only 46 percent of the chemist respondents strongly affirmed collective responsibility for colleagues' behavior.[37] Only approximately one half of faculty respondents in the Swazey, Lewis, and Anderson survey were familiar with the content of their disciplinary code of ethics.[38] Dismissals of tenured faculty for incompetence or unethical conduct have been rare. In the period 1970–1990, the AAUP reported 1,589 dismissals. Eighty-four percent (1,334) were for financial exigency, retrenchment, or restructuring; 6.5 percent (104) were civil liberties cases involving freedom of speech or political or religious activity; 4.0 percent (63) were dismissed for union or faculty senate organizational activity, criticism of the administration, or employment grievances; and the remaining 5.5 percent (87) of the cases involved miscellaneous causes, including incompetence or unethical conduct. Thus, at most, four to five reported terminations a year in the period 1970–1990 involved dismissal for incompetence or unethical conduct. The tenured professorate numbered more than 200,000 in this period.[39]

Professor William Van Alstyne has emphasized that academic tenure, accurately defined, carries no claim whatsoever to a guarantee of lifetime employment or insulation from a fair accounting for performance. Rather,

> the price of an exceptional vocational freedom to speak the truth as one sees it, without penalty for its possible immediate impact upon the economic well-being of the employing institution, is the cost of exceptional care in the representation of that truth, a professional standard of care. Indeed, a grave ethical failure in the integrity of a teacher's or a scholar's academic presentation ... is precisely the kind of offense to the contingent privilege of academic freedom that states a clearly adequate cause for a *faculty* recommendation of termination.[40]

It is the correlative obligation of the faculty as a collegial body to enforce the duties when individual professors do not observe them. Professor Fritz Machlup also stressed that the faculty has a moral obligation to initiate action against professors who falsify evidence or distort the truth in the presentation of readily verifiable facts.[41]

Early in the last century, in championing the concept of peer review, AAUP leaders took pains to argue that peer review would not shelter the incompetent or unethical professor. For example, before an audience of university presidents, the AAUP's first president, John Dewey, maintained that peer review would "facilitate the removal of incompetents by bringing into play the resources of highly critical connoisseurs."[42] Many university presidents of the time were skeptical, fearing that professors were likely to protect each other and ignore the interests of students and the public.[43] The AAUP's 1915 "Declaration of Principles" cautioned that if the profession "should prove itself unwilling to purge its ranks of the incompetent and the unworthy, or to prevent the freedom which it claims in the name of science from being used as a shelter for inefficiency, for superficiality, or for uncritical and intemperate partisanship, it is certain that the task will be performed by others."[44]

PRINCIPLES OF PROFESSIONAL CONDUCT

The construct of the correlative duties of academic freedom and peer review assumes the existence of generally accepted principles of professional conduct. While not the only source for principles of professional conduct, the major statements of the AAUP have played a substantial role in defining the tradition of academic freedom in the United States.[45] We start by closely analyzing the AAUP's 1915 General Declaration of Principles and the 1940 Statement of Principles on Academic Freedom and Tenure.[46]

The American Association of University Professors (AAUP)'s 1915 General Declaration of Principles

The AAUP's 1915 General Declaration of Principles remains the foundational statement defining the American concept of professional academic freedom.[47] This document starts with the reality that "American institutions of learning are usually controlled by boards of trustees as the ultimate repositories of power."[48] Making no distinction between private or public universities, the 1915 Declaration takes the position that such boards are in a position of public trust to serve the public interest.[49] Universities serve the public interest by: (1) promoting inquiry and advancing the sum of human knowledge; (2) providing instruction for students; and (3) developing experts to advise government and community on the solution of problems.[50] The function of the professional scholar in realizing these purposes is

> to deal at first hand, after prolonged and specialized technical training, with the sources of knowledge; and to impart the results of their own and their fellow-specialists' investigation and reflection, both to students and to the general public, without fear or favor. The proper discharge of this function requires ... that the university teacher shall be exempt from any pecuniary motive or inducement to hold, or to express, any conclusion which is not

the genuine and uncolored product of his own study or that of fellow specialists.[51]

Based on these arguments, the 1915 Declaration built a definition of professional academic freedom. Professional academic freedom must enable the individual scholar to perform the three functions of: (1) dealing with sources of knowledge and reflecting upon them toward some result; (2) imparting those results to students; and (3) extending those results to the public. These three functions in turn relate closely to the university's three purposes set forth in the declaration: (1) promoting inquiry and the advancement of human knowledge; (2) providing instruction to students; and (3) developing expert advisers for the community.[52]

The 1915 Declaration defines the three elements of professional academic freedom necessary for scholars to perform their functions within the larger purposes of the university. These are: (1) freedom of inquiry and research; (2) freedom of teaching within the university; and (3) freedom of extramural utterance.[53] In these three areas, trustees serve the public trust by granting university teachers rights of freedom from lay interference so that neither intellectual inquiry and discourse nor decisions concerning professional competence to engage in the intellectual discourse will be distorted by lay bias.[54]

The 1915 Declaration recognizes that the granting of these rights of freedom from lay interference rests upon a professor meeting unique obligations. Each professor must observe personally and enforce through collegial action the ethical and competency constraints on scholarly inquiry and discourse. "Since there are no rights without corresponding duties, the considerations heretofore set down with respect to the freedom of the academic teacher entail certain correlative obligations."[55]

Correlative Obligations of the Individual Faculty Member in the 1915 Declaration

Inherent in the concept of professional academic freedom in the United States are correlative obligations for both individual university teachers and for the faculty as a collegial body. The principal correlative obligation of the *individual university teacher* is to comply with the ethical and competency constraints of professional scholarly inquiry and discourse.

> The claim to freedom of teaching is made in the interest of the integrity and of the progress of scientific inquiry; it is, therefore, only those who carry on their work in the temper of the scientific inquirer who may justly assert this claim. The liberty of the scholar within the university to set forth his con-

clusions, be they what they may, is *conditioned* by their being conclusions gained by a scholar's method and held in a scholar's spirit; that is to say, they must be the fruits of competent and patient and sincere inquiry, and they should be set forth with dignity, courtesy, and temperateness of language. The university teacher, in giving instruction upon controversial matters, while he is under no obligation to hide his own opinion under a mountain of equivocal verbiage, should, if he is fit for his position, be a person of fair and judicial mind; he should, in dealing with such subjects, set forth justly, without suppression or innuendo, the divergent opinions of other investigators.[56]

Extramural utterance in the 1915 Declaration includes: (1) speech that is both within disciplinary expertise and outside the walls (which the declaration sees as being covered by the same general principles as freedom of teaching); and (2) the political activities of a citizen outside the walls.[57] The 1915 Declaration imposes higher correlative obligations on extramural utterances. "In their extramural utterances, it is obvious that academic teachers are under a *peculiar* obligation to avoid hasty or unverified or exaggerated statements, and to refrain from intemperate or sensational modes of expression."[58]

The 1915 Declaration does not specifically address freedom for intramural speech other than teaching and research. However, freedom of teaching includes intramural speech relating to the education of students, and freedom of inquiry and research includes intramural speech that involves critical inquiry. For example, the protection of intramural speech clearly extends to decisions involving curriculum, procedures of student instruction and assessment, faculty appointments and status, and admissions. Any intramural speech involving critical inquiry is protected.

Correlative Obligations of the Faculty as a Collegial Body in the 1915 Declaration

Within the American tradition of professional academic freedom, the principal correlative obligation of the *faculty as a collegial body* is to enforce in the first instance the ethical and competency constraints of the academic profession when individual professors do not observe them. "[T]he power of determining when departures from the requirements of the scientific spirit and method have occurred, should be vested in bodies composed of members of the academic profession."[59] Only members of the profession have the competence to judge these requirements, and they "must be prepared to assume this responsibility for themselves ... The responsibility cannot ... be rightfully evaded."[60] The 1915 Declaration conditions

the rights of academic speakers on the performance of the correlative obligation to comply with the strictures of inquiry and discourse established
by their discipline. Collegial responsibility to sanction departure from professional modes of inquiry and discourse is implicit in the statement's admonition that university teachers must have the capacity "for judicial
severity when the occasion requires it."[61]

The 1940 AAUP/AAC Statement of Principles on Academic Freedom and Tenure

The 1940 Statement of Principles adopted by the AAUP and the Association of American Colleges (now the Association of American Colleges
and Universities) incorporates in summary terms the rights and correlative obligations of professional academic freedom set forth in the 1915 Declaration. It sets up a framework of norms concerning rights and duties. This
1940 Statement has been endorsed by almost all major educational disciplinary organizations in the United States,[62] is commonly adopted by reference in academic employment contracts and faculty handbooks,[63] and
is often cited in judicial opinions.[64]

Rights of Academic Freedom

For Research and Teaching.   In its introductory paragraphs, the 1940
Statement reasons that universities are established for the common good,
and the common good depends upon the free search for truth and its free
exposition.

> Academic freedom is essential to these purposes and applies to both *teach-
> ing* and *research*. Freedom in research is fundamental to the advancement of
> truth. Academic freedom in its teaching aspect is fundamental for the pro-
> tection of the rights of the teacher in teaching and of the student to free-
> dom in learning. It carries with it *duties correlative with rights*.[65]

Immediately following the introductory paragraphs, under the heading
"Academic Freedom," the 1940 Statement sets forth three paragraphs that
further define the concept. In paragraph (a), the statement provides that
"teachers are entitled to full freedom in research and in the publication of
the results, subject to the adequate performance of their other academic
duties."[66] In paragraph (b), the statement provides that "teachers are entitled to freedom in the classroom in discussing their subject, but they
should be careful not to introduce into their teaching controversial mat-

ter which has no relation to their subject."[67] Paragraph (c) of the 1940 Statement concerns extramural utterance.

For Intramural Utterances (other than Teaching and Research) and Extramural Utterance. There is no specific reference in the 1940 Statement to "freedom of extramural utterance and action" as there is in the 1915 Declaration. Paragraph (c) under Academic Freedom provides that

> college and university teachers are citizens, members of a learned profession, and officers of an educational institution. When they speak or write as citizens, they should be free from institutional censorship or discipline, but their special position in the community imposes special obligations. As scholars and educational officers, they should remember that the public may judge their profession and their institution by their utterances. Hence they should at all times be accurate, should exercise appropriate restraint, should show respect for the opinions of others, and should make every effort to indicate that they are not speaking for the institution.[68]

An interpretation adopted by both the AAUP and the AAC (now the AACU) and issued contemporaneously with the 1940 Statement refers to the "admonitions of paragraph (c)" as applicable to the "*extramural* utterances of the teacher."[69]

The question whether paragraph (c) of the 1940 Statement, creating rights of academic freedom for extramural utterance, was also intended to create rights of academic freedom for intramural utterance other than teaching and research—thus essentially creating rights of academic freedom for all professorial speech, either inside or outside the walls—has been difficult to resolve because of ambiguity in the text. The literal words of paragraph (c) of the 1940 Statement focus on speech outside the walls of the university. The second sentence of paragraph (c) refers to speaking or writing "as a citizen," recognizing that a teacher's special position "in the community" imposes special obligations. It is possible that "citizen" and "community" refer to citizenship in the university community inside the walls as well as citizenship in the community outside of the walls. However, the third sentence of paragraph (c) urges teachers to remember that "the public" may judge their profession and their institution by their utterances; and the fourth sentence urges teachers to make every effort to indicate that they are "not speaking for the institution." The contemporaneous interpretation comments that paragraph (c) deals with "extramural utterance." This evidence heavily favors reading paragraph (c) as referring only to speech outside the walls.[70]

In addition, the 1940 Statement is building on the tradition of the 1915 Declaration where extramural utterance included: (1) speech that is within disciplinary competence outside the walls; and (2) political activities of a citizen outside the walls.[71] The emphasis on faculty speech outside the walls also appears in the statement issued by a 1925 conference of major higher education organizations.[72] The conference adopted language drafted by university presidents:

a. a university or college should recognize that the teacher in speaking and writing *outside* the *institution* upon subjects beyond the scope of his own field of study is entitled to precisely the same freedom and is subject to precisely the same responsibility as attach to all other citizens.

b. If the extra-mural utterances of a teacher should raise grave doubts concerning his fitness for his position, the question should in all cases be submitted to an appropriate committee of the faculty of which he is a member.[73]

Considered together the 1915 Declaration and the 1925 Conference Statement demonstrate that the governing boards and administrators were most concerned about faculty speech outside the walls that would endanger the institution.[74]

The 1940 Statement specifically grants rights of academic freedom to teaching and research, which are types of intramural utterance, but the Statement does not specifically address whether other types of intramural utterance constitute teaching or research, leaving them with no academic freedom protection if they do not. However, the interpretation of "teaching" and "research" in the 1940 Statement must be consistent with the policy rationale for academic freedom developed in the 1915 Declaration and reflected in the 1940 Statement. Thus, "academic freedom in its teaching aspect" includes intramural utterance relating to the education of students, and academic freedom "in research" includes intramural speech that involves critical inquiry.[75]

There are differences of opinion about how broadly to construe these rights of academic freedom for intramural speech other than teaching and research. Professor Finkin fears that any restrictions on intramural speech will place a professor in the position of having to guess where his or her utterance lies on a spectrum from purely professional to purely nonprofessional.[76] Because he believes that this may harm the quest for knowledge within the university, he would protect practically all utterances of a professor within the walls.[77] Texas Chancellor Mark Yudof believes that there must be a reasonable connection between a professor's speech and the ac-

ademic work of teaching or research, or the concept of professional academic freedom will become indistinguishable from the general demands
for professional autonomy common in progressive labor relations today.[78]
Thus, Yudof argues, inadequate salaries, uncomfortable offices, inadequate
insurance, or lack of parking space typically affect all university employees, and in the case of professors, may stifle creative impulses, but academic
freedom must not be stretched too far to give special license to professors
to comment on these matters.[79]

Shedding further light on what intramural utterance should be protected
by academic freedom, the 1966 "Statement on Government of Colleges
and Universities" outlines the allocation of governance responsibilities.[80]
The AAUP, the American Council on Education, and the Association of
Governing Boards (AGB) originally jointly formulated the statement.[81]
The AGB in its 1998 "Institutional Governance Statement" took a substantially different position, essentially disconnecting shared governance
from academic freedom, and importing the idea of stakeholder analysis
from the business ethics literature where the faculty becomes one stakeholder among many the governing board should consider.[82] Rights of academic freedom would clearly protect those areas of shared governance outlined in the 1966 "Statement on Government" since the practice of shared
governance is a corollary of academic freedom and peer review. In the 1966
"Statement on Government," the voting faculty has primary authority
over: curriculum; procedures of student instruction; standards of faculty
competence and ethical conduct including faculty appointments and
tenure; policies for admitting students; standards of student competence
and ethics; maintenance of a suitable environment for learning, judgments
determining where within the overall academic program terminations for
financial emergency should occur; and decisions to terminate a program or
department when no financial exigency is declared.[83] The governing board
is to consult with the voting faculty on the following issues: the determination of mission; strategic decisions and comprehensive planning; physical and fiscal resources; budgeting and distribution of funds; the decision
to create a program, department, school, college, or division; the decision
to declare a financial exigency, and the selection and assessment of the
presidents and deans.[84]

If rights of academic freedom extend to all intramural utterance relating to the education of students or critical inquiry and to all intramural
speech relating to shared governance, the remaining subset of intramural
utterance, such as faculty complaints over parking or an uncomfortable office, is small. Professor Rabban notes that few of the AAUP reports or legal

cases on violations of academic freedom involve such cases.[85] Moreover, such speech may be protected by the First Amendment or university grievance procedure.[86]

Correlative Duties of the Individual Faculty Member in the 1940 Statement

The 1940 Statement also sets up a framework of norms concerning duties.[87] It provides that academic freedom "carries with it duties correlative with rights."[88] The phrase "duties correlative with rights" is left open-ended in the 1940 Statement, listing several specific duties and mentioning two more general duties.[89] There is no indication the listing is exhaustive on the concept of "duty."

The Statement does define several specific duties. With respect to the right of academic freedom in research, the 1940 Statement provides that such freedom is granted "subject to the adequate performance of their other academic duties."[90] It also imposes a duty that "research for pecuniary return should be based upon an understanding with the authorities of the institution."[91] With respect to the right of academic freedom in teaching students, the 1940 Statement imposes a specific duty that teachers "should be careful not to introduce into their teaching controversial matter which has no relation to their subject."[92] With respect to the right of academic freedom for extramural utterances, the 1940 Statement includes a specific duty that professors should: "at all times be accurate," "exercise appropriate restraint," "show respect for the opinions of others," and "make every effort to indicate that they are not speaking for the institution."[93] In the contemporaneous interpretation of the 1940 Statement, administrators are given permission to file charges, if "the extramural utterances of the teacher have been such as to raise grave doubts concerning the teacher's fitness for his or her position."[94]

Describing more general correlative obligations, the 1940 Statement provides that tenured professors may be dismissed for "adequate cause," which may include "charges of incompetence" or reasons "involving moral turpitude."[95] These two general duties of professional competence and ethical conduct, referred to in passing in the text of the 1940 Statement, are not further defined in the text of the 1940 Statement or the contemporaneous interpretation. They only partially define the elements of the open-ended term "duties correlative with rights" used in the 1940 Statement.

A number of other AAUP statements and scholarly commentaries help clarify the definition of "duties correlative with rights" in the 1940 Statement. It is critical first to visualize the framework of norms for the individual professor in the 1940 Statement.

1. Rights of Academic Freedom
   a. Research
   b. Teaching
   c. Intramural Utterance Relating to the Education of Students or Involving Critical Inquiry
   d. Extramural Utterance
2. Correlative "Duties" of the Individual Faculty Member. The 1940 Statement does not exhaustively define the open-ended term "duties." It lists several specific duties and mentions two general duties.
   a. Duties Relating to Research, Teaching, and Intramural Utterance
      i. Specific Duties
         1. Professors must provide "adequate performance of their other academic duties" (meaning professors cannot neglect assigned duties of teaching and service).
         2. Research for pecuniary gain should be based upon an understanding with the authorities of the institution.
         3. Teachers should be careful not to introduce into their teaching controversial material that has no relation to their subject.
      ii. General Duties
         1. Professional competence.
         2. Ethical conduct.
   b. Duties Relating to Extramural Utterance. Speech as a citizen is to be free of institutional censorship or discipline but subject to "special obligations." Teachers speaking as citizens should:
      i. at all times be accurate;
      ii. exercise appropriate restraint;
      iii. show respect for the opinions of others; and
      iv. make every effort to indicate that they are not speaking for the institution.

The most important statement further clarifying the meaning of "duties correlative with rights" is the 1970 AAUP "Interpretive Comments for the 1940 Statement."

The Association of American Colleges [now the AACU] and the American Association of University Professors have long recognized that membership in the academic profession carries with it *special responsibilities*. Both associations either separately or jointly have consistently affirmed these responsibilities in major policy statements, providing guidance to professors in their utterances as citizens, in their exercise of their responsibilities to the institution and to students, and in their conduct when resigning from the institution or when undertaking government-sponsored research. Of particular relevance is the Statement of Professional Ethics, adopted in 1966 as Association policy.[96]

The AAUP's 1970 "Interpretive Comments for the 1940 Statement" recognizes "special responsibilities" incumbent on members of the academic profession.[97] These "special responsibilities" themselves are further defined by reference to the AAUP's major policy statements, particularly the 1966 "Statement of Professional Ethics," which also recognizes the "special responsibilities" placed on members of the profession.[98]

In this framework, other major AAUP policy statements and academic tradition give more precise definition to the 1940 Statement's general duties of professional competence and ethical conduct in teaching, research, intramural utterance, and extramural utterance. What defines academic tradition? The AAUP is the one association whose mission for over eighty-five years has focused on the rights and corresponding duties of academic freedom for the entire academic profession, not just one discipline. However, a number of the disciplinary associations in more recent decades have also sought to formulate codes of ethics or standards of professional conduct. Some disciplines have comprehensive codes of ethics.[99] Some have statements that touch on only a few areas such as sexual harassment and discrimination.[100] There is strong agreement on principles of conduct between the AAUP documents and the disciplinary codes of ethics and among the disciplinary codes themselves. This indicates the existence of a commonly understood academic tradition. There is also scholarly commentary on the rights and responsibilities of academic freedom, and significant consensus within this scholarship supports the existence of a commonly understood academic tradition.

The discussion to follow is sometimes quite technical, but close analysis is necessary to define clearly the outer limits of professional academic freedom. Vagueness in this area will chill speech that actually serves the university's mission. If a principle of professional conduct appears in several sources defining academic tradition, the essay discusses each of them. This may seem redundant, but the source of a principle of conduct and the number of times the principle is articulated indicate its strength in academic tradition.

Further Definition of the General Duty of Professional Competence. The academic profession has struggled in the effort to define the duties of professional competence. The 1940 Statement refers to incompetence and moral turpitude in the discussion of termination for cause, but does so in a procedural context and without elaboration.[101] It also refers to the duty of professors to provide "adequate performance of their other assigned duties."[102] This is neglect of assigned duties of teaching and service. In 1958, the joint AAC-AAUP "Statement on Procedural Standards in Faculty Dismissal Proceedings" acknowledged that

> one persistent source of difficulty is the definition of adequate cause for the dismissal of a faculty member.... [C]onsiderable ambiguity and misunderstanding persist throughout higher education ... concerning this matter. The present statement assumes that individual institutions will have formulated their own definitions of adequate cause for dismissal, bearing in mind the 1940 statement and standards which have developed in the experience of academic institutions.[103]

Since the 1940 Statement gives such modest guidance, it is the developed academic tradition of duties in higher education that provides the definition of professional competence.

The 1970 "Interpretive Comments for the 1940 Statement" specifically refers to the AAUP's 1966 "Statement on Professional Ethics" to define a professor's "special responsibilities.[104] The AAUP's 1966 "Statement on Professional Ethics" begins, "Professors, guided by a deep conviction of the worth and dignity of the advancement of knowledge, recognize the special responsibilities placed on them."[105] The Statement defines *professional competence* for professors to include the following special responsibilities: "to seek and to state the truth"; to "devote their energies to developing and improving their scholarly competence"; to "exercise critical self-discipline and judgment in using, extending, and transmitting knowledge"; to "practice intellectual honesty"; to "hold before students the best scholarly and ethical standards of their discipline"; to "ensure that their evaluations of students reflect each student's true merit"; to acknowledge academic debt"; "to acknowledge significant academic or scholarly assistance from [students]"; "to seek above all to be effective teachers and scholars"; "to accept their share of faculty responsibilities for the governance of their institutions"; and "to observe the stated regulations of the institution, provided that the regulations do not contravene academic freedom."[106] The 1966 Statement does not further define "effectiveness" as a scholar and teacher, "scholarly competence," "best scholarly standard," the exercise of "critical self-discipline and judgment in using, extending, and transmitting knowledge," or "intellectual honesty."

The 1915 Declaration, from which the 1940 Statement's concept of a correlative duty of professional competence is drawn, lends some help. It provides that academic freedom for teaching may *only* be asserted by "those who carry on their work in the temper of the scientific inquirer."[107] Academic freedom for a scholar's conclusions "is conditioned by there being conclusions gained by a scholar's method and held in a scholar's spirit."[108] The 1915 Declaration further defines the phrases "temper of the scientific inquirer," "a scholar's method," and "a scholar's spirit" to mean that conclusions must: (1) be the fruit of "competent and patient and sincere inquiry"; and (2) especially on controversial matters, be the product of "fair" deliberation where the divergent opinions of other investigators are "set forth justly, without suppression or innuendo."[109] Richard Hofstadter and Walter Metzger, examining the development of academic freedom in the United States, describe these traditions incorporated into the 1915 Declaration as "norms of neutrality and competence."[110]

In 1971, the Association of American Colleges (now the AACU) and the AAUP established a Commission on Academic Tenure in Higher Education to evaluate the operation of the tenure system in higher education.[111] The Commission reported its views that were officially adopted by the AAC and the AAUP in 1973.[112] The Commission found that a professor must demonstrate teaching effectiveness, scholarly competence and promise, and academic citizenship at a professional standard determined by the faculty.[113] Academic tradition should guide the faculty in defining these standards.[114] The Commission defined "adequate cause" for dismissal as: (1) demonstrated incompetence or dishonesty in teaching or research; (2) substantial and manifest neglect of assigned duty; and (3) personal conduct that substantially impairs the individual's fulfillment of his or her institutional responsibilities.[115]

These principles of professional competence are easier to visualize when reorganized around duties in teaching, in internal governance, and in scholarship. In teaching, both the 1966 Statement and the 1973 Commission Report require faculty members to be effective teachers. The 1966 Statement further requires that faculty members, in teaching: (1) hold before students the best scholarly and ethical standards of the discipline; (2) ensure that their evaluations of students reflect each student's true merit, practice intellectual honesty, exercise critical self-discipline and judgment in transmitting knowledge, and acknowledge academic debt.[116] The 1973 Commission Report provides that substantial and manifest neglect of assigned teaching duties would be adequate cause for dismissal.[117]

With respect to internal governance responsibilities of academic citizenship, the 1966 AAUP "Statement in Professional Ethics" requires that faculty members "accept their share of faculty responsibilities for the governance of their institution."[118] The 1973 AAUP/AAC Commission Report provides that a professor must demonstrate academic citizenship at a professional standard determined by the faculty.[119] A professor also cannot neglect assigned service duties.

Finally, both the 1966 AAUP "Statement on Professional Ethics" and the 1973 AAUP/AAC Commission Report require a professor to demonstrate competence in scholarship. The 1966 statement further provides that faculty members should: (1) devote their energies to improving their scholarly competence; (2) hold before students the best scholarly standards; (3) practice intellectual honesty; (4) exercise critical self-discipline and judgment in using, extending, and transmitting knowledge; and (5) acknowledge academic debt.[120] A "Statement on Plagiarism," adopted during the AAUP's annual meeting in 1990, reaffirms that "professors must also be vigorously honest in acknowledging their academic debts."[121] In 1990, the AAUP's Committee B on Professional Ethics also urged that scholars involved in collaborative work explain forthrightly the respective contributions of each author.[122]

This is still not a complete definition of professional competence for a faculty member. The meanings of "best scholarly standards," "intellectual honesty," and "critical self-discipline and judgment" rest on common understandings of professional competence. A good example is the fabrication or falsification of evidence in teaching, research, and intramural utterance.

Accuracy in the recording and use of evidence and nonfalsification are simply so fundamental as to be assumed in the common understanding of "intellectual honesty" and "best scholarly standards."[123] The major canon of academic work has been honest and accurate investigation, and the cardinal sin has been stating or presenting a falsehood. This includes omission of a fact so that what is stated or presented as a whole states or presents a falsehood. It also includes misrepresenting the strength of one's findings or credentials, plagiarism, or improper attribution of authorship. With respect to extramural utterance, where this duty was not so fundamental and clear, the 1940 Statement does state that teachers speaking as citizens shall "at all times be accurate."[124] The standard of care for the duty of accuracy is high. "'The price of exceptional freedom to speak the truth as one sees it,' Professor David Rabban observes, 'is the cost of exceptional care in the representation of that "truth," a professional standard of care.'"[125]

There is, as former Harvard President Derek Bok has observed, a common definition of professional competence used to evaluate the academic work of faculty.[126] The common definition of professional competence can be gleaned from the AAUP statements and the long tradition of the academic profession. A faculty member cannot neglect any of the responsibilities assigned by the university employer: teaching, research, and academic citizenship. In satisfying these duties, the faculty member must meet a professional standard defined by faculty, which in turn is guided by academic tradition. In all academic work, a faculty member must meet general duties of both practicing "intellectual honesty" and exercising "critical self-discipline and judgment in using, extending, and transmitting knowledge."[127] In teaching in particular, a professor is "to hold before students the best scholarly standards and ethical standards of the discipline."[128] This includes staying well informed about developments in the discipline.[129] The traditions of the profession further define intellectual honesty, critical self-discipline and judgment, and best scholarly standards;

1. to gather the evidence relevant to the issue at hand through thorough and painstaking inquiry and to preserve the evidence so that it is available to others;
2. to record the evidence accurately;
3. to show the evidence and methodology so that other investigators can replicate the research;
4. to set forth without misrepresentation or distortion the divergent evidence and propositions of other investigators;
5. to give careful and impartial consideration to the weight of the evidence;
6. to reason analytically from the evidence to the proposition;
7. to seek internal consistency;
8. to acknowledge when the evidence contradicts what the scholar and teacher had hoped to achieve;
9. to present evidence and analysis clearly and persuasively;
10. to be rigorously honest in acknowledging academic debt;
11. to correct in a timely way or withdraw work that is erroneous; and
12. to provide open access to the results of research conducted within the university.[130]

In research, the faculty member must develop and improve scholarly competence. The tradition of the profession is that the faculty member is to use this competence to develop and improve some area of knowledge. In *Scholarship Reconsidered: Priorities of the Professoriate*, Ernest Boyer argues for a broader, more capacious understanding of scholarship.[131] The work of the professorate has four separate, yet overlapping functions: the scholarship of discovery; the scholarship of integration; the scholarship of application; and the scholarship of teaching. In *Scholarship Assessed: Evalu-*

ation of the Professoriate, the Carnegie Foundation returns to the topic, proposing the following standards for scholarship.

1. Does the scholar identify important questions in the field?
2. Does the scholar adequately consider existing scholarship in the field?
3. Does the scholar use appropriate methodology recognized in the field? This includes the rules of evidence and the principles of logical reasoning.
4. Does the scholarship add consequentially to the field?
5. Does the scholar make an effective presentation of the work?[132]

In the 1940 Statement, the AAUP articulated for an exceptional vocational freedom to inquire, to teach, and to publish without lay interference. The principal price of this exceptional freedom is that professors must meet corresponding duties of professional competence in their academic work.[133]

Further Definition of the General Duty of Ethical Conduct.   In defining the open-ended term *duties* correlative with rights, the 1940 Statement provides that tenured professors may be dismissed for "adequate cause," which may include charges "involving moral turpitude."[134] The AAUP's 1970 "Interpretive Comments for the 1940 Statement" provide that "moral turpitude" is "behavior that would evoke condemnation by the academic community generally."[135] The 1970 Comments also recognize special responsibilities incumbent on professors, particularly those in the AAUP's "Statement on Professional Ethics."[136] The 1966 "Statement on Professional Ethics" defines the general duty of ethical conduct for professors to include the following obligations: to "demonstrate respect for students as individuals" and to "adhere to their proper roles as intellectual guides and counselors"; to "make every reasonable effort to foster honest academic conduct"; to "respect the confidential nature of the relationship between professor and student"; to "avoid any exploitation, harassment, or discriminatory treatment of students"; not to discriminate against or to harass colleagues; "[i]n the exchange of criticism and ideas ... [to] show due respect for the opinions of others"; "to strive to be objective in professional judgment of colleagues"; to defend the academic freedom of students and colleagues; to "avoid creating the impression of speaking or acting for the university"; not to permit outside interests to compromise their freedom of inquiry; to "give due regard to their paramount responsibilities within their constitution in determining the amount and character of the work done outside it"; and to recognize the effect of their interruption or termination of service upon the academic program and to give due notice of their intentions.[137]

A 1970 statement by the AAUP's Council entitled "Freedom and Responsibility" affirms several of these duties of ethical conduct. The 1970 Statement provides that "membership in the academic community imposes on students, faculty members, administrators, and trustees an obligation" to do the following: "to respect the dignity of others"; "to acknowledge their right to express differing opinions"; "to foster and defend intellectual honesty"; *not* to express dissent or grievances in ways that (i) injure individuals or damage institutional facilities; (ii) disrupt classes or speeches; or (iii) "significantly impede the functions of the institution"; to provide an atmosphere "conducive to learning" with "even-handed treatment in all aspects of the teacher-student relationship"; *not* to force students "by the authority inherent in the instructional role to make particular personal choices as to political action or their own part in society"; *not* to persistently intrude material that has no relation to the subject or to fail to present the subject matter of the course as announced to the students and as approved by the faculty; to base "[e]valuation of students and the award of credit" on "academic performance professionally judged, and not on matters irrelevant to that performance, whether personality, race, religion, degree of political activism, or personal beliefs"; and to foster and defend the academic freedom of students and colleagues.[138]

The 1973 AAUP/AAC "Commission Report on Academic Tenure in Higher Education" also defined adequate cause for dismissal to include personal conduct that substantially impairs the faculty member's fulfillment of his or her institutional responsibilities. This presumably includes conduct like the commission of felonies or conflicts of interest.[139]

The 1915 Declaration urges professors to avoid conflicts of interest. "The proper discharge of [a professor's research, teaching, and public service] requires ... that the university teacher shall be exempt from any pecuniary nature or inducement to hold, or express, any conclusion which is not the genuine and uncolored *product* of his own study or that of fellow specialists."[140] The 1940 Statement does not directly address the area of conflicts of interest except to state that "research for pecuniary return should be based on an understanding with the authorities of the institution."[141] The 1966 AAUP "Statement on Professional Ethics" separates conflict of interest from conflict of commitment. On conflicts of interest, it provides that "although professors may follow subsidiary interests, these interests must never seriously hamper or compromise their freedom of inquiry." Regarding conflicts of commitment, the 1966 Statement also asks that "[p]rofessors give due regard to their paramount responsibilities within their institution in determining the amount and character of the work outside it."[142]

In 1965, the AAUP and the American Council on Education developed a statement, "On Preventing Conflicts of Interest in Government-Sponsored Research at Universities." The statement cautions that,

> [I]t is important to avoid actual or apparent conflicts of interest between government sponsored university research obligations and outside interests and other obligations. Examples of such conflicts of interest are:
>
> a. the undertaking or orientation of the staff member's university research to serve the research needs of the private firm without disclosure of such undertaking or orientation to the university and the sponsoring agency;
>
> b. The purchase of major equipment, instruments or materials for university research from a private firm in which the staff member has an interest without disclosure of such interest; and
>
> c. the transmission to a private firm or other use for personal gain of government-sponsored work products that are not made generally available.[143]

In 1990, the AAUP's Committee B on Professional Ethics approved a more general "Statement on Conflicts of Interest."[144] The statement urges university faculties to draw up conflict of interest guidelines with due regard for the proper disclosure of a faculty member's involvement in off-campus enterprises in terms of investment, ownership or consultative status, for the use of university personnel, including students, and for the disposition of potential profits.[145]

Further Definition of the General Duties of Individual Faculty Members Relating to Extramural Utterance.   The 1940 Statement grants broad academic freedom for extramural utterance as a citizen subject to the "special obligations" of paragraph (c). Teachers speaking as a citizen should at all times be accurate;[146] exercise appropriate restraint;[147] show respect for the opinions of others; and make every effort to indicate that they are not speaking for the institution.[148] These special obligations relating to extramural utterance are subject to a lower standard of care than the general and specific correlative duties relating to teaching, research, and intramural utterance.[149] The contemporaneous interpretation of the 1940 Statement specifies that administrators may file charges if "the extramural utterances of the teacher have been such as to cause grave doubts concerning the teacher's fitness for his or her position."[150]

The 1964 Committee A "Statement on Extramural Utterance" basically restates paragraph (c) of the 1940 Statement and the contemporaneous interpretation of the 1940 Statement.[151] It adds that the burden of proof on the administration to demonstrate that a particular extramural utterance shows grave doubts concerning the teacher's fitness for his or her position is a heavy one. "Extramural utterances rarely bear on the faculty member's fitness for continuing service."[152] The administration carries the burden to make a clear demonstration with weighty evidence.

The AAUP also formerly published responses from the AAUP's Washington staff to letters of inquiry. The 1940 Statement's injunction for faculty members to exercise "appropriate restraint" is defined to refer "solely to choice of language and to other aspects of the manner in which a statement is made. It does not refer to the substance of a teacher's remarks. It does not refer to the time and place of his utterance."[153] The staff cites with approval Professor Ralph Fuchs's statement that "a violation [of academic responsibility] may consist of serious intemperateness of expression, intentional falsehood offered as a statement of fact, incitement of misconduct, or conceivably some other impropriety of circumstance."[154]

Professor Matthew Finkin notes that the "special responsibilities" outlined in paragraph (c) of the 1940 Statement subject extramural utterance to "a professional standard of care."[155] While true at a general level, this fails to recognize that the 1940 Statement creates a different set of professional duties for extramural utterance than for teaching, research, and intramural utterance. The four correlative obligations of academic freedom for extramural utterance are lower than the correlative obligations of academic freedom for teaching, research, and intramural utterance described earlier.[156] The four correlative obligations applicable to extramural utterance were a compromise between the AAUP and the AAC (now the AACU). One of the most controversial issues addressed in the 1940 Statement was the AAC's desire to subject the extramural utterances of academics to institutional discipline.[157] The AAC insisted that faculty members reach a line of professional propriety long before they reached a boundary between legally protected speech and libelous, seditious, or obscene utterances.[158] The four correlative obligations for extramural utterance in paragraph (c) of the 1940 Statement were the result of prolonged negotiation over these issues.[159]

The grant of rights of academic freedom to extramural utterance was a major achievement in 1940.[160] The Supreme Court did not articulate a clear test to protect freedom of speech of those academics who were government employees until 1968 in *Pickering v. Board of Education*,[161] and ultimately restricted such protection only to speech of public concern subject to a balancing test against the employer's interest. Academics in public higher education can claim protection for extramural speech under both the Constitution and professional academic freedom. Rights under the latter doctrine are subject to satisfaction of the four correlative obligations. Academics in private higher education can assert only professional academic freedom, unless the institution grants additional rights.

Correlative Duties of the Faculty as a Collegial Body in the 1940 Statement

Professional academic freedom also imposes two correlative duties on the faculty as a collegial body: (1) the duty to determine when individual professors inadequately meet their responsibilities of professional competence and ethical conduct; and (2) the duty to foster and defend the academic freedom of colleagues. The 1940 Statement briefly outlines the faculty's role in determining whether an individual professor has inadequately performed the correlative obligations of academic freedom. The Statement provides that "service [of tenured teachers] should be terminated only for adequate cause.... Termination for cause of a continuous appointment ... should, if possible, be considered by both a faculty committee and the governing board of the institution."[162] The AAUP's 1970 "Interpretive Comments" for the 1940 Statement adds that "[a] further specification of the academic due process to which the teacher is entitled ... is contained in the "Statement on Procedural Standards in Faculty Dismissal Proceedings."[163] The 1958 AAC (now the AACU)/AAUP "Statement of Procedural Standards in Faculty Dismissal Proceedings" urges that "[t]he faculty must be willing to recommend the dismissal of a colleague when necessary."[164] The 1915 Declaration on which the 1940 Statement builds sets forth a clearer understanding of the correlative duty of the faculty, as a collegial body, to determine when individual professors inadequately meet their responsibilities. The faculty must acquire "the capacity for impersonal judgment in such cases, and for judicial severity when the occasion requires it."[165] The 1915 Declaration exhorts the profession to be willing "to purge its ranks of the incompetent and the unworthy," and "to prevent ... [academic] freedom ... from being used as a shelter for inefficiency, for superficiality, or for uncritical and intemperate partisanship."[166]

With respect to competency, specifically, the AAUP's Committee A in 1946 reported:

> [T]he position of the Association [AAUP] is clear: far from protecting the incompetent, it welcomes and facilitates their elimination from the profession.... The Association ... accepts the principle that institutions of higher

education are conducted for the common good, and the common good demands competence. But in order that incompetents may be eliminated, and incompetents only, the Association insists upon two things: The first is that department heads, deans, and personnel committees shall be honest and courageous in their duty of detecting and eliminating the incompetent during the period of probation.... The second thing is that when an established teacher is accused of incompetence, he shall frankly be charged with it, given a hearing with due process, and retained or dismissed on the findings.[167]

In 1963, Committee A of the AAUP attempted to develop the meaning of paragraph (c) of the 1940 Statement on extramural utterance in terms of "academic responsibility." The Committee stated that academic freedom can endure only if it is matched by academic responsibility, but that academic responsibility is very difficult to define.[168] While the primary source of an acceptable level of academic responsibility will always be the individual conscience, "faculty and administration have a legitimate interest in the maintenance of proper standards of faculty responsibility on the part of all members of the academic community."[169] For a judgment as to the line between expression of views and improper acts, "recourse should be had in the first instance to a committee of the faculty. Both traditionally and practically, it is the *duty* and within the particular competence of the faculty to make the distinction and to recommend any appropriate action."[170] "The policy of permitting disciplinary action to be initiated by the administration is not likely to result in impairment of free utterance by faculty members if under established academic traditions and procedures the initial and primary judgment of an accused individual's action rests with his colleagues."[171]

Similarly, the AAUP's 1966 "Statement on Professional Ethics" provides that the individual institution of higher education assures the integrity of members of the profession. "[T]he individual institution ... should normally handle questions concerning propriety of conduct within its own framework by reference to a faculty group."[172]

The 1966 Statement also states a duty of ethical conduct to foster and defend the academic freedom of students and colleagues.[173] The 1970 AAUP Council's "Statement on Freedom and Responsibility" also emphasizes, in three places, the faculty's duty as a collegial body to defend academic freedom and to uphold it by its own action.[174] The Council urged faculties, during a period of zealotry,

to assume a more positive role as guardian of academic values against unjustified assaults from its own members. The traditional faculty function in disciplinary proceedings has been to ensure academic due process and meaningful faculty participation in the imposition of discipline by the administration. While this function should be maintained, faculties should recognize their stake in promoting adherence to norms essential to the academic enterprise.[175]

The 1973 report on faculty tenure by the joint AAC (now the AACU)/AAUP Commission on Academic Tenure again emphasizes the theme of faculty responsibility to ensure that standards of competence and ethical conduct are met. "The faculty of the institution ... must be the source for the definition and clarification of standards of professional conduct and must take the lead in ensuring that these standards are enforced."[176] The Commission noted that during the late 1960s assaults upon academic freedom from within the institution, by or with the toleration of members of faculties themselves, have gone unpunished. "In this situation there is a special urgency for faculties to accept their full corporate responsibility for the integrity of the profession. That responsibility cannot be avoided, it should not be assumed by others, and it must be fulfilled."[177]

Finally, in 1998, the AAUP's Committee B on Professional Ethics approved a statement, "On the Duty of Faculty Members to Speak Out on Misconduct."[178] The AAUP Council remanded the proposal to be redrafted to require individual institutions to formulate rules for reporting misconduct.[179] The original statement urged that when a professor has reason to believe that a faculty colleague has violated standards of professional behavior, the professor should take the initiative to inquire about or to protest against apparently unethical conduct.[180] The statement emphasized that the obligation to speak out is rooted in two considerations: (1) the common good, which is higher education's purpose, is best served "when members of the academic profession effectively regulate their own affairs"; and (2) "faculty members are members of a profession, and as such should guard their own standards of professional behavior."[181] By calling attention to abuses of those standards, "faculty members promote adherence to norms essential to maintaining the integrity and autonomy of the academic profession."[182] Our tradition of peer review, the linchpin of academic freedom, requires a faculty member who has reasonable evidence of misconduct to act.[183]

THE TRADITION OF SHARED GOVERNANCE

First Principles of the AAUP Tradition of Shared Governance

The AAUP's shared governance tradition is inextricably tied to the university's unique mission of both creating and disseminating knowledge, academic freedom, and peer review. As the American tradition of academic freedom evolved over the course of this past century, university employers, acknowledging the university's unique mission of creating and disseminating knowledge, granted rights of exceptional vocational freedom of speech to professors in teaching, research, and extramural utterance without interference, on the condition that individual professors meet correlative duties of professional competence and ethical conduct. The faculty, as a collegial body, also assumed the duty of peer review to enforce the obligations to be met by individual professors, and to defend the academic freedom of colleagues. It is this tradition of faculty self-governance in peer review of professional competence and ethics that is the linchpin of academic freedom in the United States.

It is critical to understand that this tradition of academic freedom and peer review did not displace the legal authority of the governing boards with faculty control. In contrast to some European countries, Professor Walter Metzger emphasizes that governments in the United States had not monopolized higher education (indeed the earliest and most elite colleges and universities were private), and professors were not officials of the state, but employees of the public and private governing boards. Because of the discretionary legal authority granted to employers in the United States, the professorate here faced a unique problem: "No other major academic system brought the lay world so deeply into the academy or set up so elaborate a machinery of on-site administrative control. In their preoccupation with this problem, American academics came firmly to believe that the primary concern of academic freedom was what happened *in* a university, not what happened *to* a university."[184]

The early leaders of the AAUP, Metzger finds, accepted the legal and political impregnability of the college charters and employment law that dictated lay, not faculty, control. They proposed the idea of administrative restraint. In the 1915 Declaration of Principles, they called for faculty participation in the prosecutorial and judicial processes of the university. This is the concept of peer review and academic due process discussed earlier.

There remained unaddressed many other types of decisions that directly affected the knowledge creation and dissemination missions of the university. To address these decisions, later AAUP documents over the course of this century softened the idea of board legal control into a concept of shared governance in administrative decision making. Shared governance concedes that the governing board is the final institutional authority by law but urges the governing board and its administrative agents to share

that authority with the voting faculty regarding matters central to the research and teaching missions.

The practice of shared governance is a corollary of the concepts of academic freedom and peer review. What do the rights of freedom to research
and freedom to teach mean in a system where peer review in the context
of a discipline defines competence and ethical conduct? Clearly, they do
not mean the freedom to write anything and call it research or to say anything and call it teaching. Rather in teaching, for example, the peer review paradigm means that peers determine the curriculum and standards
that define competence and ethical conduct in the discipline, and peers
hold individual professors accountable for carrying out the curriculum and
maintaining academic standards. Shared governance on matters of curriculum is thus a necessary condition for effective peer review, academic
freedom, and the mission of the university to create and disseminate knowledge.

The major AAUP statement directly addressing the practice of shared
governance is the 1966 "Statement on Government of Colleges and Universities" [formulated together with the American Council on Education
and the Association of Governing Boards of Universities and Colleges
(AGB)].[185] The Statement both recognizes a spectrum of types of decisions
within a university and allocates varying degrees of responsibility to the
voting faculty as a peer group depending upon how closely a type of decision relates to the core functions of research and teaching. Table 1 outlines
the allocation of responsibility. "Consultation" in this tradition includes:
(1) delegation to a reasonably representative faculty body, (2) full information necessary for a decision, (3) reasonable time for consideration,
(4) reasonable opportunity to confer periodically with the administration
and board, (5) reasonable opportunity for oral or written presentation of
faculty recommendations, and (6) a reasoned decision that is timely given
the scope of the decision at hand.

What is a "compelling reason" that might justify a board or administration reversal of the faculty's judgement? The 1966 Statement on Government of Colleges and Universities does not define the term. The AAUP's
Committee T on College and University Government considered what
reasons should be described as "compelling." Committee members noted
in their discussion that the compelling reasons standard calls for something
much stronger than disagreement with a faculty judgment. On the other
hand a compelling reason does not mean a reason that is irresistible that
virtually commands a decision. A compelling reason should be one which
"plainly outweighs persuasive contrary reasons."[186]

Table 1
1966 Statement on Government of Colleges and Universities

TYPE of DECISION	ALLOCATION of RESPONSIBILITY

< Determination of mission
< Strategic direction and comprehensive
  planning
< Physical and fiscal resources
< Budgeting and distribution of funds
< Selection and assessment of the
  president and deans
	The governing board and its administrative agents have primary responsibility for these decisions but the decisions should be informed by consultation with the voting faculty.

< Curriculum
< Procedures of student instruction
< Standards of faculty competence and
  ethical conduct including faculty
  appointments and faculty status
< Policies for admitting students
< Standards of student competence
< Maintenance of a suitable environment
  for learning
	The voting faculty should have primary authority over decisions about such matters—that is the governing board and administration should "concur with the faculty judgment except in rare instances and for compelling reasons, which should be stated in detail."

Among the areas of tension in the application of the "compelling reasons" standard is administrative or board reversals of faculty judgments on promotion and tenure. It is difficult to imagine sufficiently compelling reasons for a board reversal of unanimous faculty judgments on the issue of academic competence for individual candidates, unless the board concludes the faculty has abandoned obligations of peer review. A divided vote of the faculty on issues of faculty status itself provides some evidence that there are debatable issues of professional standards (assuming good faith academic judgment) in a particular faculty status controversy. The greater the division of judgment among the faculty, the greater the likelihood that the administration and board can articulate a compelling reason.

Compared to judgments on faculty status, the decision whether to create a program, department, school, college, division, or university system is on the other side of the spectrum of decisions. The governing board has primary responsibility for this type of decision. The AAUP's Committee A on Academic Freedom and Tenure in 1957 (revised several times) also put decisions to declare financial exigency on this side of the spectrum. A demonstrably bona fide financial exigency is defined as an imminent financial crisis which threatens the survival of the institution as a whole and which cannot be alleviated by less drastic means.[187] However, Committee A put on the other side of the spectrum in the area of primary authority of the faculty: (1) judgments determining *where* within the overall academic program terminations for financial exigency may occur, and (2) bona fide decisions to discontinue a program or department of instruction when no financial exigency is declared.[188] Table 2 makes these additions.

All of these allocations of primary responsibility follow logically from the tradition of peer review and academic freedom except those regarding the reallocation of resources. Judgments regarding where, within the over-

Table 2
1966 Statement on Government Plus 1957 Recommended Institutional Regulations on Academic Freedom and Tenure

TYPE of DECISION	ALLOCATION of RESPONSIBILITY
< Determination of mission < Strategic decisions and comprehensive planning < Physical and fiscal resources < Budgeting and distribution of funds < Decision to create a program, department, school, college, division, or university < Decision to declare financial exigency < Selection and assessment of the president and deans	The governing board and its administrative agents have primary responsibility for these decisions, but the decisions should be informed by consultation with the voting faculty.
< Curriculum < Procedures of student instruction < Standards of faculty competence and ethical conduct including faculty appointments and faculty status < Policies for admitting students < Standards of student competence < Maintenance of a suitable environment for learning < Judgments determining *where* within the overall academic program terminations for financial exigency should occur < Bona fide decisions to discontinue a program or department of instruction when no financial exigency is declared	The voting faculty should have primary authority over decisions about such matters—that is the governing board and administration should "concur with the faculty judgment except in rare instances and for compelling reasons, which should be stated in detail."
< Research < Classroom (and other) teaching activities	Individual professor has primary authority over such matters subject to peer review for competence and ethical conduct, and ultimate review by the board described immediately above.

all program, terminations for financial exigency may occur, or bona fide decisions to discontinue a program or department of instruction where no financial exigency is declared, seem to be principally matters of resource allocation and planning similar to the decision to create a program, department, school, college, division, or university. Issues of curricular integrity and coherence are evident in the creation, termination, or reduction in staff of a program or department, but the faculty's role is consultative on these issues. These matters are not directly related to the protection of academic freedom in teaching and research through peer review *unless* the financial exigency or programmatic change masks a goal of coercion of faculty speech. The risk that programmatic change masks a goal of coercion of academic speech increases as the number of affected professors grows smaller. Nonetheless, the burden should be on faculty to make a prima facie case that the governing board's actions are a pretext for such coercion. My intuition is that the professorate's interest in employment security caused Committee A in 1957 to overreach by claiming primary responsibility for decisions to cut back or terminate programs, departments, or faculties. The professorate's proper role on such decisions is consultative.

Another much more general overextension of shared governance is implicit in the 1966 Statement on Government. The Statement applies to all colleges and universities. Under this umbrella, the AAUP includes all institutions from community colleges (two-year degree) to research universities. The justification for exceptional rights of vocational freedom of speech (academic freedom), peer review, and shared governance is that they are necessary to achieve the university's mission of the creation and dissemination of knowledge.

Knowledge dissemination in this tradition focuses on a particular type of teaching that is closely tied to the creation of knowledge. The knowledge dissemination mission, for Professor Eric Ashby, is to teach in such a manner that the student learns the discipline of dissent.[189] The student must become familiar with what is already known about a subject, and then how to question that orthodoxy. The teaching develops in the student: (1) an understanding of first principles in a discipline; (2) a critical analytical ability; and (3) an understanding of the methods for resolving disputes within and among the disciplines.

The AAUP 1966 Statement creates one model of governance for all institutions, but not all institutions have a mission of knowledge creation and dissemination as described above. Some institutions have almost no knowledge creation mission, and their teaching mission may be remedial or simply technical education.[190]

First Principles of the 1998 Association of Governing Boards' (AGB) Statement on Institutional Governance

"Much Has Changed" Since 1966

With its 1998 Statement on Institutional Governance,[191] the AGB intends a break with earlier understandings of internal governance in higher education. The statement assiduously avoids any use of the words "shared governance." It notes that "much has changed in the three decades since the AAUP issued its Statement on Government of Colleges and Universities." At that time, the AGB "recommended" to its members but did not "endorse" the AAUP 1966 Statement. This book's introduction summarizes the changing market realities to which AGB refers.

The essential argument of the AGB Statement is that much has changed since 1966 in terms of market realities *except the internal governance of higher education.* An influential 1994 report published by the American Council on Education, "Corporate Lessons for American Higher Education," captures what is implicit in the 1998 AGB Statement.[192] The Corporate Lessons report argues that higher education in the 1990s reflects the situation that existed in American corporations over a decade ago, namely:

- a well-entrenched bureaucracy;
- unwritten guarantees to employees of lifetime employment;
- compensation to some employees for just showing up; a culture where customers are irritants rather than the reason for the enterprise's existence;
- rapid change created by new technology and new competitors;
- innovation smothered by bureaucracy; and inertia causing things to be done simply because they had always been done.

Business and government leaders see higher education as having failed to reform or restructure internal governance and management the way business did in the late 80s and 90s in order to better maintain competitiveness. They believe higher education should adopt models of corporate governance and management proven successful in service-oriented businesses.

Seven First Principles

The AGB recommends seven principles to help governing boards restructure internal governance.[193]

1. "Ultimate responsibility for the institution rests in its governing board. . . . Traditionally, and *for practical reasons*, boards delegate some

kinds of authority to other stakeholders. . . . " (emphasis added, the board retains implicit or explicit rights of review.)

2. "The governing board should retain ultimate responsibility and full authority to determine the mission of the institution ... in consultation with and on the advice of the chief executive." The board is also responsible for establishing strategic direction through a comprehensive planning process involving other stakeholders.

3. "Colleges and universities have many of the characteristics of business enterprises. Consequently, boards should ensure that, as corporations, their institutions' fiscal and managerial affairs are administered with appropriate attention to commonly accepted business standards. . . . At the same time ... they do not operate with a profit motive. . . . By virtue of their *special mission* and purpose in a pluralistic society, they have a tradition of participation in institutional governance that is less common in and less appropriate for businesses" [emphasis added].

4. "The governing board should conduct its affairs in a manner that exemplifies the behavior it expects of other participants in institutional governance. . . . They should ... in appropriate instances and in consultation with the chief executive—afford contending parties an opportunity to present their views. The board should be prepared to set forth reasons for its decisions."

5. "Historically, higher education governance has included three principal internal stakeholders: governing boards, administrators, and the full-time faculty. In fact, other stakeholders exist and in increasing numbers [listing non-academic staff, non-tenure track faculty, and students]." The board "is responsible for establishing the rules by which [diverse internal stakeholders] voices are considered."

6. "All board members, regardless of how they come to the board, should feel a responsibility to serve the institution or the system as a whole and not any particular constituency or segment of the organization."

7. In multicampus systems, "the system governing board should clarify the responsibilities of the campus heads, the system heads, and institutional, quasi-governing or advisory boards. . . . "

While the AGB Statement recommends seven principles to help governing boards restructure internal governance, the seven recommendations boil down to two major principles. First, colleges and universities have many characteristics of nonprofit business enterprises. Governing boards have ultimate responsibility for the institution or system, including determination of the mission and strategic direction. Individual board members should serve the best interests of the institution or system as a whole. The board should clarify responsibilities in multilevel systems. Second, because of tradition and for practical reasons, boards have delegated some kinds of activity to other stakeholders, and have involved other stakeholders in appropriate decisions including comprehensive planning processes. Although, historically, governance has included three principal stakeholders, viz., governing boards, administrators and the full-time faculty, other stakeholders (nonacademic staff, nontenure track faculty, and students) exist in increasing numbers and the board is responsible for establishing rules by which all stakeholders' voices are considered.

Table 3 outlines a comparison of the allocation of responsibility for governance in the AAUP tradition and in the 1998 AGB Statements.

Table 3
Comparison of AAUP Shared Governance Tradition and
1998 AGB Institutional Governance Statement

TYPE of DECISION	ALLOCATION of RESPONSIBILITY in AAUP TRADITION	ALLOCATION of RESPONSIBILITY in 1998 AGB STATEMENT
1. Determination	The governing board and its administrative agents have primary responsibility for these decisions, but the decisions should be informed by consultation with voting faculty.	The governing board has ultimate responsibility to determine the mission in consultation with the chief executive.
2. Strategic decisions and comprehensive planning	Same as #1	The governing board is responsible for establishing strategic direction and comprehensive planning although the board should work towards a consensus or understanding on the part of stakeholders. (The full-time faculty is one principal stakeholder along with nonacademic staff, part-time faculty, and students.)
3. Physical and fiscal resources 4. Budgeting and distribution of funds	Same as #1	The governing board should set budget guidelines concerning resource allocation on the basis of assumptions, usually developed by the administration, that are widely communicated to interested stakeholders and subject to ample opportunity for challenge.
5. Decision to create a program, department, school,	Same as #1	The governing board should reserve the right to ratify proposals to adopt major new academic programs.
6. Decision to declare financial exigency	Same as #1	The governing board should first consult stakeholders and describe the analysis that led to the ultimate determination.
7. Selection and assessment of the president and deans	Same as #1	Governing boards have the sole responsibility to appoint and assess the chief executive. Assessment should be in consultation with other stakeholder groups, as the board may deem appropriate.

Table 3 (Continued)

8. Curriculum 9. Procedures of student instruction 10. Standards of faculty competence and ethical conduct including faculty appointments and faculty status	The voting faculty should have primary authority over decisions about such matters– that is the governing board and administration should concur with the faculty judgment except in rare instances and for compelling reasons, which should be stated in detail.	Curricular matters and decisions regarding individual faculty appointments, promotions, and contract renewal would normally fall within the delegated decision-making authority of appropriate faculty and administrative entities.
11. Policies for admitting students 12. Standards of student competence 13. Maintenance of a suitable environment for learning	Same as #10	These decisions are not mentioned specifically but presumably fall within the framework immediately above.
14. Judgments determining *where* within the overall academic program terminations for financial exigency should occur 15. Bona fide decisions to discontinue a program or department of instruction when no financial exigency is declared	Same as #10	The governing board should ask the administration to create a process for decision-making that includes full consultation and full communication with stakeholder groups.
16. Classroom (and other teaching activities) 17. Research	Individual professor has primary authority over such matters subject to peer review for competence and ethical conduct, and ultimate review by the board described immediately above.	These are not mentioned specially except for the following "just as administrators and boards should respect the need for individual faculty members to exercise academic freedom in their classrooms and laboratories, boards should avoid the temptation to micromanage in matters of administration."

Three Major Breaks from Academic Tradition in the AGB Statement

There are three major breaks from academic tradition in the AGB Statement. The sharpest break is the AGB Statement's emphasis that higher education has many of the characteristics of business enterprises (particularly nonprofit enterprises), constrained by higher education's "special mission and purpose in a pluralistic society. . . ." The "special mission" is not defined or explained. The Statement mentions academic freedom once only peripherally, noting that "Just as administrators and boards should respect the need for individual faculty members to exercise academic freedom in their classrooms and laboratories, boards should avoid the temptation to micromanage on matters of administration."[194] The AGB Statement makes no connection among mission, academic freedom, and shared governance, noting only that "*for practical reasons*, boards delegate some kinds of authority to other stakeholders [emphasis added]."[195] In contrast, academic tradition emphasizes that the mission of higher education is the creation and dissemination of knowledge (with the constraint that revenues cover costs). Academic freedom, peer review, and shared governance are necessary to achieve the mission.

The second major break with academic tradition is that the AGB Statement imports the idea of stakeholder analysis from the business ethics literature. Stakeholder analysis calls for business decision makers to consider impact on and interests of not just shareholders, but also employees, customers, suppliers, and the communities in which the business operates. With the exception of curricular or faculty status decisions, where the faculty share the board's delegation of power with administrators, the AGB statement makes the full-time voting faculty into one internal stakeholder for the governing board to consult, together with nonacademic staff; students; and nontenure track, part-time, and adjunct faculty. Academic tradition gives the full-time voting faculty primacy in areas related to research and teaching in order to realize the mission of creating and disseminating knowledge.

The third major break with earlier tradition is that, similar to the AAUP tradition, the AGB Statement advocates general principles that implicitly assume one model fits all. While the AAUP tradition creates a model of shared governance based on the assumption that all institutions create knowledge and teach the discipline of dissent, the AGB Statement creates a template for institutional governance based on the assumption that there is a limited or no knowledge creation mission. The AGB emphasizes that community colleges now enroll almost one-half of all students in higher education and that nontenure-eligible, part-time, and adjunct faculty now predominate in community colleges. To the degree that the mission of creating knowledge and teaching the discipline of dissent is limited at a community college, it is difficult to distinguish the institution from the purely teaching mission of secondary education, where there are no rights of professional academic freedom, peer review, or shared governance.

Common Ground

Mutual Commitment to Fulfill the Public Trust

No one benefits when governing boards, administrators, and the academic profession talk past one another or point fingers at one another. "Us" versus "them," a common theme in faculty and board thinking, takes us nowhere. The university serving its mission of seeking, discovery, and disseminating knowledge is one of humankind's greatest achievements. The mission can be achieved only through the joint effort of governing boards, administrators, and the academic profession. All three groups are in positions of public trust to work cooperatively to achieve the mission.

> In Restructuring American Education, Michael Katz writes that the university "should be a community of persons united by collective understandings, by common and communal goals, by bonds of reciprocal obligation, and by a flow of sentiments which makes the preservation of community an object of desire, not merely a matter of prudence or a command of duty. Community implies a form of social obligation governed by principles different from those operative in the marketplace and the state."[196]

Both the professorate and governing boards and administrators can do better to create a culture of collective understanding and communal goals in the service of higher education's mission.

The Responsibilities of the Academic Profession

The academic profession must acknowledge both the need for the socialization of its members into academic tradition and the need to respond to market realities, particularly long-term higher-than-inflation cost increases and changing enrollment patterns. Many faculty members have had no significant grounding in the tradition of academic freedom, peer review, and shared governance in the United States. They are socialized into a discipline, not into the academic profession. As a result, they poorly understand the traditions of the profession, particularly the profession's collective duties. As noted earlier, Professor Keetjie Ramo concludes that:

> The professorate has yet to find an effective, universal means through which to systematically imbue in the future and neophyte members a sense of academic culture that cuts across disciplinary lines. Individual professors fail to identify with the professorate as a professional culture.[197]

Over the last thirty years, other professions have moved toward mandatory education in professional tradition and ethics to protect and buttress peer review and professional autonomy. It is ironic that the academic profession, responsible for teaching in higher education, fails to educate its own members concerning the profession.

Education may counteract growing centrifugal forces in the academy that are undermining the commitment of individual faculty to shared governance. Faculty members have more attachments to disciplinary rewards, outside funding agencies, and off-campus consulting opportunities and political interests. Information technology, voice mail, and e-mail encourage working at home and less interaction with colleagues. University of California President Emeritus Clark Kerr observed in 1994 that:

> All over the United States, it is more difficult than it once was to get university teachers to take seriously their departmental and college responsibilities. They are reluctant to serve on committees, and more reluctant to make time readily available when they do, and more reluctant to accept the responsibilities of writing good reports. They wish to concentrate on their own affairs and not those of the institution.[198]

In each generation a profession must also educate the public about the social compact of the profession with society, and how the profession fulfills its duties to serve the common good. In the case of the academic profession, the focus of this education must be on the governing boards and business and government leaders. The shared governance tradition rests on an educated and enlightened governing board concerning the mission of the university and academic tradition. Again it is ironic that faculty members, whose profession is teaching, complain that governing boards and administrators lack knowledge about academic tradition and values. Has the profession stepped forward to provide such education?

If the academic profession fails to commit itself to what former Harvard Dean Henry Rosovsky has called "professorial civic virtue" in both peer review and shared governance, it is clear that others will assume that the authority should be theirs. Professor Arthur Lovejoy, one of the founders of the AAUP, emphasized almost eighty years ago that:

> If [those] whose essential business is teaching and investigation take no time at all for reflecting methodically upon the general problems and needs and the external relations of their profession, for discussing these things with their colleagues, and for using their collective power with respect to them, they will presently find that the forces which shape and limit the activities of their profession, which affect its efficiency, and control the general education and scientific development of the country, will be directed wholly by [those] whose essential business is *not* teaching and investigation.[199]

The academic profession must acknowledge market realities and work with governing boards and administrators to address them. At many institutions, costs to students cannot keep increasing in real terms. At some institutions, corporate for-profit and on-line enterprises are a serious threat. It is a reality that enrollment patterns shift, and that governors and legislators need assurance that public dollars are spent wisely.

Medicine, also one of the original learned professions, discovered that long-term cost increases in real terms for a critical service invite both government and business intervention to limit the profession's autonomy. Many members of the legal profession, another of the original learned professions, argue that the profession is simply a business where greed and careerism should play the same role as in the market generally. Clients respond with legal audits and the use of nonlawyers wherever possible, including alternative dispute resolution with minimal lawyer intervention. Public respect for the profession plummets. In Europe, the Big Five accounting firms are now the biggest law firms. If the academic profession responds to market changes by emphasizing self-interest and job security rather than the defense of transcendental purpose, academic tradition, and the fulfillment of its duties, we will follow the same path as our sister professions.

The Responsibilities of the Governing Board and Its Administrators

The governing board and its administrators have the fiduciary duty to educate themselves about the mission of higher education and academic tradition. The AGB's 1996 Report, "Renewing the Academic Presidency: Stronger Leadership for Tougher Times," concluded that

> unfortunately, too many trustees lack a basic understanding of higher education or a significant commitment to it. In extensive interviewing, the commission found instance after instance in which boards were either inadequately engaged with their institutions or, conversely, inappropriately involved in detail. . . . Many trustees understand neither the concept of service on a board as a public trust nor their responsibilities to the entire institution.[200]

The governing board also has a fiduciary duty to create a healthy institutional environment on governance that serves the mission. An "us versus them" environment is a major failure of the governing board. Boards should join the faculty in supporting education and engagement in academic tradition, the rights and correlative duties of academic freedom, and shared governance. In areas of the governing board's primary responsibility, boards must engage in good faith consultation with faculty, not lip service to consultation.

The most critical lesson for the governing boards and administrators to remember is that the mission of higher education and of the academic profession is the creation and dissemination of knowledge. The AGB's 1996 Report on the Academic Presidency emphasizes that knowledge is the foundation of the American future. The university and the academic profession are about the pursuit of knowledge; seeking efficiency and ensuring that revenues cover costs function to constrain the mission but they are not the mission per se. As President emeritus Kerr notes,

> The pursuit of knowledge means that everything is open for reconsideration at all times, that the conflict of mind with mind is of high value and can be pursued acceptably with intense personal commitment, and that the individual is at the heart of the enterprise....[201]

Boards and administrators must recognize that the faculty's areas of primary authority in shared governance tradition follow directly from the mission of higher education to create and disseminate knowledge. The faculty want governance ideas relating to the core mission to be subjected to the same type of informed public criticism and the give-and-take of reasoned argument that is foundational for teaching and research. However, teaching and research activities both are subject to schedules and deadlines, and the teacher/scholar does the best job possible within the time available. Faculty can also accept time constraints with regard to governance. Boards, administrators, and faculty members should work together to establish reasonable timetables for different types of decisions, timely flow of information, and optimal procedural mechanisms for debate and decision making within the time available.

The most critical support for the faculty's academic leadership in its areas of primary authority would be for boards and administrators to remember the mission of higher education: the creation and dissemination of knowledge. Knowledge creation occurs from the bottom up, not from the top down, and it infuses teaching and public service from the bottom up.

Burton Clark, in *The Higher Education System* (1983), captured how institutional change occurs in a bottom-heavy knowledge-creation organization.

> Despite the belief of many observers that academic systems change significantly only when pressured by external forces, such systems increasingly exhibit innovation and adaptation among their bottom units. Invention and diffusion are institutionalized in the work of the departments and counterpart units that embody the disciplines and professions. Universities, and many non-university units, move ahead in a somewhat self-propelled fashion in those areas of new thought that are perceived by academics as ac-

ceptable within general paradigms of academic knowledge. Such change is widely over-looked since it is not announced in master plans or ministerial bulletins and is not introduced on a global scale. It occurs in segments of the operating level that exchange with one another and is not characteristic of the larger entities. In a bottom-heavy knowledge institution, grassroots innovation is a crucial form of change.

[T]he leading false expectation in academic reform is that major results can be obtained by top-down manipulation. Such reforms are occasionally initiated and implemented, but more commonly small results follow from multiple efforts at the top, in the middle, or at the bottom that entail wrong experiments, false starts, and zigzag adjustments, a melange of actions out of which precipitate some flows of change. Dramatic examples of such flows are found in the evolutionary buildup of knowledge in first the physical sciences in the twentieth century, accompanied by an increasing dominance of these fields in resources and power within universities and national systems.[202]

Humankind sometimes creates institutions that, however imperfect, are substantial steps forward in realizing human potential compared to the alternatives. The university, the academic profession, and the 750-year-old traditions they have built are steps in this direction. Those holding the public trust should move carefully in concluding the crisis of the moment is so draconian and the university and the academic profession are so broken that both must be dramatically "fixed." Is the current market-driven crisis more serious than others in the last 750 years? Why? Have other means of change, like education itself, been tried?

One Model Does Not Fit All in Shared Governance

The AAUP model of shared governance is based on institutions with a substantial mission of creating knowledge and teaching the discipline of dissent, but the AAUP advocates the model for all of higher education, including community colleges. The AGB template of institutional governance acknowledges only that higher education has "a special mission and purpose in a pluralistic society," without reference to the university's knowledge creation and dissemination mission and the mission's relationship to academic freedom, peer review, and shared governance. Emphasizing that community colleges now enroll almost one-half of all students in higher education, and that nontenure-eligible, part-time, and adjunct faculty now predominate in community colleges, the AGB recommends a governance template for all institutions that is most suitable for community colleges with a limited or no knowledge creation mission.

Both sides should move toward the design of governance models appropriate to the mission of particular subsets of institutions within the universe of higher education. For example, to the degree that the mission of a community college is far more closely aligned with the teaching mission of secondary education than with the knowledge creation mission of research and doctoral granting universities, governance structures should be designed to reflect these differences in mission.

Conclusion

The academic profession, governing boards, and administrators all share fiduciary commitments to fulfill the public trust in seeking, discovering, and disseminating knowledge. Education in academic tradition, academic freedom, peer review, and shared governance is the single most important step for each group to undertake. From common understanding, common ground will follow.

STUDENT ACADEMIC FREEDOM

During the post–Civil War development of the modern university in the United States, the professorate borrowed heavily from the German university tradition of Lernfreiheit or the freedom to teach to define the American tradition of professional academic freedom. In those formative years, the professorate chose not to accept the complementary German university tradition of Lehrfreiheit or the freedom to learn.

Professor Hofstadter and Professor Metzger describe Lernfreiheit as the "absence of administrative coercion in the learning situation." Lernfreiheit meant that German university students "were free to roam from place to place, sampling academic wares; that wherever they lighted, they were free to determine the choice and sequence of courses, and were responsible to no one for regular attendance; that they were exempted from all tests save the final examination and that they lived in private quarters and controlled their private lives."[203]

Professor Howard Jones explains that American higher education did not adopt the Lernfreiheit tradition for four reasons: first, American law treated institutions of higher education as standing in *loco parentis* with respect to their students, particularly if they were minors; second, American higher education intentionally courted parental interest in the life of the institution; third, American undergraduate students wanted freedom but tended also not to want the responsibility that freedom entailed—the students in fact wanted more structure in advancing toward a degree than the European model; and fourth, the American university borrowed a graduate education model from the German university, but the undergraduate education model from the British undergraduate college, where students tended to be younger and less mature than the German university student.[204]

The freedom of students to learn in the United States is thus structured and restricted by requirements not evident in the German tradition.[205] Students, to earn a degree, must satisfy substantially more comprehensive and structured standards of competence set by each professor in individual courses and by the institution as a whole.

Over 50 years after the 1915 Declaration and over 25 years after the 1940 Statement, the AAUP developed a formal statement on students' academic freedom. In 1967, the AAUP, the National Student Association (now the United States Student Association), the Association of American Colleges (now the Association of American Colleges and Universities), and other groups adopted a Joint Statement on Rights and Freedoms of Students. This is reprinted in the Appendices.

The Joint Statement recognizes that students are not yet certified to participate in the scholarly discourse of a discipline leading to the creation of knowledge, and thus do not have the same academic freedom rights as the professorate. The Statement provides that, "As members of the academic community, students should be encouraged to develop the capacity for critical judgment and to engage in a sustained and independent search for truth."[206]

With respect to student academic freedom in instructional settings, the Joint Statement provides that:

> In the classroom and in conference, the professor "should encourage free discussion, inquiry, and expression. Student performance should be evaluated solely on an academic basis, not on opinions or conduct in matters unrelated to academic standards."
>
> "Students should be free to take reasoned exception to the data or views offered in any course of study and to reserve judgment about matters of opinion, but they are responsible for learning the content of any course of study for which they are enrolled."
>
> "Students should have protection through orderly procedures against prejudiced or capricious academic evaluation. At the same time they are responsible for maintaining standards of academic performance established for each course in which they enrolled."[207]

With respect to student affairs, the Joint Statement requires that,

Students "should be free to organize and join associations to promote their common interests."

"Students and student organizations should be free to examine and discuss all questions of interest to them and express opinions publicly and privately."

Students "should always be free to support causes by orderly means which do not disrupt the regular and essential operations of the institution."

Students should make clear "that in their public expressions or demonstrations, students or student organizations speak only for themselves."

"Students should be allowed to invite and to hear any person of their own choosing."

Students "should make clear ... that sponsorship of guest speakers does not necessarily imply approval or endorsement of the views expressed, either by the sponsoring group or by the institution."[208]

With respect to internal governance, the Joint Statement also provides that "students should be free, individually and collectively, to express their views on issues of institutional policy and on matters of general interest to the student body." Regarding student publications, "The student press should be free of censorship and advance approval of copy...." Students should also enjoy the same freedom of speech and assembly off-campus as other citizens.[209]

The AAUP Council adopted a Statement on Graduate Students in 2000. Recognizing both that graduate students are far closer to certification to participate in scholarly discourse in a discipline and that graduate students carry out many of the functions of faculty members, this statement urges the professorate to grant graduate students greater academic freedom. "Moreover, because of their advanced education, graduate students should be encouraged by their professors to exercise their freedom of discussion, inquiry and expression.... Graduate students' freedom of inquiry is necessarily qualified by their still being learners in the profession; nonetheless, their faculty mentors should afford them latitude and respect as they decide how they will engage in teaching and research."[210]

The 2000 Statement on Graduate Students emphasizes in particular the graduate student's right to receive credit for scholarly contributions. "Graduate students are entitled to the protection of their intellectual property rights, including recognition of their participation in supervised research and their research with faculty, consistent with generally accepted standards of attribution and acknowledgment in collaborative settings."[211]

Finally, the 2000 Statement on Graduate Students emphasizes education on academic ethics. "Departments should endeavor to acquaint students with the norms and traditions of their academic discipline...."[212]

NOTES

1. See Jonathan Rauch, *Kindly Inquisitors* 45 (1993); Mario V. Llosa, "The Importance of Karl Popper," *Academic Questions* (Winter 1991–1992): 16.

2. See Rauch, 46.

3. John R. Searle, "Rationality and Realism, What is at Stake," reprinted in Richard De George, *Academic Freedom and Tenure: Ethical Issues* (1993): 200.

4. Ibid.

5. See ibid.

6. See Rauch, 116–117; Thomas L. Haskell, "Justifying the Rights of Academic Freedom in the Era of Power/Knowledge," in *The Future of Academic Freedom* (Louis Menand, ed., 1996): 47, 63. The professorate's demand for professional academic freedom developed during the nineteenth century as higher education shifted its focus from essentially religious and moral training for the elite professions to a much broader intellectual inquiry based on the premise that trained reason, principally through the scientific method, could grasp the essentials of human activity and advance human welfare. As Georgetown law professor Byrne notes, this endeavor presupposes:

> a progressive conception of knowledge. Understanding at any one moment is imperfect, and defects can be exposed by testing hypotheses against reality, through either adducing new data or experimentation. The process of hypothesis–experimentation–new hypothesis improves knowledge and brings us closer to a complete, more nearly objective truth about the world. Error is not dangerous so long as the process is continued, because acknowledged means will expose it; in fact, it [error] is actually beneficial (and inevitable) as part of progressive discovery.... The process of theory, dispute, and experiment, rather than producing anxiety about the continuity of the community, is celebrated as intrinsic to the pursuit of truth.

J. Peter Byrne, "Academic Freedom: A Special Concern of the First Amendment," 99 *Yale Law Journal* (1989): 251, 273–275 [hereinafter Byrne, "A Special Concern"] (quoting Robert M. MacIver, *Academic Freedom in Our Time* (1955)). This awareness of the possibility of error and fallibility does not mean that knowledge is unattainable, but that, to reach it, one must always be ready to reexamine and correct one's view and to tolerate those who contest established knowledge.

7. A research ethics textbook published by the National Academy of Sciences concludes:

> The object of research is to extend human knowledge of the physical, biological or social world beyond what is already known. But an individual's knowledge properly enters the domain of science only after it is presented in such a fashion that others can independently judge its validity.... Throughout this continuum of discussion and deliberation, the ideas of individuals are collectively judged, sorted

and selectively incorporated into the consensual but ever evolving scientific worldview. In the process, individual knowledge is gradually converted into generally accepted knowledge.

Committee on Science, Engineering and Public Policy, National Academy of Sciences, On Being a Scientist: Responsible Conduct in Research (2d. ed. 1994): 3.

In the liberal intellectual system, all knowledge claims are revisable. "Scientific results are inherently provisional. Scientists can never prove conclusively that they have described some aspect of the natural or physical world with complete accuracy." Ibid. at 15. Our confidence in a knowledge claim grows as it is subjected to criticism and testing.

Frederick Grinnell explains

[A]t every step of the process, researchers continually reshape their work to anticipate and respond to the criticism that they expect to receive from their peers. Only when others validate the observations—often modifying them at the same time—will the new work become accepted. Objectivity is embedded in the group, not the individual....

Returning to the analogy of the baseball umpire, it should now be clear that in the everyday practice of science, individual researchers call things as they see them. Calling things as they are is reserved for scientists acting collectively, and even those calls are tentative. That is, scientists are satisfied with credibility in the present, reserving truth for the future.

Frederick Grinnell, "The Practice of Science at the Edge of Knowledge," Chronicle of Higher Education (March 24, 2000): B11–12.

Analyzing John Dewey's work, Professor Thomas Bender observes that,

Dewey did not expect to arrive at universal reason, at absolute truth. His truths would be contextual, specific to time and place, always experimental, rooted in history but continually refined, reduced of their subjectivities through a process of public discussion.

If Dewey developed a philosophical anthropology that accepted historical contingency and uncertainty, he did not thereby embrace subjectivity. He acknowledged the difference that social position produced in politics and philosophical outlook. He granted a role to interest and difference. But if he never denied the inevitability of subjectivity, his aim was always the reduction of subjectivity in the forming of public truths.... Dewey did not offer the prospect of permanent truth, nor even rational certitude. What his participatory community of truth makers may achieve is a reasoned truth. Such truth will not be objective in any absolute sense, although the content it implies will at once accommodate interest and reduce subjectivity. What he proposes for us is the possibility of ever more secure but never completely secure truths.

Thomas Bender, "Intellectual and Public Life: Essays on the Social History of Academic Intellectuals in the United States" 139 (1993).

8. Rauch, 116.

9. See ibid. at 68–70; see also Byrne, "A Special Concern," at 268–269. "The modern university ... is the true child of the Enlightenment. At its core stands the rational scientific pursuit of knowledge.... The value of cognitive rationality,

as Talcott Parsons pointed out some time ago, provides the modern university with its autonomy." Brigget Berger, "The Idea of the University," 58 *Partisan Review* (1991): 315, 328.

10. Since the emergence of the modern university after the Civil War, higher education in the United States has experienced seven waves of zealotry aimed at suppressing freedom of academic thought and speech. These waves originated in (1) the religious fundamentalism of trustees and administrators in the late nineteenth century; (2) the unfettered capitalism of trustees at the turn of the century; (3) patriotism in World War I; (4) anticommunism prior to WWII; (5) McCarthyism in the early 1950s; (6) student activism in the mid to late 1960s; and (7) the fundamentalism of the radical academic left in the late 1980s and 1990s. Neil Hamilton, *Zealotry and Academic Freedom*, (1995): chs. 1–4 [hereinafter Hamilton, *Zealotry*].

11. John R. Searle, "Two Concepts of Academic Freedom," in *The Concept of Academic Freedom* (Edmund Pincoffs ed., 1972): 88. Thomas L. Haskell observes that "communities of the competent" formed in the late 1800s in history, chemistry, engineering, and other fields, and these communities are the seed crystals around which the modern university formed. See Haskell, 42–43. Defending their authority to make knowledge claims is what academic freedom is about. Ibid.

12. Byrne, "A Special Concern," 258.

13. See ibid. 258–259.

14. See ibid. 259. Edward Shils notes that "[t]he range of 'reasonable disagreement' is the range over which academic freedom entitles individual academics to be free to investigate." Edward Shils, *The Order of Learning* (1997): 218 [hereinafter Shils, *The Order*].

15. See Byrne, "A Special Concern," at 275.

16. See ibid. 268–269.

17. See Hamilton, *Zealotry*, at 9–14.

18. See ibid. 196.

19. Error is inevitable in an intellectual system where even generally accepted knowledge claims may be proven wrong by future research. Errors arising from the responsible and reasonable best practice of the discipline are accepted. Even the most responsible scientist can make an honest mistake:

> Mistakes made through negligent work are treated more harshly. Haste, carelessness, inattention or any number of faults—can lead to work that does not meet the standards demanded in science....
>
> Beyond honest errors and errors caused through negligence are a third category of errors: those that involve deception. Making up data (fabrication), changing or misreporting data or results (falsification) and using the ideas or words of another (plagiarism)—all strike at the heart of the values on which science is based.

Committee on Science, Engineering, and Public Policy, National Academy of Sciences, *On Being a Scientist: Responsible Conduct in Research* (2d ed. 1994): 26–28. See Byrne, "A Special Concern," at 275–276; J. Peter Byrne, "Racial Insults and Free Speech Within the University," 79 *Georgetown Law Journal* (1991): 399, 417;

Richard Hofstadter and Walter Metzger, *The Development of Academic Freedom in the United States* (1955): 364–66.
20. See Hamilton, *Zealotry*, 13–14.
21. See ibid.
22. See generally ibid. 14, 163.
23. This book uses as synonyms the following terms: "duties correlative with rights" (from the 1940 Statement), "correlative duties," "corresponding duties" (from the 1915 Declaration), "correlative obligations" (from the 1915 Declaration), and "special responsibilities" (from the 1970 Interpretation of the 1940 Statement and the 1966 Statement on Professional Ethics).
24. Thomas L. Haskell emphasizes that "[t]he cardinal principle of professional autonomy is collegial self-governance; its inescapable corollary is that only one's peers are competent to judge one's performance." Haskell, 46.

> Historically speaking, the heart and soul of academic freedom lies not in free speech but in professional autonomy and collegial self-governance. Academic freedom came into being as a defense of the disciplinary community (or more exactly, the university conceived as an ensemble of such communities), and if academic freedom is to do the work we expect of it, it must continue to be at bottom a denial that anyone outside the community is fully competent to pass judgment in matters falling within the community's domain.

Ibid. at 54.
Professor Thomas Bender adds:

> Neither the AEA [American Economic Association] in the 1890s nor, for that matter, the American Association of University Professors (AAUP) in 1915 stood forthrightly for the freedom to express radical or controversial views. The real issue for them was professorial, not civil or intellectual. They defended expertise in its proper area, and they strenuously asserted that academic peers, not trustees of universities, were the only legitimate judges of academic performance.

Bender, 61.
Professor Rebecca Eisenberg emphasizes that the authors of the 1915 declaration did not argue for unqualified professional autonomy; to the contrary, the authors warned that the *only* way to preserve freedom from lay interference is through a system of accountability to professional peers. See Rebecca Eisenberg, "Academic Freedom and Academic Values in Sponsored Research," 66 *Texas Law Review* (1988): 1363, 1366–1367.
Professor David Rabban stresses the same point,

> Standards of scholarly inquiry and professional ethics define the extent to which academic freedom protects individual autonomy. The traditional conception makes faculty peers primarily responsible for applying these limiting standards. But it also advised administrators and governing boards to monitor the faculty peers and over-rule their substantive decisions when there are compelling grounds for concluding that the peers themselves have departed from professional standards of judgment.

David Rabban, "Does Academic Freedom Limit Faculty Autonomy?" 66 *Texas Law Review* (1988): 1405, 1407–1408 [hereinafter Rabban, "Does Academic Freedom"].

25. 354 U.S. 234 (1957).

26. 391 U.S. 563 (1968).

27. See Hamilton, *Zealotry*, 195–196.

28. For a full discussion of these differences, see Hamilton, *Zealotry*, 187–227.

29. Christine Licata, "Post-Tenure Review: National Trends, Questions and Concerns," 24 *Innovative Higher Education* (1999): 5, 7 [hereinafter Licata, "Post-Tenure Review"].

30. Ibid. 7–9.

31. Christine Licata, "Precepts for Post-Tenure Reviews," *Trusteeship* (Dec. 1999): 8 [hereinafter Licata, "Precepts"].

32. See Cheryl Sternman Rule, "After the Big Decision: Post-Tenure Review Analyzed," in *Policies on Faculty Appointment* 180 (Cathy Trower ed., 2000).

33. See ibid.

34. Licata, "Post-Tenure Review," 10.

35. Licata, "Precepts for Post-Tenure Review," 13.

36. See Judith Swazey et al., 542, 549.

37. Ibid.

38. Ibid.

39. Sheila Slaughter, "Dirty Little Secrets: Academic Freedom, Governance and Professionalism," in *Academic Freedom, An Everyday Concern* (Ernst Benjamin and Donald Wagner eds., 1994): 59, 61–62.

40. William Van Alstyne, "The Specific Theory of Academic Freedom and the General Issue of Liberty," in *The Concept of Academic Freedom* (Edmund Pincoffs ed., 1972): 59, 76 (emphasis added).

41. Fritz Machlup, "On Some Misconceptions Concerning Academic Freedom," in *Academic Freedom and Tenure* (Louis Joughin ed., 1969): App. B 177, 189.

42. Walter Metzger, "Academic Freedom in America," reprinted in *Commission on Academic Tenure in Higher Education, Faculty Tenure* (1973): 3, 143–44.

43. Ibid.

44. American Association of University Professors, "The 1915 General Declaration of Principles," reprinted in *Academic Freedom and Tenure* (Lewis Joughin ed., 1969): app. A 155, 170 [hereinafter AAUP, "1915 Declaration"].

45. The rights of professional academic freedom established in the AAUP statements are also adjudicated in individual cases. See Hamilton, *Zealotry*, 262 n.38. The AAUP receives approximately 800-1,000 complaints each year alleging violations of the rights of academic freedom. The AAUP undertakes formal investigation only on those complaints that the AAUP's general secretary believes involve a prima facie denial of academic freedom. In the event an investigation is made, ultimately an ad hoc investigating committee prepares a report that is submitted to the Association's Committee A. These reports do not constitute a coordinated and systematic body of common law similar to that of a judicial tribunal. Each report is an elaborate factual presentation by a different ad hoc committee, and there is no practice of citing prior cases as precedent. The uni-

versity or college administration may or may not participate in the investigation. There is no trial-type hearing.

The AAUP's docket has been overwhelmingly dominated by extramural or intramural utterance cases. Cases involving "conflicts over personal pride and prejudices, and charges of hierarchic insubordination and coworker friction have outnumbered disputes involving the content of teaching or research." See ibid. The principal grievance in nearly all of these extramural or intramural utterance cases is the failure of the administration or lay governing board to follow procedural due process in putting the decision to recommend appropriate action in the first instance to a committee of the faculty. See American Association of University Professors, "Report of Committee A," *Academe*, (September–October 1993): 36, 41; Thomas I. Emerson and David Haber, "Academic Freedom of the Faculty Member as Citizen," 28 *Law and Contemporary Problems* (1963): 525, 535; American Association of University Professors, "1943 Report of Committee A," 28 *AAUP Bulletin* (1943): 15–17; Walter Metzger, "Profession and Constitution: Two Definitions of Academic Freedom in America" 66 *Texas Law Review* (1988): 1265, 1276.

46. In the AAUP tradition, different weight is accorded different statements depending upon the method by which the statement was adopted. Weight is accorded in the following order: (1) statements jointly adopted by the AAUP and the American Association of Colleges (the AAC is now the American Association of College and Universities); (2) statements adopted by the annual meeting of the AAUP; (3) statements of the AAUP Council; and (4) statements adopted by an AAUP Committee.

47. See Byrne, "A Special Concern," 277; see also David M. Rabban, "A Functional Analysis of 'Individual' and 'Institutional' Academic Freedom under the First Amendment," 53 *Law and Contemporary Problems* (1990): 227, 232 [hereinafter Rabban, "A Functional Analysis"].

48. AAUP, "1915 Declaration," 158.

49. Ibid. 160.

50. Ibid. 163–164.

51. Ibid. 162.

52. Ibid. 163–165.

53. The 1915 Declaration does not define clearly the meaning of "extramural utterance." For example, does the term mean professional speech outside the walls of the university, in contrast to teaching inside the walls, or does it mean professional speech that is outside of a professor's disciplinary expertise? The 1915 Declaration sees teaching and extramural utterance as "closely related," and "often not distinguished." Ibid. 158. This recognizes disciplinary expertise as a key element in both, thus extramural utterance would refer to the use of disciplinary expertise other than in teaching. "However, extramural utterance has an importance of its own, since of late it has perhaps more frequently been the occasion of difficulties and controversies than has the question of freedom of *intra-academic* teaching. All five of the cases that have recently been investigated by committees of

the Association have involved, at least as one factor, the right of university teachers to express their opinions freely *outside the university* or to engage in political
activities in their capacity as citizens." Ibid. (emphasis added). This excerpt points
toward the location of the speech outside the university as a key distinction. It
also distinguishes expression of opinions outside the university from engaging in
political activity as citizens. Presumably the expression of opinions refers to expert opinion. Later references in the 1915 Declaration distinguish between purposes of the university "[t]o provide general instruction to the students" and "[t]o
develop experts for the various branches of the public service," or "experts for the
use of the community." Ibid. 362–363. Consideration of all these together suggests
that extramural utterance is intended to include: (1) speech that is both within
disciplinary expertise and outside the walls, and (2) political activity as a citizen
outside the walls.

This interpretation finds support in a final reference in the 1915 Declaration:

> In their extramural utterances, it is obvious that academic teachers are under a
> peculiar obligation to avoid hasty or unverified or exaggerated statements, and to
> refrain from intemperate or sensational modes of expression. But subject to those
> restraints, it is not, in the committee's opinion, desirable that *scholars* should be
> debarred from giving expression to their judgments upon controversial questions,
> or that their freedom of speech, *outside the university*, should be limited to ques-
> tions falling within their own specialties. It is clearly not proper that they should
> be prohibited from lending their support to organized movements which they
> believe to be in the public interest.

Ibid. 172.
    54. Ibid. 162–163.
    55. Ibid. 168.
    56. Ibid. 168–169 (emphasis added).
    57. Ibid. 158.
    58. Ibid. 172 (emphasis added).
    59. Ibid. 169.
    60. Ibid. 169–170.
    61. Ibid. 170.
    62. See American Association of University Professors, "1940 Statement of
Principles on Academic Freedom and Tenure with 1970 Interpretive Comments,"
Academe, (May–June 1990): 37, reprinted in *Policy Documents and Reports* 3 (8th
ed. 1995) [hereinafter AAUP, "1940 Statement"].
    63. See Walter P. Metzger, "The 1940 Statement of Principles on Academic
Freedom and Tenure," 53 *Law and Contemporary Problems* (1990): 3, 4.
    64. See "Selected Judicial Decisions and Scholarly Writings Referring to AAUP
Standards," in Policy Documents and Reports, App. I (8th ed.), 257.
    65. AAUP, *1940 Statement*, 3 (emphasis added). Note that the mission of higher
education is to create and disseminate knowledge. Rights of academic freedom are
granted to serve this mission. Dissemination of knowledge in higher education involves a unique kind of teaching that is closely related to knowledge creation but

different from teaching in secondary education. The AAUP's "Statement on the Relationship of Faculty Governance to Academic Freedom" provides that "good teaching requires developing a critical ability in one's students and an understanding of the methods for resolving disputes within the discipline." American Association of University Professors, "On the Relationship of Faculty Governance to Academic Freedom," *Academe,* (July–August 1994): 47; in *Policy Documents and Reports,* (8th ed. 1995): 186, 188.

Professor Eric Ashby calls this teaching the discipline of dissent. Eric Ashby, "A Hippocratic Oath for the Academic Profession," *Minerva,* (Autumn/Winter 1968–69): 65. The teaching of the discipline of dissent requires the student to become familiar with both what is already known about a subject, and how to question that orthodoxy. Teaching develops in the student: (1) an understanding of first principles in a discipline(s); (2) a critical analytical ability; and (3) an understanding of the methods for resolving disputes within and among the disciplines. It may be, Ashby concedes, that many university students never get further than becoming familiar with orthodoxy, but "what is important is that a university graduate should have watched his teacher exercising this attitude of skepticism [the discipline of dissent] toward the traditional and orthodox view." Ibid.

The 1915 Declaration also emphasizes that university instruction should seek "to habituate [students] to looking not only patiently but methodically on both sides before adopting any conclusion upon controversial issues." AAUP, "1915 Declaration," 170.

66. AAUP, *1940 Statement,* 3.

67. Ibid.

68. Ibid. 4.

69. Ibid. 5 (emphasis added).

70. Some scholars argue that paragraph (c) does grant rights of academic freedom to intramural speech other than teaching and research. See Matthew W. Finkin, "A Higher Order of Liberty in the Workplace: Academic Freedom and Tenure in the Vortex of Employment Practices and Law," 53, *Law and Contemporary Problems* (1990): 357, 366–367 [hereinafter Finkin, "Higher Order"] (stating that the 1940 Statement gives freedom of speech on any matter of intramural concern due an officer of the institution as a member of a learned profession).

71. See accompanying text at note 57.

72. See Walter Metzger, "The 1940 Statement of Principles on Academic Freedom and Tenure," in *Freedom and Tenure in the Academy* (William Van Alstyne, ed., 1993): 3, 53.

73. Ibid. (quoting the "1925 Statement of Principles on Academic Freedom," 18, *AAUP Bulletin* 329, 330 (1932)).

74. Professor Finkin reads this history differently, arguing that the 1940 Statement extends academic freedom to four activities: (1) teaching; (2) research and publication; (3) utterance as a citizen (which the Association later glossed as "extramural" but that was not intended to mean outside the walls of the institution,

but rather outside the walls of purely professional utterance as teacher and researcher); and (4) speech as an "officer of an educational institution." Matthew Finkin, "Intramural Speech, Academic Freedom and the First Amendment," 66 *Texas Law Review* (1988): 1323 [hereinafter Finkin, "Intramural Speech"]; see also Letter from Professor Matthew Finkin to Neil Hamilton (July 17, 2000) (on file with the author). The actual words of the 1915 Declaration define extramural utterance to include: (1) speech that is both within disciplinary expertise and outside the walls; and (2) political activities of a citizen outside the walls. The phrase "officer of an educational institution" does appear in paragraph (c) of the 1940 Statement, but its inclusion seems intended to be a limitation on the rights of professors to speak as citizens, not a grant of rights of academic freedom to speech as an officer of the institution. The full text is:

> (c) College and university teachers are citizens, members of a learned profession and officers of an educational institution. When they speak or write as citizens, they should be free from institutional censorship or discipline, but their special position in the community imposes special obligations. As scholars and educational officers, they should remember that the public may judge their profession and the institution by their utterances.

AAUP, *1940 Statement*, 4.

75. See David Rabban, "Academic Freedom, Professionalism and Intramural Speech," 88 *New Directions for Higher Education,* (Winter 1994): 77, 81, 86 [hereinafter Rabban, "Academic Freedom"] (arguing that intramural speech related to "critical inquiry" is protected by academic freedom).

76. See Finkin, "Higher Order," 377–378.

77. Ibid.; see also Finkin, "Intramural Speech," 1337. Finkin also argues that a narrow definition of academic freedom would encourage administrators to use unprotected, nonprofessional speech as a pretext for discipline when the real reason is the ideas expressed in teaching or research. Ibid. 1344–1345.

78. See Mark Yudof, "Intramural Musings on Academic Freedom: A Reply to Professor Finkin," 66 *Texas Law Review* (1988): 1351, 1355–1356.

79. Professor Rabban agrees with Yudof, noting that the initial concerns of the committee drafting the 1915 Declaration were that "academic freedom would lose its rationale if it were stretched to protect activities not performed in the course of professorial duty." See Rabban, "Academic Freedom," 80, 81, 84. Rabban also argues that "the more academic freedom is confined to its convincing justification, the greater the probability that academic decision makers and judges will take seriously the implications for academic freedom in close cases." Ibid. 86.

80. See American Association of University Professors, "Statement on Government of College and Universities," *Academe,* (July–August 1994): 47, reprinted in *Policy Documents and Reports,* 179 [hereinafter AAUP, "Statement on Government"].

81. Ibid.

82. See Neil Hamilton, *"Are We Speaking the Same Language?": comparing AAUP and AGB, Liberal Education (Fall, 1999): 24, 29.*

83. Ibid. 27.

84. Ibid. One sentence of the 1966 "Statement on Government" refers to faculty members' rights in their role as citizens. Focusing on the sentence in paragraph (c) of the 1940 Statement reading, "[C]ollege or university teachers are citizens, members of a learned profession, and officers of an educational institution," the 1966 "Statement on Government" asserts that "[t]he right of a board member, an administrative officer, a faculty member or a student to speak on general educational questions or about the administration and operations of the individual's own institution is part of that person's right as a citizen and should not be abridged by the institution." AAUP, "Statement on Government," 182 and n.2. Earlier discussion in this essay pointed out that paragraph (c) of the 1940 Statement refers to extramural utterance (holding it to professional standards), not intramural utterance. See Rabban, "Academic Freedom," 83–84.

85. See Rabban, "Academic Freedom," 86.

86. Ibid. 81.

87. Professor Metzger is uncertain whether the 1940 Statement grants academic freedom on the condition that the duties included in the statement are to be obeyed. The negotiations between the AAUP and the AAC over the duties were prolonged, volatile and acrimonious. The parties saw the duties as obligatory. See Walter Metzger (1990): 3, 9, 47, 59.

88. AAUP, 1940 Statement, 3.

89. Ibid.

90. Ibid.

91. Ibid.

92. Ibid. The 1970 AAUP Statement of the Association's Council: Freedom and Responsibility, provides that "[I]t is improper for an instructor persistently to intrude material that has no relation to the subject...." AAUP, 1940 Statement, 108.

93. Ibid. 4.

94. Ibid. 5.

95. Ibid. 4. "Moral turpitude" is used in the 1940 Statement in the following context: "[T]eachers on continuous appointment who are dismissed for reasons not involving moral turpitude should receive their salaries for at least a year from the date of notification." Ibid. It is clear that moral turpitude in this context is limited only to extreme violations of duties of ethical conduct. This is supported by the AAUP's 1970 Interpretive Comments for the 1940 Statement, stating that the concept of "moral turpitude" applies to that kind of behavior which goes beyond simply warranting discharge and is so utterly blameworthy as to make it inappropriate to require the offering of a year's teaching or pay. Ibid. 7. Thus, by implication, the duties of ethical conduct cover a spectrum from those duties whose violation is utterly blameworthy to those whose violation simply warrants discharge.

96. Ibid. 5–6 (emphasis added).

97. Ibid.

98. See ibid.

99. For example, among the most comprehensive codes are the following:

American Historical Association, Statement on Standards of Professional Conduct;
American Association of Law Schools, Statement of Good Practices by Law Professors in the Discharge of Their Ethical and Professional Responsibilities;
American Political Science Association, A Guide to Professional Ethics in Political Service;
American Psychological Association, Ethical Principles of Psychologists and Code of Conduct; and
American Sociological Association, Code of Ethics

Less comprehensive are the following:

American Chemical Society, Academic Professional Guidelines;
American Mathematical Society, Ethical Guidelines Drafted by the AMS Council; and
American Physical Society, Statement on Integrity in Physics.

100. For example, the following disciplinary associations have standards of professional conduct only on some issues like harassment and discrimination, conflicts of interest, or graduate student rights:

American Philosophical Association;
Association of American Medical Colleges; and
Modern Language Association.

Some disciplinary associations, like the American Economics Association, have no statements on disciplinary ethics. Professors Braxton and Bayer note that in an earlier 1995 study of sixty-two professional academic associations, thirty-six had written ethics policies. Of these "[r]emarkably few ... contain any policy statement whatsoever on teaching. In contrast more than half of the ethics policies address matters of authorship, conflict of interest and responsibilities to society." Braxton and Bayer, *Faculty Misconduct*, 142. They note that several of the behavioral and social science professional associations have adopted more detailed codes of ethics. Ibid. 140–146.

101. See AAUP, *1940 Statement*, 4.

102. Ibid. 3.

103. American Association of University Professors, "Statement on Procedural Standards in Faculty Dismissal Proceedings," *Academe*, (May–June 1990): 42, reprinted in *Policy Documents and Reports* (1995): 11, 12.

104. See AAUP, *1940 Statement*, 5–6.

105. American Association of University Professors, "Statement on Professional Ethics," 105.

106. See AAUP, "Professional Ethics," 105–106.

107. AAUP, "1915 Declaration," 168.

108. Ibid.

109. Ibid. 169.

110. Richard Hofstadter and Walter Metzger, 410.

111. See *Commission on Academic Tenure in Higher Education, Faculty Tenure*, ix, xi. (1973) [hereinafter *Faculty Tenure*].

112. Ibid.
113. Ibid. 34–41.
114. Ibid. 41, 44.
115. Ibid. 75.
116. See AAUP, "Professional Ethics," 105. How to define "effective teaching" or the "best scholarly standards of the discipline" in teaching. The Canadian Society for Teaching and Learning has provided a more developed definition of effective teaching that includes:

1. Content Competence. A university teacher maintains a high level of subject matter knowledge and ensures that course content is current, accurate, representative, and appropriate to the position of the course within the student's program of studies.
2. Pedagogical Competence. A pedagogically competent teacher communicates the objectives of the course to students, is aware of alternative instructional methods or strategies, and selects methods of instruction that, according to research evidence (including personal and self-reflective research), are effective in helping students to achieve the course objective....
3. Valid Assessment of Students. Given the importance of assessment of students' performance in university teaching and in students' lives and careers, instructors are responsible for taking adequate steps to ensure that assessment of students is valid, open, fair and congruent with course objectives.

Harry Murray et al., "Ethical Principles for College and University Teaching," *New Directions for Teaching and Learning,"* (Summer 1996): 57–58, 62.

Braxton and Bayer point out that few professional association codes of conduct contain policy statements regarding teaching. They analyze three that do, from the National Association of Biology Teachers, the American Psychological Association, and the American Sociological Association. These codes agree with the principles in the AAUP documents and include also the principles reflected in the Canadian Society for Teaching and Learning statement of effective teaching. The National Association of Biology Teachers code adds that evaluations of students should be timely. See Braxton and Bayer, *Faculty Misconduct*, 140–146.

117. What does the concept of assigned teaching duties include? It would comprise, for example, the following: teaching the course as described in the curriculum adopted by the faculty; meeting assigned courses at the designated times; being reasonably accessible to students outside of class; and meeting grading and other instructional deadlines set by the college or university.

118. AAUP, *Professional Ethics*, 106.

119. See Faculty Tenure, 34–41.

120. See AAUP, *Professional Ethics*, 105–106.

121. American Association of University Professors, *Statement on Plagiarism*, *Academe* (September–October 1989): 47, reprinted in *Policy Documents and Reports*, 109. Plagiarism means "taking the literary property of another without attribution, passing if off as one's own, and reaping from its use an unearned benefit from an academic institution." Terri LeClerq, "Failure to Teach: Due Process and Law School Plagiarism." 49 *Journal of Legal Education* (1999): 236, 244.

122. See American Association of University Professors, "Statement on Multiple Authorship," *Academe*, (September–October 1990): 41, reprinted in *Policy Documents and Reports*, 121. In addition, the 1966 AAUP "Statement on Professional Ethics" provides that professors must acknowledge significant academic or scholarly assistance from students. See AAUP, "Professional Ethics," 107.

123. Fundamental to the academic profession is a belief in intellectual integrity. "As Clark noted, 'In the academic lexicon, knowledge must be handled honestly, for otherwise it misinforms and deceives, is no longer valuable in itself, and certainly of no use to society.'" William Tierney and Robert Rhoads, *Faculty Socialization as Cultural Process: A Mirror of Institutional Commitment* 12 (ASHE-ERIC Higher Education Report No. 6, 1993).

124. AAUP, *1940 Statement*, 5.

125. Rabban, "A Functional Analysis," 242 (quoting William Van Alstyne, "The Specific Theory of Academic Freedom and the General Issue of Civil Liberty," in *The Concept of Academic Freedom* 76 (Edmund Pincoffs ed., 1972)).

126. See Derek Bok, "Universities: Their Temptations and Tensions," 18 *Journal of College and University Law*, 1, 2 (1991). A recent report by a panel of the National Academy of Sciences stresses that scientists rely on an honor system based on tradition to safeguard the integrity of the research process. Panel on Scientific Responsibility and the Conduct of Research, National Academy of Sciences, *Responsible Science: Ensuring the Integrity of the Research Process* (1992): ix, 1 [hereinafter *Responsible Science*].

127. AAUP, "Professional Ethics," 105.

128. Ibid.

129. See Ernst Boyer, *Scholarship Reconsidered: Priorities of the Professoriate* (1990): 27–28.

130. Clark Kerr, President Emeritus of the University of California, outlined the components of "the ethics of knowledge." The following actions are obligatory:

- the careful collection and use of evidence, including the search for "inconvenient facts," as in the process of attempted "falsification";
- the careful use of the ideas and work of others;
- the obligation to be skeptical of what is not fully proven;
- the openness to alternative explanations … ;
- civility in discourse, and reliance on persuasion rather than coercion;
- open access to the results of research conducted within the university … ;
- avoidance of drawing and advancing policy application unless the full range of considerations entering into the policy making has been the subject of the study…. Scholars should not go beyond their knowledge;
- separating personal evaluation, based on moral and political values, from the presentation of evidence and analysis; and as a corollary, making any personal evaluations explicit….

Clark Kerr, "Knowledge Ethics And The New Academic Culture," *Change*, (January–February 1994): 13.

Professor Martin Trow emphasizes the critical importance of the duty actively to search out and confront inconvenient facts and contrary opinion. "For example, a major function of quantification in the social sciences is that it embodies impersonal procedures that ensure the collection of negative as well as supporting evidence for whatever 'party opinion' we hold at the moment." Martin Trow, "Higher Education and Moral Development," *AAUP Bulletin*, (Spring 1976): 20, 23.

In *The Academic Ethic*, Professor Edward Shils emphasizes that a university teacher who proceeds without respect for evidence and argument "is committing the ultimate treason against the university. Systematic disciplined investigation is its life-blood." Edward Shils, *The Academic Ethic* (1983): 102.

In *The Order of Learning*, Shils argues that a professor should undertake careful study, be open to sound evidence, adhere to disciplinary rules in using and assessing evidence, record observations honestly, distinguish among varying degrees of certainty with respect to the evidence, and be fair in representing the arguments of others. Shils, *The Order*, 248.

A panel of the National Academy of Sciences stresses that fabrication, falsification, and plagiarism are the cardinal sins of scientific misconduct. The integrity of the research process requires adherence "to honest and verifiable methods in proposing, performing, evaluating, and reporting research activities. The research process includes the construction of hypotheses; the development of experimental and theoretical paradigms; the collection, analysis, and handling of data; the generation of new ideas, findings, and theories through experimentation and analysis; timely communication and publication; refinement of results through replication and extension of the original work; peer reviews; and the training and supervision of associates and students." *Responsible Science*, 17–18. The panel also stresses care in reporting data and adverse evidence. Ibid. 37, 47–48.

John Braxton and Alan Bayer argue that there is a normative structure for the performance of research.

> Merton (1942, 1973) described this normative structure as composed of four core patterns: communality, disinterestedness, organized skepticism, and universalism. Communality means that the research findings are the intellectual property of the research community. Scholars should, however, receive appropriate recognition for their contributions. Disinterestedness bars individuals from conducting research for personal or financial gain, merely to receive recognition, or simply to gain prestige. The desire to advance knowledge should be the primary motive for conducting research. Organized skepticism stipulates that research findings not be accepted without peer assessment based on empirical and logical criteria. Universalism prescribes that research be judged on the basis of merit and not particularistic criteria such as race, nationality, or social origin.

Braxton and Bayer, *Faculty Misconduct*, 5.

See generally (on the characteristics of scholarship) Seymour Martin Lipset, *Rebellion in the University* (1976): 203–204, 208; J. Peter Byrne, "Academic Freedom and Political Neutrality in Law Schools: An Essay on the Structure and Ideology in Professional Education," 43 *Journal of Legal Education* (1993): 315, 322. Professor Stephen Carter urges that:

> A principal focus of modern scholarship ... has been to assault the idea that one can evaluate anything without significant reference to one's own values that are

defined by one's status and culture. This is a point well taken but does not answer the question of what one should try to do. The knowledge that perfectly unbiased observation is impossible should instill in all of us a healthy degree of caution on the certainty of our rightness, but ... scholars should *strive* for dispassion.

Stephen Carter, "Academic Tenure and White Male Standards: Some Lessons from the Patent Law," 100 *Yale Law Journal* (1991): 2065, 2071 (emphasis added).

131. See Ernest Boyer, *Scholarship Reconsidered* (1980): 16–25.

132. Charles Glassick, et al., *Scholarship Assessed: Evaluation of the Professoriate* (1997): 25–36.

133. See Rabban, "A Functional Analysis," 242; see also Finkin, "Intramural Speech," 1323, 1332; Rabban, "Academic Freedom," (1988): 1405, 1409.

134. AAUP, *1940 Statement*, 4.

135. Ibid. 7.

136. Ibid. 5–6.

137. AAUP, "Professional Ethics," 105–106. The general duty to avoid any exploitation or harassment of students is emphasized in the American Association of University Professors, "Statement on Sexual Harassment," *Academe*, (July–August 1995): 62, reprinted in *Policy Documents and Reports*, 171 (prohibiting faculty member's use of institutional position to seek unwanted sexual relations with students or others vulnerable to the faculty member's authority).

138. American Association of University Professors, "A Statement of the Association's Council: Freedom and Responsibility," 56 *AAUP Bulletin* (1970): 375–376, reprinted in *Policy Documents and Reports*, 107–108.

139. See *Faculty Tenure*, 75. There may be other duties of ethical conduct not listed in the 1966 or 1970 statements. For example, the Federal Commission on Research Integrity defined professional misconduct to include breaches of duties of confidentiality associated with review of manuscripts or grant applications, an intentional taking of or damage to the research-related property of another, obstruction of investigations of research misconduct, noncompliance with research regulations, and obstruction of the research of others (including making allegations of misconduct in reckless disregard of facts). See U.S. Commission on Research Integrity, "Integrity and Misconduct in Research" (1995): 28–31.

140. AAUP, "1915 Declaration," 162.

141. AAUP, *1940 Statement*, 3.

142. AAUP, "Professional Ethics," 105

143. American Association of University Professors, "On Preventing Conflicts of Interest in Government Sponsored Research of Universities," 51 *AAUP Bulletin* 42 (1965), reprinted in *Policy Documents and Reports*, 116–118.

144. See American Association of University Professors, "Statement on Conflicts of Interest," *Academe*, (September–October 1990): 40, reprinted in *Policy Documents and Reports*, 119–120.

145. See ibid.

146. The 1915 Declaration provided that in extramural utterances, the university teacher was under a "peculiar obligation" to avoid hasty or exaggerated statements. See AAUP, "1915 Declaration," 172.

147. The 1915 Declaration also directed teachers "to refrain from intemperate or sensational modes of expression." Ibid. 172.

148. See AAUP, *1940 Statement*, 4.

149. If intramural speech is related to the education of students, critical inquiry, or shared governance under the 1966 "Statement on Government," then it is subject to the same higher professional standard as teaching and research.

150. AAUP, *1940 Statement*, 5.

151. See American Association of University Professors, "Committee A Statement on Extramural Utterances," 51 *AAUP Bulletin* 29 (1965), reprinted in *Policy Documents and Reports*, 32.

152. Ibid.

153. American Association of University Professors, "Advisory Letters from the Washington Office," 49 *AAUP Bulletin* (1963): 393.

154. Ibid.

155. See Finkin, "Higher Order," 366–367.

156. See earlier discussion of correlative duties for teaching, research, and intramural utterance. See text accompanying note 101–132. By implication, if the correlative duties of academic freedom for extramural speech include the duties: (1) to be accurate at all times; (2) to exercise appropriate restraint; and (3) to show respect for the opinions of others, the correlative duties of professional competence and ethical conduct in teaching, research, and intramural utterance include these.

157. Metzger, 51.

158. Ibid.

159. Ibid.

160. Professor William Van Alstyne has argued that the AAUP's extension of the protection of professional academic freedom to extramural utterance was a mistake. One of his reasons is that attaching a claim for protection of academic freedom to extramural utterance implies a duty of accountability by "academic" standards for such speech. "The result … is that the individual so situated is rendered less free in respect to his nonprofessional pursuits than others." William Van Alstyne, "Reply to Comments," in *The Concept of Academic Freedom* 127 (Edmund Pincoffs ed., 1972). This argument misses the point. While it is true that all citizens can exercise their First Amendment rights without coercion by government, private employers can fire them for doing so unless the speech relates to whistleblowing, harassment or discrimination claims, or some other subset of speech protected by statute. Professional academic freedom protection for professors' extramural utterance protects faculty members at private universities from adverse employment consequences for speech that an employer does not like. As Van Alstyne has argued elsewhere, such exceptional vocational freedom to speak the truth as one sees it and without penalty for its immediate impact upon the economic well-being of the employing institution, is the cost of exceptional care in the representation of that "truth," a professional standard of care. William Van Alstyne, "The Specific Theory of Academic Freedom and the General Issue of Civil Liberty," in *The Concept of Academic Freedom* 76 (Edmund Pincoffs ed., 1972). The tradeoff of rights and correlative duty for extramural speech seems reasonable.

161. 391 U.S. 563 (1968).

162. AAUP, *1940 Statement*, 4.

163. Ibid. 7.

164. American Association of University Professors, "Statement on Procedural Standards in Faculty Dismissal Proceedings," *Academe*, (May–June 1990): 42, reprinted in *Policy Documents and Reports*, 11–12.

165. AAUP, "1915 Declaration," 169–170.

166. Ibid. 170.

167. American Association of University Professors, "1946 Report of Committee A," 31 *AAUP Bulletin* (1946): 60–61.

168. See American Association of University Professors, "Academic Responsibility: Comments by Members of Committee A Incident to Consideration of the Koch Case," 49 *AAUP Bulletin* (1963): 40.

169. Ibid.

170. Ibid. (emphasis added).

171. Ibid. 41.

172. AAUP, "Professional Ethics," 75.

173. Ibid. 105–106.

174. See American Association of University Professors, "A Statement of the Association's Council: Freedom and Responsibility," 56 *AAUP Bulletin* (1970): 375, reprinted in *Policy Documents and Reports*, 107–108.

175. Ibid. The AAUP returned to the theme of attacks on academic freedom from within the faculty itself in 1994. "Even with a sound governance system in place and with a faculty active in self-government ... , dysfunctions that undermine academic freedom may still occur: subtle (or not so subtle) bullying on the part of the faculty itself, a covertly enforced isolation, a disinclination to respect the views of the off-beat and cranky among its members." American Association of University Professors, "On the Relationships of Faculty Governance to Academic Freedom," *Academe*, (July–August 1994): 47, reprinted in *Policy Documents and Reports*, 186, 188.

176. *Faculty Tenure*, 43.

177. Ibid. 43.

178. AAUP Committee B, "On The Duty of Faculty Members to Speak Out on Misconduct," *Academe*, (November–December 1998): 58.

179. American Association of University Professors, "Record of the Council, Nov. 13-14, 1999," *Academe*, January–February 2000): 52.

180. See AAUP Committee B, 58.

181. Ibid.

182. Ibid.

183. See Committee on Science, Engineering and Public Policy, National Academy of Sciences, *On Being a Scientist: Responsible Conduct in Research* 31 (2d ed. 1984).

184. Walter Metzger, "Academic Freedom and Scientific Freedom," in *Limits of Scientific Inquiry* (Gerald Holton and Robert Morison, eds., 1979): 93, 97.

185. "Statement on Government of Colleges and Universities," reprinted in *AAUP, Policy Documents and Reports* (9th ed. 2000): 215.

186. "The Standard of Compelling Reasons in the Joint Statement on Government of Colleges and Universities," *Academe* (September–October 1993): 54.

187. "Recommended Institutional Regulations on Academic Freedom and Tenure," reprinted in *AAUP, Policy Documents and Reports* (9th ed. 2000): 21, 23–25.

188. Ibid. 24.

189. Eric Ashby, 65.

190. The degree to which community colleges accept academic tradition may be dramatically different from four-year colleges and universities. For example, in the early 1980s, 25.5 percent of community colleges had tenure, whereas 97 percent of four-year institutions had tenure. Benjamin and Wagner, 63.

191. Association of Governing Boards of Universities and Colleges, "AGB Statement on Institutional Governance" (1998).

192. American Council on Education, *Corporate Lessons for American Higher Education* (1994): 2–3.

193. Ibid. 3-6.

194. Ibid. 5.

195. Ibid. 3.

196. Michael Katz, note 36.

197. Ramo, 5.

198. Clark Kerr, "Knowledge Ethics and the New Academic Culture," *Change* 1, (January 1994): 10.

199. Arthur Lovejoy, quoted in P. H. L. Walter, "The Professor as Specialist and Generalist," *Academe* (Fall, 1988): 25, 28.

200. Association of Governing Boards, *Renewing the Presidency: Stronger Leadership for Tougher Times* (1996): 11.

201. Clark Kerr, 10.

202. Burton Clark, *The Higher Education System: Academic Organization in Cross-National Perspective* (1983): 234–236.

203. Richard Hofstadter and Walter Metzger quoted in Howard M. Jones, "The American Concept of Academic Freedom" in *Academic Freedom and Tenure* (Louis Joughin, ed., 1969): 224–225.

204. Ibid. 225–227.

205. See Richard T. De George, *Academic Freedom and Tenure* (1997): 68–69.

206. "Joint Statement on Rights and Academic Freedom of Students Represented" in *AAUP, Policy Documents and Reports* (9th ed. 2000): 261.

207. Ibid. 262.

208. Ibid. 262–264.

209. Ibid. 264–265.

210. "Statement on Graduate Students," reprinted in *AAUP, Policy Documents and Reports* (9th ed. 2000): 268–269.

211. Ibid. 269.

212. Ibid.

CHAPTER

Problems on the Duties
of Individual Professors

The 49 problems that follow are designed for peer-group discussion. The discussion leader should select from the list those problems that both best fit the institutional context and provoke the most interest in the discussion group. Please reread the section in Chapter 1 at page 11 on the organization of the book. The problems assume the reader has finished Chapter 2. Appendix A, providing an outline of the Principles of Professional Conduct, will be useful in answering the questions to the problems.

TEACHING

PROBLEM 1: Lateness for class, office hours, and submission of grade

Professor Kim Paulsen teaches political science at your institution (YU). She is a tenured full professor and has been at YU for 15 years. She is well liked by both colleagues and students, and is highly respected for her scholarship. Paulsen is occasionally late to class, but never more than 5 minutes. The building where she has always taught her large classes is currently under construction so she must now walk 10 minutes across campus to the only other building that contains large lecture halls suitable for her freshman Political Science 101 class.

The first day of class she is 5 minutes late. The class meets 3 days a week. For the next two weeks, she is late once a week, usually no more than 5 minutes. In the last four weeks of the semester, at least once a week she arrives more than 10 minutes late to class. She is never late on test or quiz days. Some students are annoyed with her tardiness, but reluctant to speak up because they are freshmen, afraid that voicing their dissatisfaction might affect their final course grade. A large majority notes the problem in the student evaluations.

Paulsen teaches one large introductory class with 125 students and one small seminar with 15 students. In the past, she used to have a teaching assistant or adjunct professor help her with grading exams for the large course while she herself graded all papers for the seminar. In a recent budget decision, the administration eliminated all TAs for intro courses, saying that they needed to allocate more funds to the construction of new buildings and labs. In the fall, Paulsen submits her seminar grades on time, but is a week late with the freshmen exams. In the spring semester, she is a week late with seminar grades. A week after she submitted her seminar grades, she traveled to Chicago to give a conference paper that was very well received. When she returned, she graded the freshmen exams and submitted those grades 2 weeks later, a month late altogether. Freshmen became alarmed when their political science grades did not appear on their transcript. Concerned students flooded the registrar's office with phone calls. When the registrar contacted Paulsen, she explained that she is painstakingly meticulous when reading exams and couldn't submit the grades in good faith any sooner than 4 weeks after they are due. She also said that she had been in Chicago for an important conference. In short, she said: "It would be unfair to my students to give their papers a quick read in order to submit the grades on time. They've worked hard this term and I owe them this, at the very least."

With regard to office hours, Paulsen's syllabi explicitly state that she holds regular office hours on Tuesdays and Thursdays, from noon to 1:00, but is also available by appointment. Although she is always there the weeks that a test is to be given or a paper is due, she is frequently not in her office during scheduled times throughout the rest of the semester.

As for meetings by appointment, sometimes she is not in her office at the appointed time, and on other occasions when students who can't make her regular office hours ask to set up an alternate time she sometimes says she is too busy and can't schedule a meeting for several weeks.

1. Do the facts in paragraphs 2 and 3 present violations of your understanding of the general principles of professional conduct? Which principles are invoked here and how should they apply in this case?
2. What is the proper way to investigate the lateness issue? What might a conversation with her look like? Should she be issued a warning? If so, what are the terms of the warning?

3. Professor Paulsen's situation creates problems for both the administration and the peer collegium. How would you address each of these? Should anyone say anything to the aggrieved students?
4. Would Professor Paulsen's conduct call for formal sanctions? What level? By whom?
5. Should Professor Paulsen have accepted the invitation to present a conference paper given the timing of the conference?
6. What is the community standard at your institution for the number of office hours an instructor should hold? Does Professor Paulsen adhere to these standards?
7. Has Professor Paulsen violated any principles of conduct with regard to missed office hours?
8. At what point does her failure to keep office hours become a serious violation?
9. Who should be responsible for seeing that Professor Paulsen corrects the problem? The administration, peer collegium, or some combination thereof? How should they resolve the problem?
10. Should any sanctions be imposed on Professor Paulsen based on her office-hour problems? Should she be warned first? What happens if Professor Paulsen does nothing to correct the problem? When should sanctions be imposed for failing to correct the problem?
11. How can these issues serve to improve the peer culture? How could the peer collegium be more proactive in creating a culture that would prevent these problems from occurring?
12. What is the aspiration in your collegial group regarding being late to classes or meetings? Regarding general availability to students?

PROBLEM 2: Problems with new course; completion of only one-half of syllabus; testing material not covered in class

Professor Margaret Breaghm, a specialist in modern Irish history at your institution (YU), is teaching a new course for the first time in seven years. Having always taught the courses on World War I and World War II, British history, and the modern European survey course, she is now eager to teach a seminar for majors on the history of the IRA.

The YU grant committee awarded her a summer teaching grant to do archival work in Dublin for eight weeks. When she returned in late July she prepared the syllabus and had it approved by the department chair. She used the remainder of the summer to design the course. There were some problems at the beginning of the semester because she'd ordered the books too late in August. Students had to begin the term running around making copies of Breaghm's own heavily annotated materials until the bookstore received the texts in late September.

About four weeks into the semester Breaghm realized that her syllabus was much too ambitious in scope. The initial background readings were difficult and she needed more time than she'd originally thought to cover each assignment. When students questioned her about this in October, she told them that the readings would become more straightforward in a few weeks. In December, they had completed only half of the syllabus. In addition to being disappointed, students became outraged when Breaghm announced in the last class that in their final papers they needed to show evidence of having read everything on the syllabus.

1. As a peer collegium, did the grant committee violate an aspirational ethical duty in approving a course that would be taught so soon after the research had been conducted? If so, what duty?
2. Did Professor Breaghm herself violate any principles of professional conduct in expecting to teach a course for which she had just completed the research? Which principles?
3. In submitting book orders in August, Professor Breaghm created problems for the bookstore as well as for the students. Who should be responsible for handling the problem? Does Breaghm owe any aspirational ethical duty to the peer group who collectively relies on this essential service provided by the bookstore?
4. Professor Breaghm covered only one half of the syllabus approved by the department chair. At what point does this become a serious violation of the general principles of professional conduct? Which principles are called into question?
5. Should the syllabus for an old course taught for the first time by someone else have faculty approval? Should faculty approve the syllabus for a new course?
6. To what extent does Professor Breaghm owe an aspirational ethical duty to the administration and the peer collegium to cover the entire syllabus for a new course? Is this duty higher for a basic survey or introductory courses?
7. Is the lack of coverage more serious in introductory courses where the faculty has approved a specific set of syllabi? What if a professor consistently covers only one-half of the agreed-upon material?
8. Does Professor Breaghm's expectation that students be responsible for the entire syllabus on the examination violate general principles of professional conduct? Which principles?
9. Who should speak to Professor Breaghm about this expectation — the administration, the peer collegium, or a combination thereof?

10. How could the peer collegium prevent such problems from occurring? What is the culture at your institution with respect to these issues? What recourse do students have?

PROBLEM 3: Disorganization: Teaching irrelevant material that is important to political agenda

Professor Sylvia Becker is a tenured professor of geology at your institution. Usually well organized, Professor Becker found herself completely caught off guard last July when her mother fell ill. She devoted every free moment to her care. When school began in September, she had placed no book orders with the bookstore and had not prepared any syllabi. She was unable to clarify course requirements to her students. Around the middle of the semester she changed requirements for the final paper even though some students had already done a great deal of work that was now no longer necessary.

During the winter break, in the hope of becoming better organized, she took three Power Point classes offered by the college. The winter term continued in the same vein. In addition, on two different occasions when her first foray into Power Point presentations failed, she canceled class and let the students leave early. She made one class up at another time, but not all students were able to attend the makeup session. She did not make up the second class.

Professor Joan Tanaka is a tenured professor in the same department. Heavily involved with local grass-root politics, Professor Tanaka has gained a reputation as a campus radical. Despite the fact that her syllabi are always extremely organized, and her lesson plans both comprehensive and well thought out, Professor Tanaka routinely diverges from the material by discussing at length her political agenda. She raises issues that are unrelated to the course material. By the end of every semester, her classes have become a mere shadow of what she had promised in the syllabus.

1. Does Professor Becker's failure to adequately plan for her courses violate any general principles of professional conduct? Which ones?
2. Professor Becker faces a mother's illness. There are many other traumatic events that may affect performance. Does the existence of a traumatic event influence your analysis of question 1? Who should be responsible for discussing Professor Becker's incompetence with her: the administration or the peer collegium? As it becomes apparent that her mother's illness will become protracted, how does that change your

analysis as to what should be done? At what point does the group (administrative and/or peer) recognize that Becker's incompetence needs to be discussed with her? How should the students' grievances be handled?

3. Did she violate a principle of professional conduct or an aspirational ethical duty by changing course requirements halfway through the semester?

4. Professors frequently revise assignments for legitimate pedagogic reasons. Is there any way Professor Becker could have revised those requirements in an equitable fashion?

5. Professor Becker believed that familiarity with Power Point would help her regain her competence in teaching. Is she fulfilling any duty by learning new technology for the classroom? Which one(s)? To whom might she owe this duty?

6. Did Professor Becker violate a principle of professional conduct or an aspirational ethical duty in scheduling a makeup class that not all students could attend? Did she violate either in not making up the second class? Is there an outer bound on class cancellation?

7. Has Professor Tanaka violated any general principles of professional conduct in routinely diverging from the syllabus? Which principles?

8. How many times must she address unrelated material before it becomes unacceptable to do so? Once? Three times? Five times? Who makes this determination? What if, as in this case, the unrelated material causes the professor not to cover significant material in the syllabus?

9. What should the peer collegium and the administration do about a colleague who consistently intrudes political material unrelated to the subject into the classroom?

10. Does it matter for your analysis whether Professor Tanaka's politics are on the radical left or the radical right?

PROBLEM 4: Student evaluation problems

Professor John Morton, a tenured professor of biology, has been teaching at your institution for over 10 years. Ever the practical joker, in the last few years he has become increasingly more silly in his lectures. At the beginning of each semester, students find his humor refreshing and laugh a lot. By the fourth week, they've become indifferent to his humor; by mid-semester, they're annoyed; and at ten weeks into the semester, they are so irritated that they dread coming to class.

One semester, on the last day of class, as he is about to hand out the teaching evaluations, he jokes about his irreverent humor and announces to the students that he will not be distributing student evaluations that semester. Those are his parting words as he smiles and dismisses them.

Sherri Lomax, an untenured professor in the same department, is also known for her classroom antics. She is fully aware that some students find her irritating. During the last week of classes, when she can choose to distribute the student evaluations during any one of her last three classes, she decides to hand them out on the day when the two students most opposed to her humor are absent.

1. Assume that Professor Morton's joking did not interfere with covering the syllabus. Do his repeated practical jokes violate any general principles of professional conduct? Do they violate a duty of ethical conduct?
2. If Professor Morton's joking became so time-consuming that it prevented him from completing the syllabus, what additional principles or aspirational duties would he have violated?
3. In knowingly failing to hand out the student evaluations, has he violated a principle of professional conduct or an aspirational duty?
4. Should Professor Morton be warned? By whom? Should any sanctions be imposed on Professor Morton? What happens if Professor Morton continues to withhold the evaluations in future classes?
5. Has Professor Lomax violated a principle of professional conduct or an aspirational duty of ethical conduct in selectively distributing the evaluations?
6. Imagine that Professor Lomax confides in a colleague about this manipulation. Does her colleague have a duty to act? If so, what duty?
7. Should Professor Lomax be warned? By whom? Should any sanctions be imposed on Lomax? What happens if Professor Lomax continues this manipulation in future classes? Does it matter for your analysis that Professor Lomax is untenured?
8. What is the culture at your institution regarding student evaluations? Are they taken seriously? Too seriously? If a number of students are complaining to individual professors and in evaluations about inappropriate humor in a particular class, what would happen?
9. Does your collegial group have a culture where a professor's inappropriate humor can be discussed openly with the professor?

PROBLEM 5: Dead wood; ineffective teacher

Professor George Barone is a tenured professor of political science at your institution (YU). He has been teaching in the department for 25 years. He likes his students, but is not particularly motivated when it comes to designing new courses and revising old ones. For the last 15 years or so he has consistently been rated in the bottom 10 percent of student evaluations, and before that his rating was only a few percentage points higher. His colleagues who have visited his classes also rate him as a poor teacher.

Students think he's nice enough, calling him a "good guy" because he tells funny stories in class, but they do recognize in their evaluations that he rarely challenges them intellectually. They roll their eyes when at the beginning of every class Professor Barone pulls out his yellowed lecture notes from many years ago.

He teaches the required introductory course so enrollment is high, but every year a significant number of students withdraw from his upper-level seminar. It is well known by both faculty and students that Professor Barone is lethargic as a campus citizen and does no research.

Professor Mike Jarvis has also been at YU for 25 years. He is a brilliant individual, full of ideas and eager to discuss them with colleagues. Colleagues often joke with him that he needs to rein in the number of new courses he offers every few years because it makes them look bad. Although students find him dynamic in the classroom, they continually rate him in the bottom 10 percent of student evaluations because he seems unable to communicate the material effectively. His lectures are confusing and his mind wanders throughout the class. Students have difficulty grasping the material and even the better students are frustrated because they just aren't "getting it."

1. Has Professor Barone violated any principles of professional conduct in being a chronic low performer? Which ones?
2. Knowing that he is consistently in the bottom decile of teaching competence year after year, does he violate an aspirational ethical duty in continuing to teach at the same low level?
3. Does he violate a principle duty in using obsolete lesson plans? Does it make any difference that he has served on the faculty for 25 years as opposed to 10 years?
4. To what extent does Professor Barone owe an aspirational duty to the administration and the peer collegium to prevent majors from withdrawing from his seminars?
5. Does Barone's reputation as a "lethargic" citizen and scholar influence your analysis of his professional conduct as a teacher? Would your analysis be any different if he were weak only in the area of teaching, but still a good citizen and a strong scholar?
6. Who is responsible for improving Professor Barone's performance?
7. Does Professor Jarvis violate a principle of conduct or aspirational ethical duty in failing to communicate course material effectively?
8. How would your analysis change if Professor Jarvis were only of average intellect, rather than the brilliant mind that he is? What if he were a brilliant scholar?
9. As a peer collegium, do Professor Jarvis's colleagues violate any duty in regularly approving new course offerings that they know he cannot effectively teach?

10. What is the proper way to raise the communication issue with Jarvis? Who is responsible for helping him correct the problem: the administration or the peer collegium?
11. For both Professors Barone and Jarvis, does the peer collegium violate any principle of professional conduct or aspirational ethical duty if the collegium knows about the teaching problems but does nothing?
12. What should happen if after several years of warnings and administration and faculty offers of help, neither of these professors shows any signs of improvement? Does it matter if their attitude toward the need to improve is poor?

PROBLEM 6: Grade inflation; favoritism toward some students

Jennifer Jahn is an assistant tenure-track professor of art history at your institution (YU). In her fifth year now, she has gained a reputation as one of the most popular instructors on the campus. She regularly gives more A's and B+'s than any of her colleagues in the department. While her teaching evaluations indicate that her teaching is just above average, she receives high scores for enthusiasm and helping students prepare for exams. Those who have sought her help during office hours realize happily that, after taking her exam, she had given them a good indication in her office of what she was going to test.

As for enrollment, after Professor Jahn had been at YU for a year, students began flocking to her classes, which frequently have long waiting lists. Initially, the department tried to meet the needs of students who were wait-listed, so they opened another section of her modern French painting class by hiring an adjunct. When the new adjunct professor gave grades lower than Professor Jahn's grades, however, the administration found that enrollments in that section quickly dropped, forcing them to cancel the section.

1. Has Professor Jahn violated any principles of professional conduct or aspirational ethical duties by regularly giving an unusually high number of A's and B's?
2. Would your analysis be any different if she were also a strong teacher? Should those professors rated by students and colleagues as unusually strong teachers grade higher than other colleagues?
3. At what point should the practice of grading much higher than colleagues be recognized as a problem? After 2 semesters? 2 years? 5 years?
4. Who is responsible for handling the grading problem: the administration or the peer collegium? What should be done? Should she be warned first?

5. Would it matter if this were a multi-section course, with other sections giving lower grades?
6. Does Professor Jahn violate a principle of conduct or an aspirational ethical duty when she obliquely reveals the content of exams to her students during office hour discussions?
7. Would your analysis change if Professor Jahn had revealed this information (obliquely) during class-time rather than during office hours? What if she had revealed it only to her research assistants who were taking her class?
8. What should be done about the problem? Should she be warned first? Would your analysis of Professor Jahn's grading practices change if she were a tenured professor? How?
9. If Professor Jahn were an adjunct professor, would that change your analysis?
10. Assume that faculty colleagues are aware of both situations, what principles of professional conduct or aspirational ethical duties apply to the peer collegium as a whole?
11. If grade inflation is a problem more generally in the faculty, what should the peer collegium do about it?

PROBLEM 7: Inflated letters of recommendation; retaliation in a letter of recommendation

Professor Dan Weaver always had large enrollments in his Anthropology 101 class because it fulfilled a general education requirement for the BA. Because Anthro 101 was predominantly a lecture class, Professor Weaver had little opportunity to get to know his students. At the end of every school year, some students who had done well in the class asked him for a letter of recommendation even though he did not know who they were. Professor Weaver asked them to give him back their final exams so he would have something of substance to say. But, invariably, each time this happened he would write a letter that went beyond the scope of the exam. He also addressed issues about social skills and maturity, areas that he knew potential employers wanted to hear. He wrote glowing letters for his top students, figuring that an "A" in his class entitled them to receive praise on the personal as well as academic level. He liked his students and wanted them to succeed after graduation.

Professor Weaver also had students from smaller courses who requested letters from him. Some of these had received only average grades, but they got along well with Weaver both in and outside of the classroom so they did not hesitate to ask him for a letter. Even though these students did not do particularly well in his course, Weaver praised their academic as well as their social skills. He liked these students and he wanted them to get a good job.

Professor Florence Heely taught a small seminar in the same department so she knew her students quite well. She had two excellent students one semester — Charles and Ellen—each receiving an "A+" on their final papers. Charles was extremely intelligent, but generally bored and disinterested in the material. Ellen was the smarter of the two, genuinely inquisitive and eager to be challenged. Indeed, sometimes she would ask questions to which Professor Heely could not respond. On those occasions, Professor Heely would answer angrily and mumble an incomplete response. At the end of the year, both Charles and Ellen asked Professor Heely for letters that Professor Heely said she was only too glad to write. She wrote an outstanding letter for Charles but she wrote a letter for Ellen that made her look inappropriately assertive.

1. Does any principle of professional conduct require that professors write a letter of recommendation? Does a professor have an aspirational ethical duty to write recommendations for students? For which students?
2. What level of candor is expected by the recipient with these letters?
3. Over time, has candor in reference letters decreased? Explain. Is it an issue of liability or some other reason?
4. Should a professor worry about liability issues?
5. In paragraph 1, should Professor Weaver have agreed to write the letters? In paragraph 2?
6. In paragraph 1, did Professor Weaver violate any principles of professional conduct in writing letters that addressed more than performance on the final exam?
7. In paragraph 2, did he violate any principles of professional conduct in recommending his students so highly? Should Professor Weaver have been honest with students that his letters would assess both their strengths and weaknesses? Should he tell them what impact this may have on their future?
8. In paragraph 3, did Professor Heely violate any principles of professional conduct in recommending Charles more highly than Ellen?
9. Given the current culture regarding letters of recommendation, would it be appropriate for a professor to write a letter that includes an honest assessment of a student's strengths and weaknesses?
10. Is the current culture surrounding letters of recommendation so corrupt that professors should not agree to participate? What should the professorate do to secure integrity in this process?
11. Assume that the facts in both cases were laid out before your peer collegium. What would they do? What should they do? Would it matter for your analysis if Professors Weaver and Heely were tenured or untenured?

PROBLEM 8: Racial discrimination: Inadvertent neglect, overt hostility, excessive attention

Professor Harold Dietz is a tenured professor of French at your university. He prefers teaching the upper-level literature classes over the introductory language courses because he enjoys hearing students discuss what they find interesting in literature. In his "Survey of French Literature" this semester, Professor Dietz, who is white, assigns works written by white authors from France, while famous black writers from Africa and the Caribbean are not represented on the syllabus. During the course of the semester, students ask Professor Dietz about Francophone literature from other parts of the globe. Some students tell him that they signed up for the course because they wanted to learn about French literature from around the world. He realizes that he had overlooked important authors and tells himself that he really should revise the syllabus for next year. He had always used this syllabus and the issue had never been raised before.

Professor Louise Lassik is a white tenured professor of political science. She is very good at promoting discussion in her classes. She regularly solicits comments from the white students in the class, but almost never calls on the minority students. On the few occasions when she does, she makes disparaging remarks about their comments. These students either drop her class or refrain from raising their hand again the rest of the semester.

Professor Samuel Folz, a white professor of art history, is solicitous of the minority students in his classes. He often calls on them more frequently than the other students. When minority students answer a question, he responds very enthusiastically, but much less so when white students give comparable answers. The white students in the class complain among themselves that he shows favoritism toward minority students as a group.

1. Does Professor Dietz owe an aspirational ethical duty to represent Francophone writers from different parts of the globe in a survey class? If so, to whom? If he has failed to meet an aspirational ethical duty, what should be done about it? By whom?

2. Does it make any difference if the faculty had voted to include more diverse authors in syllabi where appropriate? What if the administration had directed professors to do so but without faculty input? Would Professor Dietz's failure then violate principles of professional conduct in either of these situations? If so, what should be done about it? By whom?

3. Does he have an aspirational duty to revise the syllabus during the course of the semester to address what students expected to be reading in a survey class?

4. Should he correct the problem in future syllabi? Must he?

5. Does Professor Lassik violate any principles of professional conduct by not calling on the minority students? By responding disparagingly to their comments?

6. At what point should Lassik's conduct be recognized as a problem? After 1 class? 2 classes? 1 semester?

7. Who is responsible for handling this problem — the administration or the peer collegium? What should they do? If the conduct were clearly proven as intentional, is this a situation where sanctions should be imposed? What sanctions? What if the conduct is unintentional?

8. Does it make any difference to your analysis that Lassik is tenured?

9. Does Professor Folz violate a principle of professional conduct or an aspirational ethical duty in calling on minority students more often than white students?

10. Does he violate either in responding to the same answers differently?

11. Should Professor Folz's "favoritism" be addressed? How? By whom? What if it is proven that his favoritism is intentional and that course grades are affected?

12. What should the peer collegium do to improve culture on these issues, yet avoid concerns about coercion of dissent?

PROBLEM 9: Self-promotion; taking advantage of students

Professor Gene Sherman wrote a book about music 2 years ago. The book has been met with moderate recognition in the field and makes some modest royalties for the professor. Since its publication, Professor Sherman has made the book required reading in all of the courses where the subject matter would be appropriate. This year he has decided to make it recommended reading only, offering extra-credit if students read it and write a short 2-page paper on it.

Professor Rose Liu is well liked by her students. She enjoys hanging out with them, inviting them over for a glass of wine, or sometimes dinner. She goes to their parties regularly. Lately she has been asking them to do small favors for her, such as walking the dog, picking up her dry cleaning, and occasional baby-sitting. She has been happy to discover that students have eagerly accepted requests to baby-sit or run errands for her, never turning her down. She pays them for all work they do for her.

1. Does Professor Sherman violate any principle of professional conduct or aspirational ethical duty in requiring his students to read his book? Does your analysis depend on how closely the book fits with the course? Is there an inherent conflict of interest in assigning one's own textbooks that a professor should at least consider?

2. If Professor Sherman's book had been widely recognized in his field, would this change your analysis? What if it had been badly received by all reviewers?

3. If he had made the book only recommended reading, without offering extra-credit, would he violate any principle or duty? How does offering extra-credit change your analysis?

4. Should this problem be addressed by the peer collegium or by the administration?

5. Does Professor Liu violate any principles of professional conduct in socializing at home with her students?

6. Does she violate any principle of professional conduct or aspirational ethical duty in asking her students to run errands for her? To baby-sit for her?

7. At what point do these requests become a problem? Who should determine this?

8. Does it make any difference if Professor Liu makes these requests of students currently taking a class with her? How about asking only former students to help her?

9. Assume that Liu makes these same requests of her teaching assistants. How would this change your analysis?

10. What is the appropriate peer culture with respect to socializing with students and asking them to do favors for professors? Should junior faculty be encouraged or discouraged to be "chums" with undergraduate students? With graduate students?

11. What if students are telling other faculty members that Professor Liu is drinking excessively? Or taking drugs?

PROBLEM 10: Sexual harassment

Professor Bob Jaeger, age 50, has become friendly with his student Marge, age 21. She is his best student in advanced physics so he frequently calls on her in class. One day after class she asks if she can make an appointment to speak with him about her final project, and he suggests that they talk about it over lunch the next day. At lunch, he is very helpful, giving her many useful suggestions. Over coffee, the conversation turns to more personal matters, with Marge asking him for advice about a relationship that she is in the process of ending.

A few days later, while Marge is in the professor's office picking up a handout that she'd forgotten to get in class that morning, one of Bob's colleagues drops by to offer Bob a couple of tickets for a basketball game that he won't be able to attend. When his colleague leaves, Bob asks Marge if she would like to go with him. After the game, Bob invites Marge out to dinner the following day. The following week they see each other again outside of school, at which point a sexual relationship develops between them. Both Marge and Bob are very happy together.

1. Does Professor Jaeger violate a principle of professional conduct in having lunch with Marge? In letting the conversation turn personal? In inviting her to the basketball game? In inviting her to dinner? In engaging in a sexual relationship with Marge?
2. At what stage does their relationship become inappropriate?
3. As their relationship progresses, does Professor Jaeger owe Marge an aspirational ethical duty not to let it become a sexual relationship?
4. Does it matter if Marge is Professor Jaeger's current student? Would your analysis change if Marge had finished taking classes with him last semester?
5. If Marge were only an average student, does the possible implication of grades become an issue in this situation?
6. Does favoritism become an issue? Even if Marge is not currently taking a class with Professor Jaeger, should the peer collegium consider the impact on the other students?
7. If Marge never voices concern about the relationship, does Professor Jaeger violate any principles of professional conduct or aspirational ethical duty? If so, to whom?
8. If neither Marge nor Professor Jaeger disclose the relationship to anyone, what issues are implicated if one night a maintenance person discovers them naked together in Professor Jaeger's office? What if they swear the maintenance person to secrecy, threatening her with adverse consequences if she tells anyone?
9. If their relationship becomes known, does it have any impact on other students' perception of the department? Of Professor Jaeger?
10. If Marge does not complain, but the relationship is widely known, does the peer collegium or the administration have any role to play in any of the circumstances described above?
11. What should be done if the relationship turns sour and Marge approaches the department chair about sexual harassment by Professor Jaeger?
12. What if she just approaches Professor Jaeger's colleagues about his sexual harassment of her? What should they do?

PROBLEM 11: Negativism and tyrannical conduct toward students

Professor Linda Bigler, a tenured professor of French at your institution, is teaching "The Development of the Novel" this semester. This is her favorite class because students always enjoy learning about the relationship between the rise of the middle-class and the evolution of the novel. Professor Bigler likes to introduce her students to the wide variety of approaches taken by critics in the field. Wanting her students to gain a certain critical awareness, she often voices her concern about some well-respected scholarship. Sometimes she demonstrates real hostility toward these ideas, calling them weak and ridiculous. At other times, she attacks these scholars personally, revealing details and gossip to students about these scholars' personal lives that she knows only because the field is so small.

Finding that students often don't respond to her questions as quickly as she would like, Professor Bigler criticizes them for lack of preparation. She is visibly angry and lashes out at the group as a whole. Sometimes she singles out individual students who have trouble following the more difficult concepts. She occasionally criticizes their intellect with statements such as "Does your elevator go the top?"

Professor Bigler's frustration with student performance carries over to her language classes. Her French 101 class traditionally has an enrollment of 30 or so. Once, when she called on three people consecutively, none of whom had the correct answer, Professor Bigler walked out of the classroom, telling the class they would suffer because of lack of preparation.

1. Does Professor Bigler owe an aspirational ethical duty to expose her students to the current range of acceptable scholarly thought on her subject?
2. Does she violate any principles of professional conduct in demonstrating hostility towards different points of view?
3. Does she violate any principles of professional conduct in attacking other scholars personally in the classroom? Would it make any difference if she were to do so in the privacy of her office with other colleagues?
4. Would it make any difference if Professor Bigler were showing such hostility in the classroom toward the scholarship of other colleagues on her faculty? What if she attacked them personally in the classroom, discussing campus gossip about her colleagues?
5. Does Professor Bigler violate any principle of professional conduct or aspirational ethical duty in her criticism of the class as a whole? At what point does her criticism cross the line you are drawing?
6. Does she violate a principle of professional conduct or an aspirational ethical duty in expressing her anger? In lashing out at her students?
7. Who are the stakeholders in this situation? Is anyone besides her students affected by her conduct?
8. Does she violate any principles of professional conduct or aspirational ethical duty in singling out certain students? At what point does a violation occur?

9. Would your analysis change if Professor Bigler had used profanity in criticizing other scholars to her literature students? What if she'd directed profanity at her students?
10. Does a professor meet professional standards when he or she walks out of a class when 3 out of 30 are unprepared? Are there alternative ways for handling this problem?
11. Assume Professor Bigler admits all of this conduct. What should the peer collegium and the administration do? Would it matter if both peers and administrators had warned her before to stop such conduct? Should sanctions be imposed?
12. Assume that students were bringing stories like these to you concerning a colleague's conduct. What would you do specifically?
13. What could the peer collegium do prophylactically to reduce the incidence of this type of conduct?

SCHOLARSHIP
PROBLEM 12: Plagiarism; authorship attribution

Professor Joan Linden is a medievalist who publishes widely in her field. As a tenured professor, she has enjoyed several sabbaticals in England. After returning from her leave last year, she came out with an article on a relatively new subject for her — the symbolic features of suits of armor in the late medieval period. The article was a huge success, even attracting the attention of modern scholars of military history who praised her work for its invaluable contributions to the field. After the article had been out about a year, it was discovered that Linden had plagiarized the work of a little known English medievalist who had died some years back. Linden had come across his papers in the library where she had spent most of her last sabbatical. She had lifted entire sections from his research, thinking that no one would ever uncover the deception.

Professor James Highsmith has collaborated on a project with Professor Kate Weil, a junior scholar, for three years. He recognizes that she does outstanding work and will be at the forefront of her field one day. As Weil is reading the first draft of the article they've been working on, she realizes that Highsmith has failed to make appropriate authorship attribution for the sections that were clearly hers. Furious, she confronts him but he feigns surprise at her accusations. The next draft that he submits to her for review contains all the necessary attributions.

1. Who is harmed by plagiarism? What is the harm?
2. What principles of professional conduct has Professor Linden violated?

3. Should any sanctions be imposed on Linden? Should her excellent past record mitigate any sanction?

4. If she had lifted only one brief section from the English medievalist's work, would your analysis be the same?

5. Had Linden been tenure-track instead of already tenured, how would your analysis differ? What would be the penalty if a graduate student did the same thing?

6. Has Professor Highsmith violated any principle of professional conduct or aspirational ethical duty in his allocation of authorship credit?

7. Does Professor Weil owe a duty to the peer collegium or administration to notify them of Professor Highsmith's conduct? What if Professor Highsmith's research assistant has strong evidence that he intentionally tried to manipulate authorship credit?

8. Does gender play a role in your analysis?

9. In light of the fact that Professor Highsmith corrected the problem, should any sanctions be imposed on Highsmith?

10. What are the responsibilities of the peer collegium with respect to education of professors and students on plagiarism and authorship attribution?

PROBLEM 13: Preparing lectures using the work of students and colleagues without attribution; using student input without attribution to write conference papers

The music department at your institution enjoys a national reputation. It attracts outstanding students and professors from all over the country. Professor Sangeeta Gupta, a recent Ph.D. in musicology, teaches an upper-level seminar on music history. Excellent students make the class a challenge to teach. The discussion on Beethoven as a patriarchal tool is particularly lively and even heated at times, with students contributing insights that Professor Gupta finds path-breaking. Some of these insights occur in class discussion and some appear in seminar papers.

In the "Introduction to Music" class that Professor Gupta teaches the following semester, she frequently uses ideas raised by the seminar students to prepare her lectures, using them without attribution. Likewise, in her class lectures she presents ideas verbatim from the published work of other scholars, proposing them as her own.

In a conference paper on Beethoven that she is preparing to give over the summer, she uses student input from the seminar to structure her analysis without acknowledging them in her footnotes. At times she takes portions of their written work and appropriates them as her own.

1. Does Professor Gupta violate any principles of professional conduct or aspirational ethical duties in using student ideas without attribution to prepare her lectures for the introductory class?
2. Would it make any difference if her lectures acknowledged their contributions? Would it make any difference if she asked her seminar students if she could use their ideas, still with no intention of acknowledging them?
3. Does she violate a principle of professional conduct or aspirational ethical duty in not acknowledging the published work of scholars in her field when presenting her class lectures?
4. Had Professor Gupta been a seasoned teacher, would your analysis in questions 2 and 3 change?
5. Does she violate a principle of professional conduct or an aspirational ethical duty by failing to acknowledge that the analysis in her conference paper has been informed by her students' work? Is her taking of portions of the students' written work more serious than taking students' ideas presented in class?
6. Should any sanctions be imposed on Professor Gupta? Does it matter for your analysis that she in untenured?
7. How do you define the line where a student research assistant's contribution to a professor's published paper must be acknowledged? When is coauthorship appropriate?
8. Does the peer collegium have a duty to educate new faculty on plagiarism?

PROBLEM 14: Errors in scholarship; lack of productivity in scholarship; manipulation of data

Professor Lou Boldt, age 50, is a tenured professor of English at your institution. He has produced no significant scholarship in the last five years. He continually produces research that does not take into account major recent scholarship. His analyses are weak; the writing is poor, and at times even incomprehensible. He never had an easy time placing an article, but now his submissions always come back rejected. Indifferent to his plight, Professor Boldt has decided not to send articles out anymore.

Professor Bob Sullivan is a tenured professor in journalism at your institution. He has not been a strong researcher, publishing very irregularly. Professor Sullivan wrote a human-interest article, published in both Chicago and Dallas papers about going to a Texas bar in a rural town where Dallas Cowboy fans watched the team lose to the Chicago Bears. After questions were raised about the article's authenticity, the managing editor of the Dallas paper accompanied Professor Sullivan to the Texas town, but

Professor Sullivan could not locate the bar. Professor Sullivan claimed that residents had given him false names and were hiding the bar because it may have had no license.

1. Professor Boldt stopped conducting meaningful research 5 years ago. At what point does production of unpublishable research become a serious problem? After 2 years? 5 years? 10 years? At what point does complete nonproductivity become a serious problem? After 2 years? 5 years? 10 years?
2. Has Professor Boldt violated any principles of professional conduct in producing flawed research?
3. Does he have an aspirational ethical duty to remain productive?
4. Does Professor Boldt violate any principle of professional conduct or as-pirational ethical duty in deciding to no longer send out any articles whatsoever?
5. Does the peer collegium owe Professor Boldt a duty to help him get past his indifference? Or is the problem Professor Boldt's alone?
6. How does a peer collegium create a culture of high aspiration with re-spect to scholarship?
7. At your institution, does Professor Sullivan have a duty to publish more than sporadically? What factors might affect your answer?
8. At what point might an irregular publication record become a serious problem? After 2 years with no publications? 5 years? 10 years?
9. Has Professor Sullivan violated any principle of professional conduct or aspirational ethical duty in writing the story?
10. Should any sanctions be imposed on him? Would your analysis change if the manipulation were discovered after retirement? What sanctions should be imposed then?
11. Should the manipulation of data be corrected in the public record?

PROBLEM 15: Conflicting evidence; conflict of interest

Professor Ann Clovis, a tenured professor of anthropology, is highly re-garded for her archeological research at a local historical site in the river valley. She has identified areas where stone tools were manufactured by people who lived at this location prior to the arrival of the Europeans. She distinguished areas of manufacture from areas where the stone debris was later deposited as garbage. Areas of manufacture contained one-millimeter stone flakes that were produced by manufacturing along with the larger flakes. Garbage deposits contained only the larger flakes that could be picked up and easily moved.

Clovis conducted a summer fieldwork program at this location for sev-eral years. The program was vital to the survival of the Anthropology Department. After Clovis published a widely read paper on her research, at-tendance at the summer program grew because students wanted to study with her. This firmly established her position in the department, and she hoped to be chair someday.

At a Midwestern archaeology and anthropology conference, Clovis had a spirited discussion with Professor Neil Flint, a tenure-track member of the department who disputes her research. He claimed that his research showed that as worms moved through the soil they displaced the one-millimeter stone flakes. Clovis ignored Flint's evidence in subsequent pa-pers and talks.

Later that year, Clovis served on a student grant committee. A student who participated in Clovis' summer program three years ago submitted one proposal. The student's proposal stated that if she could receive the ap-propriate funding she would demonstrate that one-millimeter stone flakes were too large to be moved by worms.

1. Do any principles of professional conduct or aspirational ethical duties require Professor Clovis to refer in her scholarship to studies that dis-pute her thesis?
2. Does her duty depend upon the quality of the research behind the con-tradictory findings?
3. Who are the stakeholders in this situation? If it is clear that Professor Clovis is ignoring credible opposing evidence in her scholarship, what should her peers do?
4. Should Professor Clovis abstain from voting on Professor Flint's pro-motion and tenure? Does Professor Flint's publication of research con-tradicting Professor Clovis necessarily disqualify Professor Clovis?
5. Would your analysis change if the disagreement turned personal?
6. Assuming that Professor Clovis knows the student well from having spent the summer together, should Professor Clovis abstain from voting on her grant proposal because of this?
7. Should Professor Clovis abstain from voting on the proposal because it disputes her own research?
8. Under what circumstances, if any, should an evaluator abstain from vot-ing on a student proposal? On a colleague's proposal?
9. Assume that Professor Clovis instructs her graduate student seminar to ignore Professor Flint's work. Does Professor Clovis violate any princi-ple of professional conduct or aspirational ethical duty when she tells her students to ignore Professor Flint's research?
10. Do Professor Clovis' colleagues have a duty to speak with her about ex-ploiting graduate students?
11. Should any sanctions be imposed on Professor Clovis? If so, by whom — the peer collegium or the administration?

12. Does the peer collegium have any responsibility to educate faculty members on their obligations regarding opposing evidence and evaluation of others when self-interest is apparent?

PROBLEM 16: Falsifying credentials

Professor Eric Falz, a tenured professor of communications at your institution, is a productive scholar. He has several projects going at the same time, including putting together an anthology of writings by twentieth-century American and European journalists, editing a volume on Internet journalism, and writing a book on Marshal McLuhan. He has contracts from major university presses for all three and has only to complete them for final submission.

At a meeting nine months ago with the department chair concerning a proposal for a conference on campus, Professor Falz told the chair that he had completed the edited volume on Internet journalism and wanted to design a symposium with colleagues in the department serving as respondents to the essays in the volume. Eight months later, with the conference date fast approaching and his colleagues repeatedly asking Professor Falz for the original essays, Professor Falz revealed that in fact he had not yet even received the articles for the volume, let alone edited them. The conference organizer quickly had to rearrange sessions, to the embarrassment of the entire department.

As for the anthology, he had received copyright permission for all the essays he wanted to include. The only thing preventing his sending it off to the publisher was his as yet unwritten introduction to the volume. The book on McLuhan was likewise only halfway done. Professor Falz wanted to apply for an external grant to conduct summer research abroad. The C.V. that he submitted along with his grant proposal indicated that both projects were completed. Under the "Education" section of the C.V., he included an MA in International Relations even though he had only completed one year of coursework.

1. Did Professor Falz violate any principles of professional conduct in telling his chair that he had completed the edited volume?
2. Did Professor Falz violate any aspirational ethical duties in causing his colleagues to rely upon his unfinished project?
3. Did the department chair or the peer collegium have any duty to confirm that Professor Falz had indeed completed the volume?
4. Should any sanctions be imposed on Professor Falz for inducing reliance on his completion of the volume? For wreaking havoc on the conference and embarrassing his department?

5. What principles of professional conduct did Professor Falz violate in indicating on his C.V. that his research was complete?
6. Who is affected by this conduct?
7. What principle of professional conduct or aspirational ethical duty does Professor Falz violate in saying that he earned an MA in International Relations?
8. Who does this statement affect?
9. Who should be responsible for handling Professor Falz's situation — the administration or the peer collegium?
10. Should the peer collegium or the administration impose any sanctions on Professor Falz for the false statements on his C.V.?
11. Would your analysis of Professor Falz's conduct change if he were untenured? Are the duties any different?
12. What if Professor Falz claimed he was struggling with alcohol abuse in this period? Does that change your analysis?

PROBLEM 17: Conflicts with outside consulting work; use of university resources

Troy Carter, a tenured professor of geography, launched a new project several years ago that set out to study residential housing patterns. After the data came in last year, Professor Carter published an important article that was highly respected by scholars as well as the public and private sectors. Since that time, Professor Carter has seen a high demand for her services as a consultant to real estate companies and public agencies.

Wishing to respond to this demand, she decided to open a consulting business on the side, in addition to her academic career. She has stationery and business cards printed up that list her academic affiliation and also the name "Carter Consulting Associates." She arranges for private telephone and fax lines in her faculty office. Professor Carter also pays a student research assistant to answer phones, send faxes, etc. Professor Carter usually works about 65 hours a week year-round, 12 of which she devotes to her consulting business.

1. Does Professor Carter violate any principles of professional conduct in using university space for her consulting business? Consider the indirect costs of this arrangement in your answer.
2. Does she have an aspirational ethical duty to separate university affiliation from consulting? What are the outer bounds of using university prestige for private advantage?
3. Does your analysis change if she were to work a total of 40 hours a week, 12 of which were devoted to the business? Is it possible to determine how many hours a week are appropriate for each of her two jobs? Pro-

fessor Carter makes the argument that her outstanding reputation in consulting enhances the prestige of the university and that she should devote even more time to consulting. How does this argument affect your analysis?

4. Does she violate any duties if her consulting requires her to miss class once a semester? Twice? Five times? Assume she reschedules all classes, but the students are complaining about excessive absences.

5. Assume a public agency is ready to give her a grant to implement a particular study. She can run it through either her consulting practice or the university. Which should she choose? Does she violate any principles of conduct or ethical duties in choosing the former?

6. Who are the stakeholders in the dilemma posed in Question 5?

7. At your institution, how far can a professor go in pursuing private consulting before members of the peer collegium speak up about the issue? At what point would sanctions be imposed?

8. What are typical areas where professors use university resources for private advantage? Do they violate any ethical duties in doing so?

9. Imagine that a student reports to Professor X that she has observed Professor Y (untenured) using university resources for personal monetary advantage. Does Professor X have a duty to investigate? What is the nature of this duty? What boundaries must Professor Y cross that would warrant investigation into this matter? Does your analysis change if Professor Y is tenured?

PROBLEM 18: Correction of previously reported results

Greg Mendel is a tenured professor of biology specializing in plant biotechnology. After fifteen years of relentless study and experimentation, he has now discovered a way to improve the nutritional quality of cassava plants via genetic modifications that pose no health risks to humans. Because cassava is a major food source for third world countries, this scientific breakthrough has been hailed as an important step for all humankind. Professor Mendel's discovery has brought great recognition to the university, including a dramatic rise in the number of both undergraduate and graduate applicants, new-found benefactors, and the promise of international prizes awarded to Professor Mendel. Professor Mendel has recently learned that he is being considered for a Nobel Prize in physiology or medicine.

Shortly before the Nobel winner is to be announced, Professor Mendel receives a heated e-mail communication from Cooper, a scientist in Nigeria, saying that repeated duplications of Professor Mendel's experiment have not yielded the same remarkable results. In addition, Professor

Mendel's research did not account for a particular climate condition that El Niño was, by all predictions, certain to bring in the next ten years. According to the Nigerian scientist, if meteorological forecasts proved true, Professor Mendel's research would become superfluous, and indeed, obsolete before it could be of any use to anyone.

1. Does Professor Mendel violate a principle of professional conduct if he chooses not to investigate the validity of this contradictory evidence?
2. Does he have an aspirational ethical duty to investigate this claim?
3. Assume that Professor Mendel shows the e-mail to a colleague in the same field named Kolmes. Does Kolmes have a duty to investigate? How does Kolmes determine if investigation is warranted?
4. It turns out that other investigators support Cooper; no one can duplicate Mendel's results. Does this mean that Mendel is professionally incompetent?
5. Assume that Professor Mendel had considered the effects of climate on his experiment, but had neglected to consider this particular area before publishing his results. Does this mean that Professor Mendel was professionally incompetent? Assume that it was a deliberate oversight on his part because investigation into this area was costly and so time-consuming that it could add 5 or 6 more years to his research. Does this mean he was professionally incompetent? Should he have disclosed this choice in his published research?
6. Before confirming or disproving Cooper's results, does Professor Mendel have an aspirational ethical duty to notify anyone that the results may be in question?
7. If he learns that Cooper is right, does Professor Mendel have a duty to correct his work? Do the relevant principles of professional conduct require him to correct his work?
8. Who are the stakeholders in this situation?
9. Change the facts above. Assume that Professor Mendel has not yet published any results and now discovers that the climate problem is a valid one. He includes this issue in his published work. Should he generously credit Cooper with the discovery in a footnote? Should he invite Cooper to be listed as a coauthor?
10. Would your analysis be any different if Professor Mendel's research had not produced a scientific breakthrough, but had simply been a minute step forward in an already small area of genetic modification?
11. At what point should previously reported results be corrected? Does your answer depend on the magnitude of the original discovery?
12. What if Professor Mendel subsequently learned that some data he had discussed was in fact erroneous but that it did not matter for the project as a whole. Does he have a duty to correct it?

PROBLEM 19: Response to fraud of a colleague

Michelle Viti is a newly tenured professor of music. Her research analyzes the relationship between history and music tempo. Scholars regard her work as cutting edge. She recently received tenure for publication of a book on Beethoven that examines whether Beethoven's metronome markings on his piano sonatas indicated that he really wanted them to be played so fast. Her conclusion that the markings were the result of a broken metronome has led musicians and conductors to perform new experiments with time in Beethoven's works and has opened the door to a productive new kind of Beethoven scholarship.

An untenured professor in the department, Anthony Rollins, enjoys an occasional coffee with Professor Viti after work. Professor Rollins also writes on tempo, but in contemporary music. After a few months of these casual meetings, Professor Rollins notices some inconsistencies in Professor Viti's statements about Beethoven. When he questions her, Professor Viti replies that her book "stretched a few things here and there" and that the metronome in question was in fact not always used by Beethoven in his piano sonatas. She explains that her book makes an important contribution to the field because it helped inspire new performances of Beethoven's work, sometimes even creating jobs for young musicians. Likewise, it helped develop a scholarly field that was sorely in need of some "livening up."

At their next meeting for coffee, Professor Rollins informs Professor Viti that he is going to tell the department chair what she has told him about her book. Professor Viti tells Professor Rollins that the chair is a close friend of hers and that he already knows all about this. Professor Viti then threatens to see to it that Professor Rollins's contract not be renewed next year if Professor Rollins makes this information public. Professor Rollins backs down and does nothing.

1. Does Professor Viti violate any principles of professional conduct or aspirational ethical duty when she "stretched" her research?
2. Who is affected by Professor Viti's conduct?
3. Who should be responsible for determining whether Professor Viti's conduct is research fraud?
4. Do Professor Viti's motives redeem her conduct in any way? How does one distinguish honorable from dishonorable motives?
5. Should any sanctions be imposed on Professor Viti? Who should handle this—the administration, the peer collegium, scholars in the field, or a combination thereof?
6. Say that Professor Viti instead used the "publish or perish" argument to justify her conduct to Professor Rollins. How does this reasoning com-

pare to the "helping the field" argument that she makes to Professor Rollins? Is there any place for a weighing of justifications on these facts?

7. Does Professor Rollins have an aspirational ethical duty to speak with the chair, despite Professor Viti's admonitions? Does he violate any principles of professional conduct if he decides to do nothing?

8. If Professor Rollins learns firsthand from the chair that the chair will indeed do nothing, does Professor Rollins have a duty to pursue this further? Should he go to the faculty itself?

9. Say that Professor Viti, upon discovering that Professor Rollins intends to blow the whistle on her, retaliates by making sure he gets a bad schedule next term. Does this act of retaliation violate any principles of professional conduct?

10. Professor Rollins is untenured. How does this affect your analysis or your recommendation of what should be done? How would it affect your analysis and recommendations if Professor Rollins were tenured?

11. What institutional steps can a faculty or department take to prevent fraud and to encourage responsible whistle-blowing?

PROBLEM 20: Conflict of interest with a corporate funding source

Carol Wardin, a tenured professor of pharmacology, has received funding for the last 10 years from TDH Pharmaceuticals to conduct research on four asthma medications developed by the company. Professor Wardin signed an agreement with TDH that required her to obtain their consent before naming the drugs in any studies she may publish. The company also recommended that she provide them with the complete manuscript in which the drugs would be mentioned. The company promised further funding if all went well. Professor Wardin found that mice were particularly responsive to compounds in two of the drugs and wrote an article to this effect. She showed it to TDH before submitting it to a journal in her field. The article was very well received. As a Christmas present, TDH gave Professor Wardin an all-expenses-paid trip to Paris for two.

1. Did Professor Wardin violate any principles of professional conduct in signing the consent agreement with TDH?

2. Since TDH only recommended, rather than required, Professor Wardin to send them any manuscripts referencing the drugs, should she have sent them her article for their review?

3. Does Professor Wardin owe an aspirational duty not to comply with TDH's demands with regard to naming the drug in published work? To whom? What is the nature of her duty when TDH only recommends,

rather than requires, that she provide them with the complete manuscript?

4. Who is affected by her compliance?

5. Is there a conflict of interest in accepting funding from a corporation to conduct research? What are the outer bounds of this conflict? Would it be suitable to accept funds from a company that neither requires consent nor asks the researcher to submit any manuscripts for their review? Is it a violation of the principles of professional conduct if the grant recipient does not reveal the funding source for published research?

6. What if the article specially found that all four compounds were in fact harmful to mice, and after reviewing the article, TDH asked the professor not to publish it. She did not. Has the professor violated any principles of professional conduct? Any aspirational ethical duties?

7. Does Professor Wardin violate any principles of professional conduct in accepting the Christmas gift from TDH? Would your analysis be any different if the gift was of no substantial significance? What constitutes an acceptable gift?

8. Does the peer collegium have any obligation to provide clear guidelines on conflicts of interest with funding sources?

INTERNAL GOVERNANCE

PROBLEM 21: False allegations of misconduct against a colleague

Theresa Skillman is an assistant professor of sociology who specializes in work patterns of young rural Americans. She is exasperated with the comments of her senior colleague, Carl Upton, who occasionally makes disparaging remarks about her "pedestrian" subject. Professor Upton works on philanthropic patterns in Europe and the United States.

Aware that the two of them are being considered for the same external grant, Professor Skillman contacts a colleague at another institution whom she knows is a good friend of one of the grant reviewers. She tells her friend that Professor Upton is "just coasting on the excellent reviews of his first book" and that his research now cuts corners. She even goes so far as to tell her friend that he has fabricated data for his current work. Professor Skillman knows, however, that Professor Upton's work is as rigorous as ever.

Professor Skillman is also concerned that Professor Upton will be difficult at her tenure review. Not wanting him to participate in her promotion decision, Professor Skillman tells the chair that he has sexually harassed her by calling her names at a private meeting in her office when she knows he hasn't.

1. What principles of professional conduct does Professor Skillman violate in the grant situation? In the tenure scenario? Go through each step Professor Skillman takes. How serious is each individual action? Standing alone, would any individual action be a basis for a sanction?

2. Does Professor Skillman's colleague at another institution violate any principles of professional conduct if she conveys the information to the grant reviewer without doing any investigation?

3. Assume that a student informs you of rumors that a colleague has fabricated data. Do either the principles of professional conduct or aspirational ethical duties compel you to do a reasonable investigation before making public charges against a colleague?

4. Does the chair have a duty to investigate Professor Skillman's accusation of sexual harassment? What should the investigation look like?

5. What if the matter goes to a hearing? Should Professor Upton have the usual protections of a full hearing, including cross-examination? Who should decide the issue; Professor Upton's peers or administrators?

6. What sanctions should the peer collegium impose on Professor Skillman?

PROBLEM 22: Poor department service

Julia Wilson and Denise Kirby were good friends who attended graduate school together at a top-ranked university. Both got jobs at your school.

Denise had a reasonable teaching load and was happy to be teaching a seminar on her dissertation topic. Her colleagues found her teaching adequate. When she wasn't in class, she was always home working on books. She completed several books that were very well received. When it came time to complete her tenure dossier, she had not served on one committee before coming up for tenure. Either she refrained from volunteering or she turned down almost every request to serve. For those committees that she had been assigned to, she never showed up for meetings, infrequent as they were. Denise hardly knew her colleagues because she spent so little time at the department.

Julia, for her part, was feeling overwhelmed by the teaching load in her department. The students were incredible and she found herself over-preparing for class just so she could keep up with their intellectual curiosity. Her colleagues found her teaching excellent. Between this and preparing her manuscript for publication, she found little time to act collegial. She did what was asked in the way of service, but nothing more. Her department chair was careful to remind her every now and then that her service was minimal. Julia just barely submitted her manuscript on time for a tenure decision, and when it came back a few months later, complete with a contract and rave reviews, all she felt was relief.

1. As an untenured person, does Denise violate any principles of professional conduct or aspirational ethical duties in not volunteering to serve on committees? In turning down almost every request to serve? In not showing up for meetings? Should any colleagues talk to her about her service contributions?
2. Compare Denise with Julia, who attends meetings but does nothing more than asked. Does she violate any principles of professional conduct or aspirational ethical duties?
3. Is it possible to weigh outstanding scholarship and/or teaching against service?
4. What are the outer bounds of minimum acceptable service with relation to excellence in scholarship and teaching?
5. Would both of these individuals receive tenure at your institution?
6. Should a senior colleague tell untenured colleagues to back off of service in favor of scholarship?
7. What can the peer collegium and/or administration do to prevent conflict surrounding tenure due to minimal or no service?
8. What if both individuals were tenured at your institution. Do either of them, as tenured faculty members, violate principles of professional conduct or aspirational ethical duties with this little service?
9. What is the impact on the peer collegium and the institution if some tenured faculty members do no service? What should be done?

PROBLEM 23: Hiring decisions and contradicting schools of thought in a discipline

Dan Cleff, a tenured professor of musicology, is on the search committee for a position that will be shared with the Cultural Studies department. The departments are conducting an open search because they are interested not so much in the actual field of study as they are in finding someone whose work is genuinely interdisciplinary. Two candidates look especially promising: Fried, who works on popular music, and Berg, who works on classical music.

Professor Cleff and some of his colleagues are contemptuous of anything that looks "popular." They thus favor Berg's candidacy. When the two candidates came for campus visits, Professor Cleff actually found Fried more scholarly, but as a matter of principle would not consider him as a viable candidate.

1. Assume that both schools of thought are within the legitimate bounds of the discipline. Should the department be able to exclude scholars from the other school of thought? Should students be exposed to the range of accepted thought in a field? Should a department be able to build a critical mass of scholars around one field of thought?
2. If Professor Cleff and those who agree with him are in the minority on this issue, should they form a vociferous blocking minority to prevent hires they do not want? What if the difference of opinion in the department is over the importance of scholarly potential in candidates?
3. Who is affected by the department's decision? Should a candidate be hired over the opposition of a significant minority of the faculty?
4. Assume that both favored candidates are from the same school of thought. The department realizes that one is more scholarly, but (a) in Professor Cleff's words, "we don't like her style," or (b) they don't like her politics. They choose the less qualified candidate over her. Do they violate any principles of professional conduct in each situation? Do they violate any aspirational ethical duties?
5. Should the peer collegium try to prevent decision-making based on vague personal characteristics in cases such as this? Is there a risk to diversity if opposition is based on "style"? What if the opposition is based on irritating personal characteristics like interrupting others' comments?
6. Is your analysis of questions 1 and 5 affected by the size of the department?
7. Assume that Berg would be up for tenure in a few years, but in the interim Professor Cleff realizes he made a terrible mistake in voting to hire Berg. He thinks Berg is not "collegial." What are the appropriate and inappropriate aspects of "collegiality" that a senior faculty member should consider?

PROBLEM 24: Confidentiality

Curtis Snipes is chair of the math department. At last month's chairs' meeting with the dean, the dean discussed some new additions to the strategic plan. After the meeting, Snipes walked back with the dean to their respective offices. On the way, Snipes questioned him about the additions to the strategic plan and the dean told him some confidential information that could be potentially damaging to the administration. Snipes agreed to keep it confidential. That night at dinner, Snipes relayed this information to his wife, who works in the biology department.

Snipes has a colleague, Bill, going through a difficult divorce. Bill tells him something in confidence that Snipes later reveals to his best friend, who works in the same department as Bill.

Snipes' best student, Alice, tells him in confidence that she is pregnant and will be absent for a few days because she is having an abortion. A week later Snipes tells a colleague, Robin, whose class he knows Alice is currently taking. Robin knew nothing of the reasons for Alice's absence.

1. What is the nature of the aspirational ethical duty to maintain confidentiality when the information comes from the administration, colleagues, and students? Is there a heightened duty for one, but not the others?
2. What principles of professional conduct are implicated in each of the three situations?
3. Is it acceptable for Professor Snipes to tell his wife what the dean had told him in confidence?
4. Had Snipes' wife not worked at the same institution, would it have been acceptable to tell her?
5. When a colleague tells confidential information to another colleague who then reveals it to a third colleague, what aspects of professional life are placed in jeopardy?
6. Assume that Snipes revealed information about Bill's divorce to a student. How does this change your analysis of handling confidential information?
7. Did Snipes violate any principle of professional conduct in revealing the student's confidential information to a colleague? Any aspirational ethical duty? Can Snipes in any way justify revealing a student's confidential information? What if the student's confidential information relates to student misconduct like cheating under the school's conduct code? What if the student's confidential information relates to the student's substance abuse?
8. Assume that Snipes told other students about Alice's situation. How does this change your analysis?

PROBLEM 25: Condescending and tyrannical conduct toward colleagues

James Wilder, a tenured professor of economics, is becoming increasingly unpleasant at faculty meetings and in the hallways. He is continually negative about any proposed changes in curriculum and is down on the department. He continually interrupts colleagues and staff to make his points. He swears at colleagues and is tyrannical toward staff. He is especially condescending toward untenured faculty. Students say he talks about colleagues in his classes and verbally abuses them. He also makes demeaning demands of and comments about people who rank low in the administrative hierarchy. During interviews with potential faculty candidates or potential students, Professor Wilder goes out of his way to cast the depart-ment in a negative light.

1. What principles of professional conduct or aspirational ethical duties does Professor Wilder violate in acting this way toward staff, colleagues, administration, and students? Analyze each type of conduct.
2. Should persistent negativism about governance issues be analyzed dif-ferently from personal negativism directed toward colleagues?
3. In your analysis, is personal hostility toward administrators under a different standard than personal hostility toward colleagues? Are ad-ministrators "fair game"? Should there be a different standard for per-sonal hostility directed toward untenured faculty? Staff? Teaching assis-tants?
4. What do you think of Professor Wilder's argument that the university is about robust public criticism, and if you can't take the heat, get out of the kitchen?
5. Who should be responsible for handling this situation — the peer col-legium, the administration, or both? Who should make the decision that this conduct is not permitted?
6. At what point should someone step in to handle this situation? After a few weeks, 2 months, a semester, a year? What should they do? Should Professor Wilder be sanctioned for his conduct?
7. If substance abuse were the cause of Professor Wilder's behavior, how would this change your analysis?
8. What can the peer collegium do to build and monitor a healthy posi-tive culture directed at achieving the mission? Is it inevitable that fac-ulty culture will exhibit personal hostilities and "difficult" conduct?

EXTRAMURAL UTTERANCE AND CONDUCT

PROBLEM 26: Criminal conduct

The *New York Times* recently did a series on civil liability and criminal con-duct in higher education. The articles on civil liability included racial dis-crimination, sexual harassment, suspension of a medical license for in-competence by the state licensing board for a professor of medicine, suspension of a law license for taking a client's money for a professor of law, and failure to pay child support. Criminal activity ranged from failure to pay taxes to rape. In between these two extremes the article also addressed repeated DUI, shoplifting, perjury, fraud, and domestic violence including spouse and child abuse.

Many fine faculty and administrators across the country criticized the series for painting a negative picture of academia. They feared that it would produce yet another excuse for politicians, the public, and the media to disparage academics.

1. Consider each of these instances of civil and criminal misconduct and analyze whether this conduct by one of your colleagues would violate any principle of professional conduct or aspirational ethical duty:
   (a) civil liability
      • race discrimination;
      • sexual harassment;
      • suspension of professional license for incompetence or unethical conduct by a state licensing board; and
      • failure to pay child support.
   (b) criminal conviction
      • failure to pay taxes for 5 years;
      • repeated DUI;
      • shoplifting;
      • perjury;
      • fraud;
      • domestic violence including spouse and child abuse; and
      • rape.
2. Should the peer collegium and administration impose sanctions on a faculty member for any of these violations of the law? Would it matter for your analysis if the faculty member were tenured or untenured?
3. If any of these occurred on your campus, would any principles of professional conduct be violated in trying to keep this information from reaching the students and the public?
4. Is there an aspirational ethical duty to allow access to such information on campus? Should criminal conduct be revealed, but not civil liability?
5. Should certain individuals, such as a university president, dean, or law professor, be held to a higher standard with regard to such conduct?
6. Assume that a theme of the newspaper's series was that other professions, like law and medicine, are including a wider range of conduct, including conduct that does not directly affect clients or patients, in professional discipline. The academic profession has not done so. Should the academic profession move in this direction? What are the benefits and costs of doing so?
7. What can peer collegia do prophylactically to address these issues? What if a colleague has a DUI, or two DUIs? Should colleagues say something?
8. If the profession is criticized, should a negative be turned into a positive? Should academic leadership use the occasion to educate the public on the social compact of the profession and how the profession is addressing its obligations?

PROBLEM 27: Testimony inside and outside the discipline

Daniel Reinhardt is a torts (civil wrongs like personal injuries) professor at your state law school. He recently testified at the state legislative hearings to consider revisions of the No-Fault Act. Hoping to shape the law on liability as he believed it should read, Professor Reinhardt knowingly misrepresented the strength of his research on accidents involving taxi drivers and their passengers to favor injured persons. He also failed to acknowledge strong opposing evidence in his statements. He was not under oath.

Eric Ranger is a professor of engineering who conducts research that has been favorable to sports utility vehicles. He has been recently subpoenaed by a plaintiff to testify about recent lab findings concerning roll-over rates. It turns out Professor Ranger knowingly misrepresented his data and failed to present conflicting evidence in his court testimony under oath.

1. Does testifying outside the walls of the university but within your discipline mean you should be held to the same professional standard as scholarship or to the lower professional standard of extramural utterance?
2. How would you characterize the difference between misrepresenting research and failing to recognize strong opposing evidence?
3. Did Professor Reinhardt violate any principles of professional conduct in his testimony? Any aspirational ethical duties?
4. Did Professor Ranger violate any principles of professional conduct in his testimony? Any aspirational ethical duties?
5. Does it matter for your analysis that the court testimony was under oath but the legislative testimony was not? Does it matter that in the first case, the testimony favored injured persons but in the second case, it favored industry?
9. When a professor, using his or her institutional affiliation, testifies at a court or a legislature, do you think the listener is expecting an advocacy brief where half-truth by omission is acceptable?
10. Does a scholar who adopts advocacy ethics in such a situation, without informing his or her listeners, undermine the public's trust in the professorate? Would this also be true with respect to media interviews and other public statements on topics within the professor's discipline?
11. What should the peer collegium and the administration do about Professor Reinhardt and Professor Ranger's conduct? Should sanctions be imposed? Should sanctions be imposed for the same deceptive conduct in a media interview?
12. What if the professor is testifying at the legislature or in court but the topic is outside of the professor's discipline, and the same conduct oc-

curs? What principles or aspirational ethical duties apply? What if it occurs in a media interview on a topic outside of the professor's discipline? What should the peer collegium do?

13. Must a professor in all of these circumstances indicate that he or she is not speaking for the institution?

PROBLEM 28: Failure to perform disciplinary commitments

Diane Lilianthal, a tenured professor of English, agreed to serve a three-year term as executive committee chair of the Shakespeare section of International English Studies. Her responsibilities included overseeing a newly-annotated version of Othello, founding a new series on how to teach the tragedies, and serving as respondent for the Macbeth session at the annual IES conference. For a variety of reasons, she followed through with none of these responsibilities, including failing to notify the Macbeth panelists that she would not be present at the session.

Six months ago, Tracy Washington, a tenured professor of psychology, was selected to serve on a national board that helps at-risk adolescents graduate from high school. Professor Washington is in charge of allocating funds for after-school activities. To date, she has called no meetings and has failed to meet every deadline proposed by the national board. The national board is calling for her resignation.

1. What principles of professional conduct or aspirational ethical duties apply to Professor Lilianthal? Are her commitments to the professional association in the nature of scholarship?

2. Did Professor Lilianthal violate any principles of conduct or aspirational duties?

3. Do her colleagues on campus have a duty to do anything about her conduct? What should they do?

4. What reasons could Professor Lilianthal give for her failure that would mitigate the situation? Over-commitment? Ill health? Death of a family member? Substance abuse? How much do the reasons mitigate the situation?

5. How does Professor Lilianthal's agreement to accept disciplinary commitments off campus change the nature of her duties to the institution? Can she now claim that she must have a light internal governance load? Who should decide this type of question? Based on what criteria?

6. Assume that Professor Lilianthal had hired two teaching assistants to help with the tragedies series. She gave them little guidance and didn't follow through with the work she assigned them. The TAs were unable

to put in the hours they were promised and had a difficult time paying living expenses as a result. What principles of professional conduct or aspirational duties are implicated?

7. What principles of professional conduct or aspirational ethical duties apply to Professor Washington? While her commitment is not to a disciplinary association, the national board presumably selected her because of her disciplinary competence. Does this mean that her commitments are in the nature of scholarship? If not, and her commitments are not teaching or internal governance, is she subject only to the standards for extramural utterance? Or is this situation within the general duty of professional competence within the meaning of the 1940 Statement of Principles on Academic Freedom and Tenure?

8. Does it matter if Professor Washington claimed credit for these activities on her annual report to the dean?

9. Does it matter if Professor Washington's colleagues have legitimate concerns on how her failure reflects on the department and the institution?

10. Did Professor Washington violate any principles of professional conduct or aspirational ethical duties? If so, what should her colleagues do about it?

11. Assume that Professor Washington meets all her campus obligations. Does this affect your analysis?

12. Would your analysis change if Professor Washington did not have tenure, but was up for promotion in 1 year? In 2 years? In 4 years?

PROBLEM 29: Careless scholarship; plagiarism; inflation of credentials

Caryl Tenzel, a tenured professor of economics, has published widely on the effects of NAFTA on the Mexican rural economy. She has been so busy that she sometimes borrows whole portions of a recently given talk to local and national community groups and cuts and pastes them into the current presentation. She tells herself that it doesn't matter since it's all her own work anyway.

Professor Tenzel is also active outside the college community. She is regularly invited to give talks to both local and national groups that range from the regional library to the National Press Club. She receives so many invitations that she occasionally does not have time to check the sources she refers to in her speeches. She cites them based on what she has been told. Last week, in a speech before the National Press Club, she knowingly borrowed ideas from scholars in the field without citing them at all.

David Vaquero, a tenured professor of history, specializes in American military history. At academic conferences, Professor Vaquero has decided to use his experience as a platoon leader and paratrooper in Vietnam to engage his audience before launching into a talk about his research. As a result, he has earned a reputation as a dynamic academic who can mix the personal and professional in a productive way. He has become so well-known that he is now the keynote speaker at conferences in his field, receiving a substantial honorarium in the process. He also receives regular invitations to present his work at nonacademic venues. Last month he delivered a speech at a symposium sponsored by National Public Radio that ended with rousing applause and a standing ovation. Professor Vaquero, a creative soul, has neglected to reveal to his various audiences that he never served in Vietnam.

1. Is the professional standard higher, lower, or the same when presenting work within the discipline, but to lay groups?
2. Does Professor Tenzel violate any principles of professional conduct or aspirational ethical duties in cutting and pasting her own past work into current talks to be given at another institution? Should she tell those who select her to speak that the speech may be recycled material?
3. Would your answer be any different if she were to present these talks on her own campus? What if the talk is identical to previous talks but she does not tell the organizer of this fact?
4. Who might be affected by this practice?
5. What principles of professional conduct or aspirational ethical duties does Professor Tenzel violate in not verifying her sources?
6. Who are the stakeholders in this situation?
7. Does the speech at the National Press Club violate the principles of professional conduct or aspirational ethical duties?
8. If it is only one time that she borrows without citing scholars, is there a violation? What about 2 times? Five times? Is there a threshold limit in this case?
9. Had she *unknowingly* failed to cite her sources because of poor note-taking on her part when she read the original source, would your analysis be any different?
10. Does Professor Vaquero violate any principles of professional conduct or aspirational duties by fabricating a Vietnam experience?
11. Compare the use of such fabrication when employed at academic vs. nonacademic settings. Does it matter?
12. Does one have an ethical duty to keep imagination out of the academic endeavor? What are the outer bounds of such activity?
13. Does receiving an honorarium influence your analysis of the gravity of this situation? What if Professor Vaquero donated all honoraria to charitable organizations?

14. Should either of these professors be sanctioned in any way? If so, by whom—the peer collegium, the administration, the public, the media?
15. Assume that Professor Vaquero is running for local city councilman and uses his Vietnam experience as an important part of his campaign strategy. Compare this to the use of such information at a disciplinary conference and the National Press Club.

CHAPTER 4

Problems on the Rights
of Academic Freedom
for Individual Professors

TEACHING

PROBLEM 30: References to professor's faith and social or political ideology in the classroom

Norm Buckley coaches men's basketball at your institution and teaches the basic three-credit course in physical education for undergraduates. He is tenured.

This past semester, two students complained to the department chair that Professor Buckley, who does not dispute the facts, stated in class three times that one could not understand the miracle of human physiology without acknowledging a divine presence.

On two occasions, Professor Buckley stated his conviction that a strong faith was highly beneficial for physical health and overall well-being. On three other occasions, Professor Buckley mentioned his faith in class and called on students to remind him if, in his relationships with and assessments of students, he did not live up to his aspiration of living a "Christian life." Total class-time for these comments was roughly ten minutes.

Professor Angela Sunfish teaches a three-credit course in the psychology of education in the education department. She is tenured. She is extremely active in a radical environmental organization and organizes media coverage for her organization's protests of World Trade Organization meetings. Two students complained to the department chair that Professor Sunfish spends at least five minutes of each class talking about her organi-

zation's ideology, positions, and activities. She reviews which political candidates support these positions and how she will vote. She urges students
to vote similarly, and to join her in the organization.

1. Does academic freedom in teaching grant both professors freedom to
   teach what they wish in the classroom?
2. Does it matter whether the personal views expressed by a professor relate to the subject matter of the course? Should a professor introduce
   controversial material that has no relation to the subject taught?
3. Whose personal views have more relation to the subject matter of the
   course; Professor Buckley's or Professor Sunfish's? Are Professor Buckley's comments about faith not competent within the discipline? Would
   it matter if Professor Buckley were a biologist?
4. If the professor's personal comments are not related to the subject taught,
   does the amount of time spent on such comments matter? Is the standard whether such asides are persistent or whether inclusion of the ex-
   traneous material prevents the professor from covering the content of
   the course assigned by the faculty? Did either professor cross this line?
   At what point?
5. Whether or not the professor's personal views are related to the subject
   matter, is it appropriate for a professor to express his or her personal
   views on a topic or to advocate for his or her views?
6. When does a professor's advocacy of a personal position in the classroom
   cross over to indoctrination or unprofessional conduct? Must the professor's advocacy be conducive to the intellectual inquiry of students in
   the classroom? Must it be based on the professional competence of the
   professor? Must the professor's position be presented with evidence and
   argument that the students are invited to assess? Did either professor
   here cross over to indoctrination? At what point? Is either of them using
   the authority inherent in their instructional role to coerce students to
   make particular political choices? Is the absence of opportunity for open
   discussion an issue in either Buckley's or Sunfish's case?
7. Are some (many?) students intimidated by a professor's passionate argument for a personal position? Do some (many?) students fear bad
   grades if they disagree? What could be done under these circumstances
   to facilitate students to think for themselves? Is professorial advocacy
   necessarily circumscribed in the classroom because of the power differ-
   ential?
8. Is the solution to hire faculty in each department representing the full
   spectrum of political and social views on major issues and expect each
   to advocate aggressively in the classroom for his or her views?
9. What difference does it make to your analysis if Professor Sunfish states
   openly that she is not constrained by principles of academic tradition
   in her advocacy of causes in the classroom. She states, "these limitations

are simply masks for Eurocentric capitalist oppression." She proceeds to use ten minutes of each class for her advocacy. What if Professor Buckley makes a similar claim of secular humanist oppression based on his faith?

10. Who should make the decision whether either professor has exceeded his or her rights of academic freedom? The department chair? The dean? The departmental colleagues?
11. What courses of action should be taken to address the issues? By whom?

PROBLEM 31: Causation of events ascribed to astrology and channeling; denial of the Holocaust

Cheryl MacLaine is a tenured professor of political science at your institution. She is recognized as an outstanding scholar and teacher. Lately, she has become deeply interested in astrology and channeling and has studied both fields. At a recent faculty lunch, she tells a number of colleagues, including you, that she is increasingly convinced that these two fields provide answers for recent conduct in Washington D.C., and that she believes they can predict the future political events. She intends to include significant material on these fields in her Selected Topics in Political Theory seminar.

Bill Aryan is a tenured professor in engineering at your institution who has an international reputation as a scholar and lecturer in his specialty. In remarks in class, totally unrelated to the subject matter, Professor Aryan states that, based on his research, Jews in Europe in the period from 1936 to 1945 did not die from the Holocaust but from a combination of a type of plague and mass suicide. The remarks lead to student complaints and demonstrations on campus.

1. Does Professor MacLaine have academic freedom to include whatever topics she wishes in her seminar?
2. Is her teaching of astrology and channeling to explain causation and to predict political events within the range of reasonably competent disagreement within the discipline?
3. What if she includes evidence and argument supporting her theories in the seminar materials and encourages open discussion and criticism of both?
4. Would it matter for your analysis if she were a physics professor teaching a physics seminar using astrology and channeling to explain causation and to make predictions?
5. Who should make the decision whether Professor MacLaine's choice of topics is competent and thus protected by academic freedom? The board

of trustees? The president? Colleagues in the department? Her colleagues in other disciplines?

6. Does Professor Aryan have academic freedom to make such unrelated comments in his class?

7. Does it matter that the remark is on a topic outside of Professor Aryan's discipline? If such a remark on a topic outside the professor's discipline is made while teaching, should it be held to the higher professional standard of teaching and research or the lower professional standard of extramural utterance?

8. Say that the topic of the particular class in which the comment occurs is heating technology, and Professor Aryan asserts, based on his research, that the killing technologies and ovens alleged to be used by the Nazis could only have been one-tenth as efficient as the Holocaust scholarship claims. He proposes an alternative theory focusing on plague and mass suicide to explain what occurred. Does this change your analysis of the extent of his academic freedom? Which standard of professional competence applies? Would it matter if Professor Aryan provides all of his evidence and analysis to the class and makes them critique his work as a class exercise?

9. Who should make the decision whether Professor Aryan's comment is protected by academic freedom? The board of trustees? The president? The dean? His colleagues in the department? His colleagues in other departments? The institution's harassment and discrimination officers?

10. Should Professor Aryan have the opportunity to present the evidence and argument for his position or should abhorrence for his position be sufficient to force the conclusion that academic freedom does not protect the remark? Must peer assessors exercise all care to make their assessment based on scholarly grounds, regardless of the assessors' personal abhorrence for the argument?

11. Should campus demonstrations and possible disruption matter in the determination of the extent of Professor Aryan's academic freedom?

12. What course of action should be taken to address the issues? By whom? Assume this event occurs late in the semester after the drop/add period. Should faculty peers support a change in policy so that any student who wishes can drop out or even receive a passing grade for the course?

13. What if Professor Aryan's discipline is Twentieth Century European History and his teaching and writing are impeccable except for this topic?

14. Would it matter to your analysis if Professor Aryan's comments were made in a nondisciplinary speech to a Rotary Club outside the walls? In a presentation to a disciplinary organization? Does it matter if he refers to his institutional affiliation in the presentation or not?

PROBLEM 32: Hostile or insensitive environment created by professor or by other students

Sally Young is a tenured professor teaching the required introductory psychology course at the Nursing School. Twenty percent of the course deals with adult sexuality. Professor Young stated at the beginning of the course that sexually explicit material including pornography would both be shown and discussed in an open, scholarly manner. In this part of the course, she is liberal in her use of sexual imagery and plainspoken in her description of psychological theories, for example stating that "when Freud talks about castration anxiety, he is saying that little boys worry their penises and testicles will get cut off."

In several discussions on issues of adult sexuality, some students in Professor Young's class get into heated arguments. They trade angry insults to the effect that "all white men think with their dicks about sexuality." There are similar comments with respect to African-American women and other gender and racial groups. Professor Young thinks robust, frank debate is excellent and says nothing to control the class.

Three women students, an Evangelical Christian, a Moslem, and a strong feminist, complain to other faculty members and the department chair about an insensitive and hostile environment in the classroom.

1. Does Professor Young have academic freedom to present material on adult sexuality in the manner she thinks is most effective?
2. Would it matter to your analysis if in her classroom presentations the professor substitutes common slang words when referring to sexual organs? What if she uses other profanity in the classroom?
3. Would it make any difference in your analysis if Professor Young had students sign an informed consent stating that the class would cover sexually explicit material to be discussed in an open scholarly manner? It also states, "If you decide to stay in class and you experience distress, you can leave the room and see the professor after class to discuss the material. We will find a mutual way to cover any significant material missed."
4. What should be done in this situation and who should carry it out?
5. Should the student discomfort described here be sufficient to trigger an investigation into Professor Young's teaching? Does an investigation itself threaten academic freedom? Does the convening of a tribunal? Who should investigate whether Professor Young's teaching is protected by academic freedom? How should it be done?
6. Who should decide if the investigation should lead to formal charges and tribunal? Who should serve on the tribunal to decide if Professor

Young's teaching is protected by academic freedom? Her colleagues? The institution's harassment and discrimination officers? What should the hearing look like?

7. What if Professor Young aggressively questions all students, including students who are reticent and sensitive, about issues of adult sexuality? What if she selectively uses aggressive questioning only on the reticent and sensitive students to draw them out?

8. Would it matter to your analysis if Professor Young were untenured?

9. Does Professor Young have any duty to create a respectful classroom environment? Should she have sought both to make clear that the students' hostile exchanges cause harm and to restore civility and tolerance in the classroom?

10. Taking into account the issues of academic freedom involved, are the matters of professorial speech or student speech here a proper matter for investigation, tribunal, and sanction, or are they more properly a matter for private remonstrations by her colleagues to encourage her to ensure civility and student-centered learning?

PROBLEM 33: Tough-grading professor; student appeal of low grade

Professor Shirley Mansfield in the Math Department is known as an outstanding teacher, but she is also the toughest grader on your campus. She teaches one of the required multi-section large enrollment courses for math majors, and awards an average grade that is a full point lower than any other section of the course. The department does not have a required curve. The students in Professor Mansfield's class appeal to the department chair and the dean to adjust the grades.

Professor Mansfield also supervises a number of senior honors theses. She routinely writes sharp comments on some papers, for example stating that the analysis is "embarrassing," "hopeless," "a joke," or that the research materials were "something my 6th grader could have done." A student receiving a "C" on the thesis claims Professor Mansfield's grading was gratuitously nasty and personal and appeals to the department chair and dean to permit the student to drop the thesis course and to expunge the grade.

1. Is student assessment and grading part of a professor's academic freedom?

2. What if the department has agreed on a mandatory curve? Must a professor follow it? In this situation, there is no mandatory curve; does that matter?

3. What procedures should be followed if a student wishes to protest a grade?

4. Should the student be required to visit first with the professor? Is a professor required to meet with the student to give a reasoned explanation of the grade?
5. Should a student have an additional right to appeal a grade? To whom? On what grounds should an appeal be permitted? How deferential should the reviewer(s) be toward faculty grading decisions?
6. When does a professor cross the line toward abuse or arbitrary and capricious decision-making in evaluation and grading? Has Professor Mansfield crossed that line in either of these cases? In either case, should peers informally chat with her? Should they do more than that?
7. What if Professor Mansfield had written obscenities on the honors thesis?
8. What if a student could show that a professor had personal animosity or bias toward him or her? What sort of evidence would demonstrate this?
9. What should the peer collegium do if the administration unilaterally changes a grade without peer evaluation of a professor's grade? What if the administration changes a grade for the child of a major donor? Or because poor grades threaten grants or student recruitment?

SCHOLARSHIP

PROBLEM 34: Scholarship on alien abduction and intelligent design

Dr. James Leary, a psychiatrist on your medical school faculty, is noted for his research on the philosophy of medicine from a strong theoretical perspective. He recently published a book on alien abduction listing his institutional affiliation. The book asserts that based on his case studies of 20 patients who claim alien abduction for sexual experiments, he concludes that none of the patients are mentally ill and that all of them are honestly reporting the trauma they experienced. He states in the book and on talk shows that his theoretical analysis undermines previous scholarship that debunked alien abduction. While his evidence does not prove the existence of alien abduction for sexual experimentation, it strongly supports the hypothesis that people have experienced alien abduction. To contradict their experience compounds the oppression of society toward them and their alienation from society.

Professor Elizabeth Schweitzer, an untenured mathematician, has published more books and articles to scholarly acclaim for technical merit in her first five years than any other untenured professor in your institution's history. Her most recent article, listing her institutional affiliation, has generated much controversy outside the discipline. In this article, Professor

Schweitzer applied mathematics to the biochemical structure of cells and concluded that blind natural selection could not have created them, thus calling into question Darwinian mechanisms of random mutation and natural selection. Critics in the media and public immediately labeled Dr. Schweitzer a creationist, while proponents of intelligent design immediately proclaimed her as a new ally. Intelligent design acknowledges evolution up to a point, but disputes the idea that Darwinian natural selection is fully sufficient to explain the complexity of life, thus suggesting the possibility of other causes for the complexity, such as life on earth may have been seeded by meteorites or life may reflect the work of an intelligent designer (God).

1. Assume that in both cases, the professor's scholarship has generated much unwanted media and public attention and criticism (and controversial support) for the department and the institution. Many faculty administrators and board members are concerned about damage to institutional prestige and the impact on grants and gifts to the department. Are these concerns relevant to the question whether the scholarship of the two professors is protected by academic freedom? Would public demonstrations or disruption in favor of or opposed to their scholarship be relevant?

2. In both cases the scholarship is outside of the mainstream of the discipline. Does academic freedom give a professor the freedom to research and to publish any idea in his or her scholarship?

3. Who should decide whether this scholarship deserved the protection of academic freedom? The peer collegium? Just members of the department or members of the wider faculty? The administrators? The board of trustees?

4. If the peer collegium should decide, on what basis should it make the decision? Who should carry the burden of proof that the scholarship falls within the range of reasonably competent disagreement within the discipline?

5. Note that Professor Leary states that his evidence strongly supports the hypothesis that alien abduction for sexual experimentation exists, while Professor Schweitzer's analysis restricts itself to calling into question the comprehensiveness of Darwinian theories of evolution. Does this make any difference in your analysis?

6. If the peer collegium should decide that the scholarship is not competent and therefore is outside the protection of academic freedom, can the administration and board then factor in the amount of damage it causes to the department and institution in determining what course of action to take with respect to the professors?

7. If the peer collegium concluded that the scholarship is marginal, but is within the envelope of reasonably competent discourse in the discipline,

what should be done? Could peers informally talk to the professor about the value of the scholarship? Could peers and the department chair support giving fewer scarce departmental research dollars for scholarly projects that are considered marginal? Professor Schweitzer is untenured. Is this relevant in your analysis?

8. Would it matter if either professor publishes the work in question *without* indicating an institutional affiliation? Would it matter if either professor does not claim scholarly credit for the work? Would this mean that the proper standard of professional competence is the lower standard applicable to extramural utterance?

9. Would it matter if Professor Leary was a tenured art historian and Professor Schweitzer was an untenured music professor, so both are publishing these works outside their disciplinary expertise? Would claiming or not claiming institutional affiliation matter under these circumstances?

10. What if the dean, with the concurrence of the department chair, publicly censored both professors and denied them salary increases and research or travel support until they repudiated their questionable scholarship? What should the peer collegium do?

11. Must these professors make clear in their publication that they are not speaking for the institution?

PROBLEM 35: Hostile environment created by publication

Professor Linda McCarriston, a tenured creative writing professor, published a poem, "Indian Girls," in a poetry journal.

Indian Girls

I.
They come down all the ways
waterways or over snow and
frozen river, or come down
roads in pickups, getting
away, getting to town.
Many clans, tribes,
the Snail, the Raven,
many complexions, the thick
black hair. They learn
they are not my sisters
for I am white
though I would tell them—have—
that my road into
this town, too, was long

and bitter and began
breathlessly, silently,
under a chief still
called wise one.

II.
Out in the low and
wind-shriven villages
winter is warming its
hands on the flat roofs.
Women are making
fire inside, and food, and
mukluks for the babies.
Women are making
light, trying, trying
to shine it over the
whole house, even
to the dark, rooms of
cold, where savage
rights of the old
body over the
young, the great
body over the small
are preserved
as the oldest charter.

III.
They swagger out of the
Avenue Bar at midnight with
some tonight's Honey
laughter that's a dare to
make them scared of
you or any buddy. They
wear wallets on chains
and cowboy boots worn to
the cardboard heels
and their hair wants
washing. A few still
young—too ripe too
early—figure even
this picking is better
than being handed
over without so
much as beer. Who

might any of them
have become
in even the least
of the villages
had Christ not
come with his cross
and bottle
of vodka, his father's
god-awful rights
to
the daughter,
the sister,
the son?
    —Linda McCarriston

Native American students and local Native American community groups demanded an apology from the professor, filed a complaint with the president of the institution asking for an investigation, and organized protests outside the administration building and the professor's classes for the past several weeks. Their complaint is that the poem stereotypes Native American men concerning child abuse and creates a hostile environment for Native Americans.

Tenured law professor William Sowell, who teaches a required contracts course, published an essay in the state bar journal on affirmative action at the law school. He states that African-American students are entering the law school with substantially lower LSATs and undergraduate grade-point averages than Caucasian or Asian students and the academic average and bar passage rates of the African-American group of students are also significantly lower. Professor Sowell asks why this is. He writes that statistics indicate Asian students on the average spend the most time studying and in school, followed by Caucasians, Hispanics, and African Americans. The most reasonable explanation for this statistical difference in average study and school time, Professor Sowell concludes, seems to be cultural difference in encouragement and rewards for academic achievement. A focus on culture would alleviate the differences in the averages.

Professor Sowell does not mention those views in class and there have been no complaints from students in his classes. The published remarks lead to public allegations by on-and off-campus advocacy groups that Professor Sowell is a racist and should be treated as a pariah. Students not in his class file a complaint of hostile environment. Some politicians and funding sources threaten to withhold funds from the law school. None of the complaints dispute the accuracy of the data.

Drama department tenured professor Stanley Rushmore has published a play that parodies the excesses of monotheistic religions throughout history. The major characters in the play are Jehovah, Allah, and Jesus Christ. The dialogue is extremely demeaning to each faith. Religious groups on and off campus file complaints against Professor Rushmore asking for an investigation and demonstrate against the president of the institution and Professor Rushmore.

1. Does academic freedom protect Professors McCarriston, Sowell, and Rushmore from any adverse employment consequences for their published scholarship?
2. Would initiating an investigation of the charges against any of the professors itself chill academic speech? Should published scholarship, the competence of which is not challenged, ever be the subject of such investigations? Would convening a tribunal to hear the complaints chill academic speech?
3. Does academic freedom insulate a scholar from robust public criticism including nondisruptive demonstrations against the ideas?
4. What is the duty of the peer collegium and the administration with respect to academic freedom in situations like these? What if some members of the peer collegium or administration disagree with the ideas expressed? How should they proceed? Does a peer have a duty to protect a colleague's academic freedom if he or she abhors the idea expressed? Are peers bound to make their assessments solely based on scholarly grounds?
5. Assume the demonstrations move from being nondisruptive to being disruptive of the professor's teaching. Do the administration and peer collegium have a duty to protect the professor from such disruption?
6. Should the administration and peer collegium allow any religious or minority students to transfer from these professors' courses even after drop/add?
7. What if Professor Rushmore was on the faculty at a religiously affiliated college or university? Would that make any difference in your analysis?
8. Professor Sowell is writing in a professional legal journal but is not an expert on educational testing. Does this matter for your analysis? Is he thus subject to the lower standard of professional competence for extramural speech outside of the discipline?
9. Would it matter for your analysis if Professor Rushmore were Islamic, Christian, or Jewish; if Professor Sowell were African American; and if Professor McCarriston were Native American? Would it matter if any of them were untenured?
10. Would it matter for your analysis if Professor Sowell went further in his article and stated that the inquiry into biological foundations for human

behavior is a promising field and may ultimately explain these differences in genetic terms? What if Professor Sowell wrote that he believes the Bell Curve by Richard Herrnstein and Charles Murray presents evidence that should be considered on this issue?

11. Must these professors make clear that they are not speaking for the institution? What if they do not?

PROBLEM 36: Corporate pressure on scholars' publication or research

Professor Westington Carver, a tenured member of the medical school, published findings that showed some toxic reaction to an experimental hemoglobin treatment. The corporate sponsor of the research, Mediplex, complained to the university that the professor was forbidden to publish this essay because he had signed an agreement that publication could only occur with corporate consent. The corporation called off talks with the university for a 20-million-dollar endowment gift to the medical center that was to support the research center Dr. Carver headed. In response to the corporate complaint and suspension of discussions over the gift, the dean of the medical school asked for Dr. Carver's resignation as director of the research center and reassigned him to a small laboratory with a smaller staff.

Professor Susan Nader, tenured in Environmental Studies, has been scouring local lakes for years for an outlawed pesticide called toxaphene, a dangerous environmental toxin. The research has been funded by a grant from the federal Environmental Protection Agency. She discovered substantial amounts in some local lakes and published her findings in an environmental journal. A large New York law firm on behalf of an anonymous client has asked Professor Nader and the university to turn over copies of all her toxaphene research and everything ever written about her or by her. This includes all public personal data, all applications and supporting documents, memoranda, correspondence, reports, meeting minutes, calendars, telephone logs, and documents relating to the grant. The requests, made under the Federal Freedom of Information Act and the state's open-records law, include document demands that range from some that are clearly lawful to some that are highly questionable. Professor Nader estimates that she will have to send over 10,000 pages of documents to the firm to comply with all the requests. Collecting and copying the documents will take many days of her time. She also does not want to share her data prematurely and considers the raw data to be her intellectual property.

1. If Professor Carver has signed a contract to do research for a corporate sponsor that contains a nondisclosure agreement without corporate consent, should the university play a role in helping the corporation to enforce such an agreement? Should the university support academic freedom in the publication of such scholarship and argue that such agreements are bad public policy?

2. Is the loss of a potential 20-million-dollar gift to the institution because of a professor's controversial publication a relevant consideration for the university in this situation?

3. Is the university's removal of Professor Carver from an administrative position as a research center director different from negative consequences for his teaching and research as a professor? If an administrator's controversial publication causes the person to lose substantial fundraising capability, is this a factor to be considered with respect to the administrative post?

4. Should the university support Professor Carver's legal defense that the restriction on publication of important health data is an unreasonable restriction contrary to public policy?

5. With respect to Professor Nader, should the institution defend her by paying for counsel to litigate all questionable document requests? Why or why not?

6. Even if many of the document requests are lawful, should the peer colleagues and administrators publicly condemn such requests and seek to discover who is funding these strategies?

7. Note that a few corporations are using defamation actions against professors who criticize them. Subsequent to filing such an action, the corporation subpoenas all research notes and data including those documents identifying confidential sources. Should the peer collegium and the university respond to these actions? How?

8. If the institution fails to assist Professor Nader in defending herself, what should her peer collegium do?

INTRAMURAL UTTERANCE

PROBLEM 37: Retaliation against campus reformer; complaints about parking and other personal issues

Professor Betty Juarez, tenured in Philosophy, is a campus reformer active in organizing the faculty senate against the policies of the current president of the institution. The administration wants to shift resources and emphasis away from the liberal arts toward distance learning in applied subjects. Professor Juarez writes a series of internal white papers showing the flaws in the administration's data and analysis, and she speaks force-fully against the administration at meetings around the campus. With her leadership, the faculty senate votes against the president's plans. The ad-ministration finds itself embarrassed and frustrated. The dean of her fac-ulty suggests to Professor Juarez that she should spend more time on her scholarship. Her department chair increases her teaching load and com-mittee assignments.

Tenured anthropology professor George King is extremely dissatisfied with his perks of office. In a series of memoranda and meetings, he com-plains bitterly to the department chair and dean about the distance to his parking space, the location, size, and comfort of his office, and the inade-quacy of his support staff. He brings this up regularly at departmental meet-ings. The department chair and dean instruct Professor King to stop wast-ing their time and the faculty's time with these complaints, or they will take his conduct into account in determining salary increases.

1. Is the conduct and speech of Professor Juarez protected by academic free-dom? Is the conduct and speech of Professor King?
2. Should academic freedom cover whatever a professor says or does within the walls of the institution or must the speech or conduct be reasonably related to teaching, scholarship, or the faculty's role in shared gover-nance?
3. Who should decide if the conduct and speech is protected by academic freedom? What should the peer collegium do in these cases? Does it have a role to play?
4. Does the tone and manner of the speech or conduct matter? If Profes-sor Juarez conducts herself in an angry and threatening manner, or uses insulting or abusive language or personal attacks, does that change your analysis? What if Professor Juarez uses obscenities?
5. Would it matter to your analysis if either Professor Juarez or Professor King were untenured? Would the type of speech or conduct outlined in the initial paragraphs bring into question their collegiality? Is collegial-ity a proper factor to consider in evaluation of a faculty member? Is it relevant whether a faculty member can work reasonably harmoniously on teams? Should academic freedom protect the curmudgeon on gov-ernance matters?
6. What if Professor Juarez writes a memorandum totally undermining the administration's data and analysis of the benefits of distance learning, but she intentionally neglects to include all evidence and argument fa-vorable to the administration's position? In other words, she writes a lawyer's brief, but dose not inform the reader that it is an advocacy brief. Is this a violation of her duties of professional conduct?

PROBLEM 38: Advancing individual causes; speeches and organized disruption on and off campus by professor

Tenured political science professor Melissa Ruud is a member of a militia recently formed to resist perceived FBI, DEA, and ATF coercion. Professor Ruud organized students to join the militia, speaking at a number of rallies on campus at which she wore a militia uniform and was protected by militia "guards" as she spoke. When the Attorney General of the United States visited campus to speak, Professor Ruud organized and participated in demonstrations against the attorney general. She led a two-day sit-in at the president's office to protest the invitation to speak. On the evening of the speech, Professor Ruud led the militia students into the lecture hall, waving flags and shouting down the attorney general, who ultimately gave up without speaking that evening. Professor Ruud also organized and participated in off-campus demonstrations for her cause. On one occasion, she organized and led a group to block traffic at the local FBI office, and pled guilty to trespass charges. She was photographed throwing a rock over a fence toward a group of FBI officers and is under investigation for that incident. Finally, during a law enforcement conference involving FBI speakers, she led a demonstration that overturned an FBI vehicle outside the hall. This is also under investigation. Professor Ruud does not dispute these facts.

1. Are the on-campus activities and speech of Professor Ruud in behalf of her cause protected by professional academic freedom? Which activities, if any, crossed the line to become unprotected speech or conduct subject to discipline? Why? Who should decide?
2. Are her off-campus speeches and conduct protected by professional academic freedom? Which activities, if any, crossed the line to become unprotected speech or conduct subject to discipline? Why? Who should decide?
3. Should off-campus speech and conduct be assessed by a different standard? Should a misdemeanor occurring off campus matter? Should a felony?
4. Does it matter whether Professor Ruud announces her institutional affiliation in these activities? Does she have an affirmative duty to indicate she is not speaking for or representing the institution in these activities?
5. What should the peer collegium do under these circumstances? Specifically, does it have a role to play when a professor prevents a speaker from speaking on campus? When students do so?
6. If Professor Ruud's conduct violates principles of professional conduct, what sanctions are appropriate?

7. Would your analysis be different if Professor Ruud were untenured?

8. Does the administration bear any responsibility for ensuring that speakers can speak on campus without harassment? What action should it take regarding the students led by Professor Ruud?

9. What if Professor Ruud only incited the students to organize an act disruptively but was not personally present at any of these events?

10. Assume Professor Ruud is president of the Progressive Student and Faculty Organization. Would it matter to your analysis if these same on-campus events involved protests against a speaker who questioned aspects of affirmative action?

11. Assume that the institution's president summarily fired Professor Ruud for these activities. What should the peer collegium do? Does it matter whether individual faculty colleagues agree or disagree with Professor Ruud's ideology with respect to their duties regarding a summary termination?

EXTRAMURAL UTTERANCE AND CONDUCT

PROBLEM 39: Off-campus press conference on administration's competence and conduct

Your institution is at a particularly sensitive moment in its development. You are about to be visited by a major accrediting agency, legislature funding for a major project is hanging in the balance, and next week the president intends to publicly announce the largest capital campaign in the institution's history.

Professor Helen Mencken, who is tenured in statistics and also holds a CPA certification, calls a press conference off campus. She presents a letter to the people of your state alleging first, that the president is a totally incompetent manager unable to focus the resources of the institution on the educational mission; second, that the president, who travels a great deal serving on various international committees, has been spending enormous amounts of institutional money on "junkets" at international vacation spots unrelated to the institution's mission; and third, that she has reason to believe the president has been falsifying expense vouchers for his personal benefit. She signs the letter showing her institution affiliation and position.

1. Does academic freedom cover Professor Mencken in her remarks at the off-campus press conference?

2. What standard of professional competence and ethical conduct applies to remarks at an off-campus press conference? Does it matter that Professor Mencken is in fact both a statistician and an accountant and thus

within her disciplinary competence? What if she were a professor of linguistics?

3. Do you think Professor Mencken's first two allegations, which are her opinions that the president is an incompetent manager and is taking "junkets," are different from her allegation that the president is falsifying expense vouchers? Does the difference matter for your analysis?

4. Assume Professor Mencken heard the third charge from a student research assistant to the president. Must she do some investigation of these allegations before calling a press conference? Does either the duty to be professionally competent or the duty to be "accurate" presuppose due diligence with respect to reasonable investigation?

5. Would it affect your analysis if Professor Mencken knew of other mitigating or exculpatory evidence and argument, but excluded it, choosing instead to present an advocacy brief in making these charges to the media?

6. Must Professor Mencken make clear that she is not speaking for the institution? Would it make any difference if she did not mention her institutional affiliation and position to the media?

7. What if, rather than call a press conference outside of the institution's walls, Professor Mencken had written these charges in an internal memorandum to all faculty. Does this change your analysis? Should she have pursued internal processes or remedies first? What processes or remedies? Does your institution have any internal processes where such concerns can be raised?

8. Based only on the facts presented, which should act? What should they do? Does the peer collegium have any role to play? What role?

9. What if Professor Mencken did proceed with the press conference based on reasonable professional investigation and the press conference causes terrible damage to the institution. After further investigation, her allegations turn out not to be true. Does academic freedom protect her?

10. What if, subsequent to the press conference, the board and president summarily suspend Professor Mencken and initiate de-tenuring proceedings? What should the peer collegium do?

PROBLEM 40: Falsehoods and grossly intemperate remarks in a professor's political campaign

Professor Jim McCarthy, tenured in economics, decides to run for a part-time city council position. In his campaign literature, he mentions that he is an economics professor at your institution. His campaign and speeches include his economic analysis "as a scholar" of the impact of the current council's policies on the city's economic health. The analysis ignores substantial opposing evidence and indicts the current council for "self-serving stupidity" and "gross incompetence."

Professor McCarthy includes in his speeches and literature charges that his opponent has engaged in sexual misconduct with a campaign volunteer thirty years his junior and that the opponent is "immoral scum." He also claims that the current council and mayor, in complicity with the police chief, are running "a concentration camp" in the city jail by intentionally arresting and incarcerating political opponents without cause. Professor McCarthy states that he cannot disclose the source of these allegations because of potential retaliation to the whistleblower. He has done no other investigation and has no other evidence.

Professor McCarthy's conduct is causing serious embarrassment to his department and the institution. Influential alumni and city leaders are calling the president asking why the institution employs such a destructive, incompetent professor.

1. Does academic freedom cover Professor McCarthy in his written and spoken remarks during the campaign?
2. What standard of professional competence and ethical conduct apply to the professor's written and spoken remarks? Does it matter that the economic analysis "as a scholar" is within the discipline but fails totally to meet standards of scholarship within the discipline?
3. Professor McCarthy did no further investigation of the charges (by an unnamed source) of wrongful conduct. Does this meet his professional duties with respect to extramural utterance?
4. Does the serious intemperateness of Professor McCarthy's personal attacks create any issues for his claim that his speech is protected by academic freedom?
5. What if there is no unnamed source and the allegations are intentional falsehoods?
6. Must Professor McCarthy make clear that he is not speaking for the institution? Would it make any difference if, in his literature and speeches, he did not claim his institutional affiliation?
7. What if Professor McCarthy's allegations are found by a court to be violations of the fair campaign legislation?
8. Based just on the facts presented, who should act? What should they do? Does the peer collegium have any role to play? What role?
9. What if the president and board, responding to community outrage, summarily suspend Professor McCarthy for six months. What should the peer collegium do? Can peers defend academic freedom while distancing themselves from Professor McCarthy's conduct?

CHAPTER

Problems on the Duties of the Faculty as a Collegial Body

ADJUNCT FACULTY

PROBLEM 41: Program for education and assessment of adjunct, part-time, and temporary professors; firing these professors for controversial speech

Your institution is relying on adjuncts, part-time, and "temporary" full-time faculty to do a significant amount of teaching. President Rosa de Santa Ana wants to improve the quality of the teaching by this group of faculty. Pointing out how busy tenured faculty are, she proposes that a team of assistant deans create and carry out a teaching improvement and teaching evaluation program for adjunct, part-time, and temporary professors. The program would involve: (1) education on teaching methodology and student evaluation, (2) regular review and evaluation of these faculty members by the administrative team, and (3) the development of a handbook for these faculty members to clarify administrative expectations.

President de Santa Ana has decided not to rehire several of the part-time adjunct and temporary faculty members for the following reasons:

First, adjunct professor Henry Crazy Horse in the forestry school conducted a survey for his outside employment on resident attitudes toward tourism in the state. The majority of respondents wanted the hotel taxes the state collects to go toward environmental concerns. Only twenty percent wanted the money to go to promoting tourism. He published the results. Major tourist interests urged President de Santa Ana to terminate Professor Crazy Horse. He enjoyed large enrollments and excellent teaching evaluations.

Second, business school part-time professor Mary Fonda spends much of her nonteaching time supporting the campaigns of former communists in elections in Eastern Europe. Her classes on the European Community have large enrollments and excellent teaching evaluations. A number of colleagues suggested to President de Santa Ana that Fonda's political views were extreme and embarrassing for the business school. Professor Fonda also uses a case study in her class that is embarrassing for a large local corporate donor. The donor asks President de Santa Ana to terminate Professor Fonda's connection to the university.

1. Is President de Santa Ana correct that higher education should move toward a "let managers manage and faculty teach and research" model?
2. In American academic tradition, who is responsible for the definition and clarification of the standards of the academic profession and for maintaining those standards within the peer collegium? Who, in the first instance, is to judge the professional competence of teaching?
3. Are adjunct, part-time, and temporary professors part of the peer collegium for these purposes?
4. Should the core tenured and tenure-track faculty do better at the peer collegium's correlative duties with respect to the improvement and assessment of the teaching of adjunct, part-time, and temporary faculty? Should these noncore faculty be more intentionally included in the institution's academic culture?
5. If the core faculty of tenured and tenure-track faculty are in fact too overburdened to carry out these responsibilities, should they press persistently for greater balance in academic staffing to increase the proportion of tenure-track faculty?
6. With respect to President de Santa Ana's decisions to terminate Professors Crazy Horse and Fonda, do adjunct, part-time, and temporary professors have academic freedom in scholastics and teaching? If so, who has the responsibility to protect it? The core tenured and tenure-track faculty as a peer collegium?
7. Do untenured tenure-track professors have academic freedom? Who is responsible for protecting it?
8. What processes would be appropriate to provide the protections of academic freedom to these groups?
9. Should adjuncts, part-time, and temporary faculty have contracts that provide procedural protection for academic freedom?

FULL-TIME FACULTY

PROBLEM 42: Board ignorance concerning academic tradition and academic freedom; faculty failure to maintain academic standards

The governing board of your institution recently announced the appointment of a number of new board members who are exceptionally wealthy business people. Several new board members are quoted as saying that it is about time higher education woke up to business realities. The students are "customers." They deserve whatever they want in terms of curriculum, course content, techniques of instruction, and evaluation. "The customer is always right." Another group of new board members said that the time for the security of tenure is over. "It protects troublemakers and deadwood."

You learn of another institution where the governing board members stage a rebellion against the president and the faculty, voting to replace the president and vice president and a number of deans and department chairs. They want a full review by prestigious outside academics of the productivity of individual faculty members. This board is reacting to a petition from the student body association and the alumni association pointing out the following over the past five years: (1) the institution's declining enrollment and falling academic quality of students, (2) the institution's falling ranking in its mission cohort, (3) falling student evaluations of teaching and falling scholarly output, (4) the loss of significant faculty members and outside funding, and (5) an increase in the faculty's outside consulting.

1. What should the faculty collegium and faculty leadership do in the first situation? Should they do nothing?
2. Who is responsible for educating each generation of faculty, students, administration, governing board, and the public about the tradition of the academic profession, the benefits of the tradition, the meaning and value of academic freedom and peer review, and their benefits to society? Must the social compact be renewed in each generation? Why? How?
3. Who is the most qualified to provide such education?
4. In the second situation, do you think it is reasonably possible that the professorate in a particular institution or particular department so ignores their individual and collegial duties that the social compact of the profession with society is broken and the governing board must exercise its legal authority to restore it?
5. What is the fiduciary duty of the board in the second situation?

6. Is it legitimate for board members to focus on the problems enumerated in the second situation and to ask about the peer collegium's responsibility in these matters? Who is responsible for an academic culture of high aspiration?

7. Assume a faculty at an institution of higher education produces little or no scholarship. Is it a legitimate question whether such a faculty is more like a faculty in secondary education, thus presenting no compelling justification for exceptional vocational freedom of speech and rights of peer review and shared governance?

8. What if a board member observes that almost no faculty member in the humanities, and few in many of the social sciences any longer believe in the epistemology on which academic freedom, peer review, and shared governance rest. The board member asks why the board should continue to honor an arrangement based on an epistemology that many faculty disavow. What is your answer?

CHAPTER

Problems on the Rights
of the Faculty
in Shared Governance

MISSON AND STRATEGIC PLANNING

PROBLEM 43: Change in mission/vision toward teaching excellence and technology in learning

The governing board and president of your institution want to shift the institution's mission, strategic vision, and strategic goals to give more emphasis to technology in learning (including distance learning). They also want to lower costs and tuition, and to increase budgetary and programmatic flexibility by relying more heavily on part-time faculty.

In order to realize the strategic goal of teaching excellence and increased use of technology in learning, the president and board want each faculty, department, and faculty member to provide a written assessment of how the entity or individual currently allocates time and energy to this mission emphasis, and what will be done to improve current efforts. The president and board would like each faculty and department to include this new mission focus in annual faculty assessment, and in determinations of salary increases and other resource allocation decisions like research assistance, faculty travel funds, and sabbaticals.

1. Many administrators and board members complain about faculty inertia and resistance that undermine the institution's ability both to respond to changing societal and student needs and market realities and to develop institutional priorities that allocate resources accordingly. Do you think members of your faculty and department could do better to

address these concerns? If so, what specifically do you think should be done? If not, why not?

2. Is it healthy for institutions of higher education to have high degrees of reciprocal frustration among governing boards, administrators, and the faculty? Is this an issue at your institution? Are the administration and board solely the problem or does the faculty have joint responsibility for the problems? What should be done specifically to address the problem? To the degree the problem is lack of education and thus understanding about academic tradition and the responsibilities of shared governance, which is responsible for correcting this lack of education?

3. With respect to the president's and board's interest in shifting the mission, vision, and strategic goals to place more emphasis on teaching excellence and the use of technology in learning, who is primarily responsible for these areas? Is the strategic mission and vision to be an institution known for teaching excellence primarily the board's responsibility? And is the execution of this mission and vision more a matter of curriculum, methods of instruction, and environment for learning the responsibility of the faculty? Does the board or the faculty have primary responsibility for the emphasis on the use of technology in learning?

4. With respect to the president's and board's interest in lower costs and tuition increases and increasing budgetary and programmatic flexibility by relying more heavily on part-time faculty, who has primary responsibility? Is the decision to lower costs and tuition increases and to increase budgetary and programmatic flexibility primarily a board decision? Does such a decision have a direct impact on standards of faculty appointment, standards for faculty competence, the environment for learning, curriculum development, and the development of new methods of instruction? Does the move to part-time faculty affect the full-time faculty's other responsibilities for research, teaching, and internal and external service?

5. For decisions in this problem which are the administration's and board's primary responsibility, academic tradition calls for consultation with the voting faculty. What would a consultation on these issues look like at your institution? Which stakeholders should be included in the process? Should untenured and part-time professors be included? Staff? Students? Should the voting faculty have the primary voice? How would you ensure that the faculty carries out its consultative role in a timely and efficient manner?

6. Administration and board members often complain that faculty decision making is highly time-consuming and that delay often results in missed opportunity. They also complain that faculty decision making is vulnerable to blocking minorities who inappropriately use procedure necessary for collegial decision making so that delay and high transaction cost to others determine the outcome, not the merits. Do you think

these are realistic problems at your institution? If so, what can be done to mitigate the problems?

7. What if a decision in the problem is in the administration and board's area of primary responsibility, but they provide limited or no consultation by the faculty? What should the peer collegium do?

8. What if a decision in this problem is in the faculty's area of primary responsibility, but the faculty does nothing or is not timely. What can the administration and board do?

9. What if the administration and board properly consult with the faculty in an area of the faculty's primary responsibility, but the administration and board disagree with the faculty on major issues. How should the administration and board proceed?

10. What if the faculty in a professional and timely manner gives the administration and board its reasoning and decision on a matter in the faculty's area of primary responsibility but the administration and board adopt a different decision? What burden do the administration and board carry to reverse or substantially modify such a faculty decision? Is it important that the faculty observe the administration and board to have listened carefully to and understood the faculty's evidence and argument in making the final decision? How do the administration and board demonstrate this? Are hearings important? Are written reasons and findings important?

11. Assume the administration and board, after faculty consultation and faculty endorsement, have adopted a mission and vision change placing more emphasis in teaching excellence and use of technology in learning. To what degree must individual tenured faculty members lean into these mission and vision changes and allocate their time and energy accordingly? What if an individual tenured professor's portfolio of interests is significantly out of line with the institution's mission and vision? What should happen? To what degree can the institution force a tenured professor to align with the institution's new mission and vision in the allocation of his or her time and energy? In the adoption of teaching methodology? What if the faculty endorses more diverse authors in the curriculum? Must an individual faculty member comply? Does tenure mean that individual faculty members can pursue his or her individual portfolios of interest regardless?

12. Can the administration and board withhold approval of hiring, promotion, and tenure decisions by the faculty that do not serve the mission and vision?

13. Would your analysis of the previous two questions change if the board and administration had properly consulted with faculty on the decision, but had gone ahead with these proposals over the faculty's objection? What if the board and administration had not consulted with the faculty at all in these decisions?

14. Once the mission and vision are determined, what is the role of the peer collegium in developing a culture that realizes them? How can the faculty create a peer culture that aspires to excellence at the mission? How can the faculty foster leadership toward the mission from within the peer collegium?

15. Does one size fit all on these shared governance issues? Should there be any difference in the decision making regarding the issues in this problem whether the institution is a community college with a limited scholarship mission or a major research university?

PROBLEM 44: Change in mission/vision toward national and international recognition in identified fields; creation of a new department

The president and governing board want to shift the mission, vision, and strategic goals toward national and international recognition in certain fields. They believe these fields offer the most promise for increasing student quality, student tuition revenues, and grants and gifts to the institution. They also believe that achieving excellence in certain fields has a "halo" effect on the rest of the institution, raising its overall reputation.

The plan they propose is for the next ten years: the university will increase resources, including focusing fund-raising efforts to certain departments, but hold all other departments to increases sufficient to cover inflation only. They also have a donor prepared to give $20 million to fund a new department for New Age Spiritual Studies. This includes four fully endowed chairs. This new department is one of the fields the board and administration wish to emphasize.

1. Many administrators and board members complain about faculty inertia and resistance that undermine the institution's ability to respond to changing societal and student needs and market realities, and to develop institutional priorities that allocate resources accordingly. Do you think members of your faculty and department could do better to address these concerns? If so, what specifically do you think should be done? If not, why not?

2. Is it healthy for institutions of higher education to have high degrees of reciprocal frustration among governing boards, administrators, and the faculty? Is this an issue at your institution? Are the administration and board solely the problem or does the faculty have joint responsibility for the problems? What should be done specifically to address the problem? To the degree that the problem is lack of education and thus understanding about academic tradition and the responsibilities of shared governance, which is responsible for correcting this lack of education?

3. With respect to the president's and board's interest in shifting the mission, vision, and strategic goals to place more emphasis on teaching excellence and the use of technology in learning, who is primarily responsible for these areas? Is the strategic mission and vision to be an institution known for teaching excellence primarily the board's responsibility? And is the execution of this mission and vision more a matter of curriculum, methods of instruction, and environment for learning the responsibility of the faculty? Does the board or the faculty have primary responsibility for the emphasis on the use of technology in learning?

4. Who should select the identified fields of emphasis? By what process?

5. The decision to create a new department is in the board's area of primary responsibility. A new department is created around a field, which is a set of reasonably interconnected ideas that generate a set of research programs and methodologies for carrying them out. Should the faculty have a role in this determination? Who carries the burden to present evidence that the new field and department meet these criteria?

6. Does it matter if a donor gives a large gift to establish the new department? Should it matter if off-campus religious groups lobby assiduously for the new department?

7. Change the facts. What if the board created a new department solely to satisfy on-campus and off-campus political groups? What if this is a dominant, but not the sole reason?

8. If the facts of either question 6 or 7 were true, what should the peer collegium do?

9. For decisions in this problem which are the administration's and board's primary responsibility, academic tradition calls for consultation with the voting faculty. What would a consultation on these issues look like in your institution? Which stakeholders should be included in the process? Should untenured and part-time professors be included? Staff? Students? Should the voting faculty have the primary voice? How would you ensure that the faculty carries out its consultative role in a timely and efficient manner?

10. Administration and board members often complain that faculty decision making is highly time-consuming and that delay often results in missed opportunity. They also complain that faculty decision making is vulnerable to blocking minorities who inappropriately use procedure necessary for collegial decision making so that delay and high transaction cost to others determine the outcome, not the merits. Do you think these are realistic problems at your institution? If so, what can be done to mitigate the problems?

11. What if a decision in the problem is in the administration's and board's area of primary responsibility, but they provide limited or no consultation? What should the peer collegium do?

12. What if the administration and board do properly consult with the faculty in an area of the board's primary responsibility, but they disagree with the faculty on major issues. How should they proceed?

13. If the faculty supports the mission change toward internationally recognized scholarship, can the administration and board pressure a tenured faculty member to align his or her portfolio to activities within the mission? What if the tenured professor does not have the ability to do such scholarship? Can the administration take this into account in decisions on further promotions?

14. Assume a department is selected for emphasis. Who decides which subject areas merit more faculty positions within the department? Who decides the criteria for the searches? What if the board wants only terminal degrees from prestigious institutions?

15. Once the mission and vision are determined, what is the role of the peer collegium in developing a culture that achieves them? How can the faculty achieve a peer culture that aspires to excellence in the mission? How can the faculty foster leadership toward the mission from within the peer collegium?

PERSONNEL DECISIONS

PROBLEM 45: President and board reverse faculty decision on promotion and tenure under existing standards; president and board propose changing standards in a promotion decision

Based on existing promotion and tenure criteria, the president and governing board reverse a tenure recommendation that had the unanimous recommendation of the candidate's department, department chair, dean, and provost.

Based on existing promotion and tenure criteria, the president and governing board reverse a second tenure recommendation that had majority support from the department and the recommendation of the department chair and provost, but not the dean.

Facing a downturn in applications, the president and governing board wish to increase the institution's reputation and attractiveness to students. They propose to increase the criteria for promotion and tenure and to apply the criteria to recommendations for new appointments, promotion, and tenure. They also propose to change the faculty salary policies to reflect the change in mission and vision.

1. Who has primary responsibility over questions of faculty status and professional competence? For the president and board to reverse a unani-

mous vote of all levels of faculty and administrative review in the first tenure decision, what does academic tradition require? In such a situation, should the president and board give the faculty a chance for further argument to take into account the concerns of the president and the board?

2. Some institutions have an interdisciplinary advisory committee to the president and board on promotion and tenure issues. A few consult with scholars from various disciplines from outside the institution on promotion and tenure issues. Would it matter for purposes of the first paragraph if the president and board had the advice of a committee of scholars from a number of disciplines within the institution and that committee had recommended against tenure? What if the president and board had a standard procedure of consulting with a committee of scholars from various disciplines from outside the institution and that committee had recommended against tenure?

3. For purposes of the situation presented in the second paragraph, what, if any, is the relevance of the divided internal votes on tenure? What if only a handful of votes were opposed to tenure, but they consisted of all of the most productive scholars in the department? Would that matter?

4. Can the president and board, faced with decreasing applications, change the criteria for promotion and tenure in an effort to increase institutional reputation? Is this a mission and vision decision or a faculty status decision? How should the president and board proceed with their proposal to satisfy the tradition of shared governance? Should untenured professors participate in decision making on these issues? Should any other stakeholders?

5. Assume the faculty endorses the mission and vision change as it relates to promotion and tenure criteria. Can a change in institutional mission and vision regarding promotion and tenure affect those hired under different criteria? Must implementation of the new mission and vision in effect be delayed for as many years as the tenure process takes for those already hired? Doesn't this lock the institution into lifelong commitments to individuals who do not serve the new mission and vision? Is it generally understood in the hiring and promotion process that criteria for tenure may be increased?

6. With respect to the decision to change faculty salary policies to reflect the change in mission and vision, what is the role of the faculty? Is the salary policy a matter within the faculty's or the administration's and board's primary responsibility? Would a process involving faculty in setting policies to determine salary increases help the peer collegium focus on the mission and how to create a peer culture of high aspiration with respect to the mission? Is it important as a means to achieve the mission that the salary policy and criteria be open and clearly understood? Should untenured professors be part of this consultation?

PROBLEM 46: Search process and performance assessment of the president and dean

The president of the institution and the dean of the faculty are both re-tiring at the same time next year. The governing board has asked the fac-ulty for its input, first on the question of an optimal search process for both positions, and second on the question of the optimal process of assessment of performance for both positions.

1. Who has primary responsibility for the search process for the president and for the dean?
2. Who are the stakeholders who should be involved in each selection pro-cess? Should a search committee for a president look different from a search committee for a dean? Should the search committee include staff, alumni, students, adjunct/part-time/temporary faculty as well as board members and voting faculty?
3. Should the overall makeup of the committee reflect the primacy of the voting faculty's concerns? How? How should the committee members be selected?
4. How should the process of consultation between governing board and search committees be structured? Is regular information to the board and to other stakeholders in the search process critical for the legitimacy of the process?
5. How important is clarity of mission and vision in conducting a search process for either position? Should mission and vision work precede the search process itself or should the institution hope that the candidates will clarify on the institution's mission and vision?
6. Can the board insist that the search committee recommend more than one candidate? If the search committee recommends several candidates, can the board select a candidate the search committee ranks lower than first on the list?
7. Can the board select a candidate not recommended by the search com-mittee? What if the search committee fails to recommend a candidate after several searches?
8. Who has primary responsibility for the assessment of the performance of the president and the dean? Who has primary responsibility for the assessment of the performance of the board itself?
9. How often should assessment occur? Should there be both routine pe-riodic assessment and then a more infrequent intensive assessment? Should the assessment process for the president look different from the assessment process for a dean?
10. Who are the stakeholders who should be involved in the assessment process? Outline what the process should look like.

11. Are clarity of mission, vision, and strategic goals critical for assessment to be effective? Should assessment occur against an agreed time frame for achieving the strategic goals?
12. If the assessment process leads to a unanimous recommendation or retention and the renewal of the contract, must the board follow the recommendation? If not, and the board does not wish to follow the recommendation, how should the board proceed?
13. Who has primary responsibility for creating a culture among faculty of high aspiration toward the mission and vision? The board? The president? The peer collegium itself? Does leadership of a peer collegium come from outside the collegium or from within it?

FINANCIAL PROBLEMS

PROBLEM 47: Declining enrollments and restructuring and retrenchment; mission change and restructuring

The president and governing board observe that: (1) overall revenue from tuition and grants is declining, (2) the institution is in a deficit position for this fiscal year, (3) several departments have increasing enrollments and grants and high student teacher ratios, and (4) several departments have significantly decreasing enrollments and grants and very low student teacher ratios. The institution is not yet in financial exigency threatening its survival because it can dip into quasi-endowments (unrestricted funds set aside from excess tuition dollars in previous years).

The board and president are considering options to balance revenue and costs: (1) an across-the-board reduction in staff and faculty or (2) a selective reduction in faculty and staff in the departments with declining enrollment and grants. The board wants to focus its fundraising capabilities to raise endowments to increase the institution's academic excellence in those departments with increasing enrollment and grants.

1. Who should have primary responsibility for deciding to make cuts in academic programs?
2. Who should have primary responsibility for deciding where reductions should be made within the overall academic program? Note that AAUP tradition on this question is to place primary responsibility for this decision with the faculty, whereas the AGB places primary responsibility with the board but urges the board to consult fully with stakeholders and to communicate the analysis that led to ultimate determinations.
3. Unless the reduction in staff is a pretext masking a hidden objective of penalizing faculty speech the board or president does not like, how does

the AAUP position relate to academic freedom in teaching and scholarship? Is there a legitimate concern that the institution retains a viable and coherent academic program both across the curriculum as a whole as well as within an individual department? For example, is there some minimum critical mass of professors below which a department cannot deliver a viable and coherent academic program?

4. What process should the board follow to determine whether to reduce the academic program? Assume that a decision to reduce the program is made, what process should the board follow to determine *where* within the overall program the reduction should occur? Which stakeholders should be included? Should the process reflect the primacy of the voting faculty's concerns? The primacy of the tenured faculty's concerns?

5. Within a department identified for faculty reduction, who bears primary responsibility for deciding which faculty members are to be terminated? What decision-making process do you recommend? Which stakeholders should be included?

6. In all three levels of decision making above, the decision to downsize the overall academic program, the decision where to make the reduction, and the decision on which specific faculty are to be terminated, time will be of the essence. If the institution is experiencing financial deficits, delay will be costly. How will your recommended process ensure timely decisions?

7. Should all untenured members of a department be terminated before any tenured member? Should termination of tenured faculty members occur in reverse order of seniority? Would these two approaches ensure academic excellence and increasing enrollments and grants for the department?

8. Is a faculty member tenured in the institution (meaning that if the professor's department is downsized, he or she still has tenure in the university) or is a faculty member tenured in a department? Academic freedom, peer review, and shared governance rest on the mission of knowledge creation. In the usual case, can a faculty member in one department become a knowledge creator in another department in a reasonable time? In a reasonable time, can such a faculty member achieve academic excellence in the second department? On the other hand, should an institution make a reasonable effort to determine if a tenured member in one department could make a contribution to the academic excellence of a second department? Should the faculty members in the second department have a voice in this decision?

9. The shift in focus of the board's fundraising should follow from a shift in mission, vision, and strategic goals. Problems 43 and 44 explore the consultative process that leads to such as mission, vision, or strategic goals change. What should be the process a board follows to make such changes?

10. The peer culture of the faculty is critical if the institution is to address successfully the challenge of declining enrollments, grants, and revenue. What can be done in these circumstances to maintain morale and encourage the peer collegium toward a culture of commitment and high aspiration to the mission?

CHAPTER

Problems on the Rights of Academic Freedom for Students

UNDERGRADUATE STUDENTS

PROBLEM 48: Undergraduate student's regular disagreement with a professor in class; widespread student cheating in the department; faculty and administrative anger at student organization's speaker

In roughly every other class session in a Sociology 101 class, a student asks questions that take well-reasoned exception to the professor's position. The questions are brief, respectful, and to the point, but they frustrate the professor, who occasionally struggles with an answer. By mid-semester, the professor either will not call on the student or attempts to browbeat the student with hostile remarks and a threatening demeanor.

Many professors and students know that a number of departments on campus are acquiescing in substantial student cheating on take-home examinations and papers. Nothing is being done to correct the problem.

A student organization uses university-supplied funds to bring to campus an extremely controversial speaker who favors abortion, euthanasia, and the death penalty. A number of other groups organize peaceful demonstrations. The event draws negative media attention and alumni reaction. Several faculty speak to the student president of the organization, expressing their anger over the selection of the speaker, and the dean of students indicates to the student group he may reduce funding for the student group next year.

1. In paragraph 1, is the professor's classroom conduct toward the student a violation of the student's academic freedom? Would your answer be different if the student's questions were dominating the discussion, taking the discussion away from the point of the professor, or showed disrespect? If a student shows anger or disrespect toward the professor or other students, should the professor retaliate in kind? Are there conditions where a professor could ask a student to leave a class?

2. If on the examination, the student writes a well-reasoned answer from an alternative school of thought accepted in the discipline but not part of the professor's approach to the discipline, does that professor violate the student's academic freedom by giving the student's analysis a low grade? Would it matter if this were a graduate class in the discipline?

3. If a student makes clear in class questions and comments that she strongly disagrees with the professor's political views, what are the outer limits of a professor's response? Does control of the podium put some restraint on the intensity and passion with which the professor can disagree? Does a professor in a graduate class have fewer constraints because of the maturity of the students? What if the professor shows anger toward the student in written comments on the student's papers?

4. Should the faculty offer workshops to help professors deal with frustrating classroom situations?

5. With respect to a culture of widespread cheating, who bears primary responsibility for creating a culture of academic integrity: the faculty or the students? Is it a violation of a student's rights of academic freedom to subject the students knowingly to an evaluation system that is arbitrary and capricious because of widespread cheating?

6. Under these circumstances, what should a faculty do to restore a culture of academic integrity?

7. With respect to the third paragraph, do students and student organizations have academic freedom to use the institution's funds to bring in speakers of their choice? Does the amount of disruption or institutional embarrassment or alumni dissatisfaction matter in your analysis? Can faculty members express robust disagreement with a student organization's decision about speaker selection? At what point would such disagreement cross the line toward coercion? What if faculty disagreement was expressed in class? Or in comments on a student's paper?

8. Does the dean violate the students' academic freedom by threatening to reduce funding for the next year?

9. Must the student organization make clear that institution sponsorship does not mean approval of the speaker's view by the organization or by the institution?

GRADUATE STUDENTS

PROBLEM 49: Graduate student teaching assistant expresses controversial views in class, in governance activities, and in the media outside of the institution's walls

A professor teaching a large class of Principles of Micro Economics 101 has four graduate teaching assistants who teach smaller sections and who grade all the papers. One of the TAs, Jasmine Truth, teaches her section the professor's analysis of the subject under discussion as well as critical race theory to give an alternative analysis of the topic. The professor is angered by this deviation from his syllabus and threatens to fire the TA. The grades Ms. Truth awards are also higher than those of the other three TAs and the professor again threatens to fire her if she does not bring her grades in line with the others.

Ms. Truth also serves as a graduate student representative on the department's hiring committee. She is outspoken in critical comments about the department's culture of lack of accessibility of professors and lack of adequate advising and mentoring for graduate students. She consistently raises with faculty candidates these issues and votes only for candidates who give assurances they will devote substantial time to graduate students. The department chair is personally offended by Ms. Truth's criticism and gives her a recommendation for a job that questions whether she is a team player on governance. The qualified recommendation kills her chances for the job.

Ms. Truth also is quoted by the major newspapers in the town as questioning the commitment to diversity of the department chair. She is quoted as wondering if the chair has dealt with issues of unconscious racism. When the chair does not recommend for appointment a minority candidate Ms. Truth supported, she organizes a peaceful demonstration outside the department's building. This leads to an embarrassing article for the department in the Chronicle of Higher Education.

1. Does a graduate teaching assistant have less academic freedom in the classroom than a professor? If yes, how much less? Must the TA teach the section according to the professor's school of thought on the subject? Can a TA introduce her own analysis in addition? If she identified it as her own and not as the professor's? If it is within the range of reasonable disagreement in the discipline?
2. Does a TA have academic freedom in grading? Does it violate the undergraduate students' rights to nonarbitrary grading for there to be a

large inter-sectional grading disparity? Does a TA have academic freedom to introduce personal views unrelated to the subject into her teaching? Under the same constraints as would apply to a professor? See problems 30 and 31 in the Rights of Academic Freedom for Individual Professors.

3. Does a graduate student have academic freedom to express his or her opinions about institutional policy while serving on committees? Did the department chair violate the student's academic freedom in writing a qualified letter of recommendation?

4. What if Ms. Truth were to have conducted herself disrespectfully or otherwise unprofessionally in her work on the committee?

5. Does a graduate student serving on the recruitment committee have any outer limits on her criticism of the institution when she is dealing with candidates for appointment? Does a faculty member? Should both take care accurately to distinguish personal views from the position of others in the department?

6. Does a graduate student have the same academic freedom with respect to intramural and extramural utterance as does a faculty member? And the same duties?

7. Were Ms. Truth's comments to the media about the department chair protected by academic freedom? Must she make it clear in her media interviews and demonstrations that she speaks only for herself and not for the institution?

8. Was her leadership of the peaceful demonstration protected by academic freedom? Is this true regardless of the damage it causes to the department? Would her demonstration have been protected if it occurred in the office of the department chair and disrupted his or her work?

APPENDIX A

Summary of the Principles of Professional Conduct

The following summary uses **bold faced** to identify the framework of principles in the 1940 AAUP *Statement of Principles on Academic Freedom and Tenure*, and *italics* to identify the clarification added by the 1966 AAUP *Statement on Professional Ethics*. Sources for other principles are indicated in parentheses.

I. **Rights of Academic Freedom Relating to:**
   A. **Research**
   B. **Teaching**
   C. **Intramural Utterance Relating to the Education of Students or Involving Critical Inquiry**
   D. **Extramural Utterance**
II. **Correlative "Duties" of the Individual Faculty Member. The 1940 Statement does not exhaustively define the open-ended term "duties." It lists several specific duties and mentions two general duties.**
   A. **Duties Relating to Research, Teaching, and Intramural Utterance**
      1. **Specific Duties**
         a. **Teachers are entitled to full freedom in research ... , subject to the adequate performance of their other academic duties.**
         b. **Research for pecuniary gain should be based upon an understanding with the authorities of the institution.**
         c. **Teachers should be careful not to introduce into their teaching controversial material that has no relation to their**

subject. [Also in 1970 AAUP Statement on Freedom and Responsibility where the modifier "persistently" is added.]

2. **General Duty of Professional Competence**

    a. *In Teaching*

    i. *"As members of an academic institution, professors seek above all to be effective teachers and scholars."*[1]

    ii. *In teaching, a faculty member:*
    holds before students the best scholarly and ethical standards of the discipline;
    ensures that the evaluation of students reflects each student's true merit;
    exercises critical self-discipline and judgment in using, extending, and transmitting knowledge; and practices intellectual honesty.

    iii. In teaching, a faculty member must base evaluation of students and award of credit on "academic performance professionally judged, and not on matters irrelevant to that performance, whether personality, race, religion, degree of personal activism or personal beliefs." [Freedom and Responsibility]

    iv. Substantial and manifest neglect of assigned teaching duties would be adequate cause for dismissal (or by implication, lesser sanctions). (1973 AAC/AAUP Report of the Commission on Academic Tenure in Higher Education.)[2]

    b. *In Internal Governance or Academic Citizenship*

    i. *"As colleagues, professors have obligations that derive from common membership in the community of scholars."*

    ii. *Faculty members must "accept their share of faculty responsibilities for the governance of their institution."*

    iii. A professor must demonstrate academic citizenship at a professional standard determined by the faculty. A professor cannot neglect assigned service duties [1973 ACC/AAUP Report of the Commission on Academic Tenure in Higher Education].

    c. *In Scholarship*

    i. *"Professors' primary responsibility to their subject is to seek and to state the truth . . . "*

    ii. *"As members of an academic institution, professors seek above all to be effective teachers and scholars."*

    iii. *Professors should "devote their energies to developing and improving their scholarly competence."*

    iv. *A faculty member should:*

- *hold before students the best scholarly and ethical standards;*
- *practice intellectual honesty; exercise critical self-discipline and judgment in using, extending and transmitting knowledge;*
- *acknowledge significant academic or scholarly assistance from students; and*
- *acknowledge academic debt.* [A 1990 AAUP Statement on Plagiarism urges that professors must be rigorously honest in acknowledging academic debt, and a 1990 AAUP committee B statement urges that scholars involved in collaborative work explain forthrightly the respective contributions of each.]

v. In research, a faculty member must develop and improve his or her scholarly competence. Academic tradition is that the faculty member is to use this competence to develop and improve the account of some area of knowledge. In *Scholarship Reconsidered: Priorities of the Professorate* (1990), Ernest Boyer argues for a broader, more capacious understanding of scholarship. The work of the professorate has four separate, yet overlapping functions: the scholarship of discovery, the scholarship of integration, the scholarship of application, and the scholarship of teaching. In *Scholarship Assessed: Evaluation of the Professorate* (1997), the Carnegie Foundation returns to the topic, proposing the following standards for scholarship:

- Does the scholar identify important questions in the field?
- Does the scholar adequately consider existing scholarship in the field?
- Does the scholar use appropriate methodology recognized in the field? This includes the rules of evidence and the principles of logical reasoning.
- Does the scholarship add consequentially to the field?
- Does the scholar make an effective presentation of the work?

vi. The 1966 Statement urges: (1) devotion of energy to "developing and improving scholarly competence," (2) "critical self-discipline and judgment in using, extending, and transmitting knowledge," (3) "intellectual honesty," (4) "the best scholarly and ethical standards," and (5) contribution as an "effective scholar." The 1915 Declaration emphasizes both the importance of painstaking and thorough inquiry and the prohibition against misrepresentation or distortion of others' work. The meanings of these phrases rest on common understandings of professional competence. Accuracy in the recording and use of evidence and non-falsification are simply so fundamental as to be assumed in the common understanding of "intellectual honesty" and "best scholarly standards." The major canon of academic work has been honest and accurate investigation, and the cardinal sin has been stating or presenting a falsehood. This includes omission of a fact so that what is stated or presented as a whole states or presents a falsehood. It also includes misrepresentation of the strength of one's findings or credentials, plagiarism, and improper attribution of authorship. With respect to extramural utterance, where this duty was not so fundamental and clear, the 1940 Statement states that teachers speaking as citizens shall "at all times be accurate."

vii.   In all academic work, a faculty member must meet general duties of both practicing "intellectual honesty" and exercising "critical self-discipline and judgment in using, extending, and transmitting knowledge." In teaching in particular, a professor is "to hold before students the best scholarly standards and ethical standards of the discipline." The traditions of the profession further define intellectual honesty, critical self-discipline and judgment, and best scholarly standards to include the following duties of inquiry and argument:

- to gather the evidence relevant to the issue at hand through thorough and painstaking inquiry [1915 Declaration] and to preserve the evidence so that it is available to others;
- to record the evidence accurately;
- to show the evidence and methodology so that other investigators can replicate the research;
- to set forth without misrepresentation or distortion the divergent evidence and propositions of other investigators [1915 Declaration];
- to give careful and impartial consideration to the weight of the evidence;
- to reason analytically from the evidence to the proposition;
- to seek internal consistency;
- to acknowledge when the evidence contradicts what the scholar and teacher had hoped to achieve;

- to present evidence and analysis clearly and persuasively;
- to be rigorously honest in acknowledging academic debt; and
- to correct in a timely manner or withdraw work that is erroneous.

d. *In Teaching, Internal Governance, or Academic Citizenship and Scholarship*
" ... [P]rofessors observe the stated regulations of the institution, provided the regulations do not contravene academic freedom. ..."

3. **General Duty of Ethical Conduct.**
The 1970 Interpretive Comments for the 1940 Statement defines moral turpitude as "behavior that would evoke condemnation by the academic community generally."

a. *Duties to Students:*
- *to demonstrate respect for students as individuals and to adhere to their proper roles as intellectual guides and counselors;*
- *to make every reasonable effort to foster honest academic conduct;*
- *to respect the confidential nature of the relationship between professor and student;*
- *to avoid any exploitation, harassment, or discriminatory treatment of students;*
- *to protect the academic freedom of students;*
- to provide an atmosphere "conducive to learning and to evenhanded treatment in all aspects of the teacher-student relationship" [1970 AAUP Statement, Freedom and Responsibility];
- *not* to force students "by the authority inherent in the instructional role to make particular personal choices as to political action or their own social behavior." [Freedom and Responsibility];
- to evaluate students "based on academic performance professionally judged and not on matters irrelevant to that performance. Whether personality, race, religion, degree of political activism, or personal beliefs." [Freedom and Responsibility].

b. *Duties to Professional Colleagues:*
- *not to discriminate against or to harass colleagues;*
- *to strive to be objective in professional judgment of colleagues;*
- *to defend the free inquiry of colleagues.*[3]

c. *General Duties to the Academic Community:*
i. *In the exchange of criticism and ideas, to show due respect for the opinions of others;*

ii. to respect the dignity of others [Freedom and Responsibility];

iii. to acknowledge their right to express differing opinions [Freedom and Responsibility];

iv. *not* to express dissent or grievances in ways:
- that disrupt classes or speeches
- that significantly impede the functions of the institution [Freedom and Responsibility];

v. *not* to engage in personal conduct that substantially impairs the faculty member's fulfillment of his or her institutional responsibilities [1973 AAUP/ACC Commission Report on Academic Tenure].

d. *Duties Relating to Conflicts of Commitment:*
- **to reach an understanding with the authorities of the institution regarding research for pecuniary return;**
- *to give due regard to the faculty member's paramount responsibilities within the institution in determining the amount and character of the work done outside it;*
- *to recognize the effect of their interruption or termination of service upon the academic program and give due notice of their intentions.*

e. *Duties Relating to Conflicts of Interest:*
- *to practice intellectual honesty, in particular, not permitting outside or subsidiary interests to compromise or hamper freedom of inquiry;*
- to avoid actual or apparent conflicts of interest between government-sponsored university research obligations and outside interests or other obligations [AAUP Statement on Preventing Conflicts of Interest on Government-Sponsored Research at Universities].

B. **Duties Relating to Extramural Utterance. Speech as a citizen is to be free of institutional censorship or discipline but subject to "special obligations." Professors speaking as citizens should:**

1. **at all times be accurate;**

2. **exercise appropriate restraint;**

The AAUP also occasionally publishes responses from the AAUP's Washington staff to letters of inquiry. The 1940 Statement's injunction for faculty members to exercise "appropriate restraint" is defined to refer "solely to choice of language and to other aspects of the manner in which a statement is made. It does not refer to the substance of a teacher's remarks. It does not refer to the time and place of his utterance." The staff cites with approval Professor Ralph Fuchs's statement that "a violation [of academic responsibility] may consist of serious intemperateness of expression, intentional falsehood offered as a statement of fact, incitement of misconduct, or conceivably some other impropriety of circumstance."

3. show respect for the opinions of others; and
4. make every effort to indicate that they are not speaking for the institution [to avoid creating the impression of speaking or acting for the university].

III. **Correlative Duties of the Faculty as a Collegial Body.** "Termination for cause of a continuous appointment ... should if possible, be considered by both a faculty committee and the governing board of the institution."

The faculty has the following duties:

1. to determine in the first instance when individual professors inadequately meet their responsibilities of professional competence and ethical conduct [1940 statement, 1970 Interpretive Comments, and 1958 AAUP/AAC Statement on Procedural Standards in Faculty Dismissal Proceedings];
2. to be the source for the definition and clarification of standards of professional conduct and to take the lead in ensuring that these standards are enforced [1973 AAUP/ACC Commission on Tenure];
3. to distinguish "honest error" that peers consider within the range of competent and ethical inquiry;
4. to respect and defend the free inquiry of colleagues;
5. to assume a more positive role as guardian of academic values against unjustified assaults on academic freedom from within the faculty itself [1970 AAUP Statement on Freedom and Responsibility];
6. to be honest and courageous in their duty to detect and eliminate the incompetent during the period of probation [AAUP Committee A];
7. to strive to be objective in professional judgment of colleagues;
8. if faculty members have reason to believe a colleague has violated standards of professional conduct, to take some initiative to inquire about and to protest against apparently unethical conduct [1998 AAUP Committee B];
9. to draw up conflict of interest guidelines, with due regard for the proper disclosure of a faculty member's involvement in off-campus enterprises, including the use of university personnel, property, and the disposition of potential profits [1990 AAUP Committee B];

10. *recognizing the particular obligation of professors as citizens engaged in a profession that depends upon freedom for its health and integrity, to promote conditions of free inquiry and to further public understanding of academic freedom.*
11. to create a peer culture of high aspiration with respect to the ideals of the profession.

NOTES

1. The Canadian Society for Teaching and Learning in Higher Education describes teaching competence to include:

- Content Competence. A university teacher maintains a high level of subject matter knowledge and ensures that course content is current, accurate, representative, and appropriate to the position of the course within the student's program of studies.
- Pedagogical Competence. A pedagogically competent teacher communicates the objectives of the course to students, is aware of alternative instructional methods or strategies, and selects methods of instruction that, according to research evidence (including personal and self-reflective research), are effective in helping students to achieve the course objective.
- Valid Assessment of Students. Given the importance of assessment of students' performance in university teaching and in students' lives and careers, instructors are responsible for taking adequate steps to ensure that assessment of students is valid, open, fair, and congruent with course objectives.

Braxton and Bayer's review of the few professional association codes of ethics that cover teaching shows widespread agreement among those codes on these same principles. Braxton and Bayer, 140-146.

2. Assigned teaching duties include for example:

- presenting the subject matter of the course as announced to the students and as approved by the faculty [1970 AAUP Statement Freedom and Responsibility];
- meeting assigned courses at the designated times;
- being reasonably accessible to students outside of class; and
- meeting grading and other instructional deadlines set by the college or university.

3. The Commission on Research Integrity adds the following duties to professional colleagues:

1. Observing confidentiality associated with review of manuscripts or grant applications;
2. Not taking or damaging the research-related property of another, obstructing investigations of misconduct, or to obstructing the research of others; and
3. Complying with all research regulations.

APPENDIX

1915 AAUP General Declaration of Principles

Editor's Note[1]: Throughout its history the American Association of University Professors has sought the formulation, the recognition, and the observance of principles and procedures conducive to freedom of thought, of inquiry, and of expression in colleges and universities. At the organizational meeting of the Association on January 1 and 2, 1915 it was voted that the Association form a Committee on Academic Freedom and Academic Tenure, which should include members of a joint Committee on Academic Freedom and Tenure of the American Economic Association, the American Political Science Association, and the American Sociological Society, which had been constituted in 1913 to study and report on problems of academic freedom and tenure in teaching and research in economics, political science, and sociology. Pursuant to this action Dr. John Dewey, the Association's first President, appointed a Committee of fifteen members as follows: Edwin R.A. Seligman (Economics), Columbia University, Chairman; Charles E. Bennett (Latin), Cornell University; James Q. Dealty (Political Science), Brown University; Edward C. Elliott (Education), University of Wisconsin; Richard T. Ely (Economics), University of Wisconsin; Henry W. Farnam (Political Science), Yale University; Frank A. Fetter (Economics), Princeton University; Guy Stanton Ford (History), University of Minnesota; Charles A. Kofoid (Zoology), University of California; James P. Lichtenberger (Sociology), University of Pennsylvania; Arthur O. Lovejoy (Philosophy), The Johns Hopkins University; Frederick W. Padelford (English), University of Washington; Roscoe Pound (Law), Harvard University; Howard C. Warren (Psychology), Princeton University; Ulysses G. Weatherly (Sociology), Indiana University.

The Association's first Committee on Academic Freedom and Academic Tenure was established primarily to formulate principles and procedures, the observance of which would ensure intellectual freedom in colleges and universities. It was not anticipated that the Committee would be called upon to engage in extensive investigatory work. In this connection it is pertinent to note Dr. Dewey's statement as Chairman of the organizational meeting of the Association in reference to the Association's interest in academic freedom.

> The defense of academic freedom and tenure being already a concern of the existing learned societies will not, I am confident, be more than an incident in the activities of the Association developing professional standards.

The Committee had scarcely been formed, however, when a number of alleged infringements of academic freedom were brought to its attention. Eleven such cases were considered during 1915. These cases were diverse in character, viz., dismissal of individual professors, resignation of professors in protest of dismissals of colleagues, dismissal of a university president, and a complaint of a university president against the institution's governing board. Apropos of these unanticipated demands that were made on the Association during 1915, Dr. Dewey spoke as follows in his Presidential Address to the Annual Meeting of that year:

> In concluding, I wish to say a word about the large place occupied in this year's program by the question of academic freedom in its relation to academic tenure. I have heard rumors of some criticism on this point. Some have expressed to me fear lest attention to individual grievances might crowd out attention to those general and "constructive" matters that are the Association's reason for existence. Let me say for the reassurance of any such that none of the officers of the Association, least of all those who have been overwhelmed by the duties incident to these investigations, regard this year's work as typical or even as wholly normal. . . . The investigations of particular cases were literally thrust upon us. To have failed to meet the demands would have been cowardly; it would have tended to destroy all confidence in the Association as anything more than a talking body. The question primarily involved was not whether the Council should authorize the investigation of this or that case, but whether the Association was to have legs and arms and be a working body. In short, as conditions shape themselves for us, I personally feel that the work done on particular cases this year turned out to be of the most constructive sort which could have been undertaken. . . . The amount and quality of energy and the time spent upon these matters by our secretary and by the chairman of our committee of fifteen are such as to beggar thanks. These gentlemen and the others who have labored with them must find their reward not only in the increased prosperity of this Association in the future, but, above all, in the enhanced security and dignity of the scholar's calling throughout our country.

Despite the unexpected volume of work incident to the investigation of individual cases during its first year, the Committee was able to complete a comprehensive report concerning academic freedom, which was approved by the Annual Meeting of the Association held in Washington, D.C., December 31, 1915 and January 1, 1916. In presenting this report to the meeting the Committee said:

> *The safeguarding of a proper measure of academic freedom in American universities requires both a clear understanding of the principles which bear upon the matter, and the adoption by the universities of such arrangements and regulations as may effectually prevent any infringement of that freedom and deprive of plausibility all charges of such infringement. This report is therefore divided into two parts, the first constituting a general declaration of principles relating to academic freedom, the second presenting a group of practical proposals, the adoption of which is deemed necessary in order to place the rules and procedure of the American universities, in relation to these matters, upon a satisfactory footing.*

Largely as a result of the interest in the principles enunciated in the 1915 Declaration of Principles, the American Council on Education in 1925 called a conference for the purpose of discussing the principles of academic freedom and tenure, with a view to formulating a succinct statement of these principles. Participating in this conference were representatives of a number of organizations of higher education. At this conference there was formulated a statement of principles known to the profession as the 1925 Conference Statement on Academic Freedom and Tenure. In the formulation of this statement, the participants were not seeking to formulate new principles, but rather to restate good academic custom and usage as these had been developed in practice over a long period of time in institutions whose administrations were aware of the nature of the academic calling and the function of academic institutions. [In both] the 1925 Conference Statement and the subsequent adaptation of the principles set forth therein—the 1940 Statement of Principles . . . the principles set forth in the Declaration of 1915 are adhered to, adapted, and strengthened. . . .

GENERAL DECLARATION OF PRINCIPLES

The term "academic freedom" has traditionally had two applications—to the freedom of the teacher and to that of the student, *Lehrfreiheit* and *Lernfreiheit*. It need scarcely be pointed out that the freedom, which is the subject of this report, is that of the teacher. Academic freedom in this sense comprises three elements: freedom of inquiry and research, freedom of teaching within the university or college, and freedom of extramural utterance and action. The first of these is almost everywhere so safeguarded that the dangers of its infringement are slight. It may therefore be disregarded in this report. The second and third phases of academic freedom are closely related, and are often not distinguished. The third, however, has an importance of its own, since of late it has perhaps more frequently been the occasion of difficulties and controversies than has the question of freedom of intra-academic teaching. All five of the cases which have recently been investigated by committees of this Association have involved, at least as one factor, the right of university teachers to express their opinions freely outside the university or to engage in political activities in their capacity as citizens. The general principles, which have to do with freedom of teaching in both these senses, seem to the committee to be in great part, though not wholly, the same. In this report, therefore, we shall consider the matter primarily with reference to freedom of teaching within the university, and shall assume that what is said thereon is also applicable to the freedom of speech of university teachers outside their institutions, subject to certain qualifications and supplementary considerations which will be pointed out in the course of the report.

An adequate discussion of academic freedom must necessarily consider three matters: (1) the scope and basis of the power exercised by those bodies having ultimate legal authority in academic affairs, (2) the nature of the academic calling, and (3) the function of the academic institution or university.

1. Basis of Academic Authority

Boards of trustees as the ultimate repositories of power usually control American institutions of learning. Upon them finally it devolves to determine the measure of academic freedom which is to be realized in the different institutions discussed below. It therefore becomes necessary to inquire into the nature of the trust reposed in these boards, and to ascertain to whom the trustees are to be considered accountable.

The simplest case is that of the proprietary school or college designed for the propagation of specific doctrines prescribed by those who have furnished its endowment. It is evident that in such cases the trustees are bound by the deed of gift, and, whatever be their own views, are obligated to carry out the terms of the trust. If a church or religious denomination establishes a college to be governed by a board of trustees, with the express understanding that the college will be used as an instrument of propaganda in the interests of the religious faith professed by the church or denomination creating it, the trustees have a right to demand that everything be sub-ordinated to that end. If, again, as has happened in this country, a wealthy manufacturer establishes a special school in a university in order to teach, among other things, the advantages of a protective tariff, or if, as is also the case, an institution has been endowed for the purpose of propagating the doctrines of socialism, the situation is analogous. All of these are es-sentially proprietary institutions, in the moral sense. They do not, at least as regards one particular subject, accept the principles of freedom of in-quiry, of opinion, and of teaching; and their purpose is not to advance knowledge by the unrestricted research and unfettered discussion of im-partial investigators, but rather to subsidize the promotion of the opinions held by the persons, usually not of the scholar's calling, who provide the funds for their maintenance. Concerning the desirability of the existence of such institutions, the committee does not desire to express any opinion. But it is manifestly important that they should not be permitted to sail under false colors. Genuine boldness and thoroughness of inquiry, and free-dom of speech, are scarcely reconcilable with the prescribed inculcation of a particular opinion upon a controverted question.

Such institutions are rare, however, and are becoming ever more rare. We still have, indeed, colleges under denominational auspices; but very few of them impose upon their trustees responsibility for the spread of spe-cific doctrines. They are more and more coming to occupy, with respect to the freedom enjoyed by the members of their teaching bodies, the position of untrammeled institutions of learning, and are differentiated only by the natural influence of their respective historic antecedents and traditions.

Leaving aside, then, the small number of institutions of the proprietary type, what is the nature of the trust reposed in the governing boards of the ordinary institutions of learning? Can colleges and universities that are not strictly bound by their founders to a propagandist duty ever be included in the class of institutions that we have just described as being in a moral sense proprietary? The answer is clear. If the former class of institutions constitutes a private or proprietary trust, the latter constitutes a public trust. The trustees are trustees for the public. In the case of our state universi-ties, this is self-evident. In the case of most of our privately endowed in-stitutions, the situation is really not different. They cannot be permitted to assume the proprietary attitude and privilege, if they are appealing to the general public for support. Trustees of such universities or colleges have no moral right to bind the reason or the conscience of any professor. All claim to such right is waived by the appeal to the general public for con-tributions and for moral support in the maintenance, not of a propaganda, but of a nonpartisan institution of learning. It follows that any university which lays restrictions upon the intellectual freedom of its professors proclaims itself a proprietary institution, and should be so described whenever it makes a general appeal for funds; and the public should be advised that the institution has no claim whatever to general support or regard.

This elementary distinction between a private and a public trust is not yet so universally accepted as it should be in our American institutions. While in many universities and colleges the situation has come to be entirely satisfactory, there are others in which the relation of trustees to professors is apparently still conceived to be analogous to that of a private employer to his employees; in which, therefore, trustees are not regarded as debarred by any moral restrictions, beyond their own sense of expediency, from imposing their personal opinions upon the teaching of the institution, or even from employing the power of dismissal to gratify their private antipathies or resentments. An eminent university president thus described the situation not many years since:

> In the institutions of higher education the board of trustees is the body on whose discretion, good feeling, and experience the securing of academic freedom now depends. There are boards which leave nothing to be desired in these respects, but there are also numerous bodies that have everything to learn with regard to academic freedom. These barbarous boards exercise an arbitrary power of dismissal. They exclude from the teachings of the university unpopular or dangerous subjects. In some states they even treat professor's positions as common political spoils; and all too frequently, both in state and endowed institutions, they fail to treat the members of the teaching staff with that high consideration to which their functions entitle them.

It is, then, a prerequisite to a realization of the proper measure of academic freedom in American institutions of learning, that all boards of trustees should understand—as many already do—the full implications of the distinction between private proprietorship and a public trust.

2. The Nature of the Academic Calling

The above-mentioned conception of a university as an ordinary business venture, and of academic teaching as a purely private employment, manifests also a radical failure to apprehend the nature of the social function discharged by the professional scholar. While we should be reluctant to believe that any large number of educated persons suffer from such a misapprehension, it seems desirable at this time to restate clearly the chief reasons, lying in the nature of the university teaching profession, why it is to the public interest that the professional office should be one both of dignity and of independence.

If education is the cornerstone of the structure of society and if progress in scientific knowledge is essential to civilization, few things can be more important than to enhance the dignity of the scholar's profession, with a view to attracting into its ranks men of the highest ability, of sound learning, and of strong and independent character. This is the more essential because the pecuniary emoluments of the profession are not, and doubtless never will be, equal to those open to the more successful members of other professions. It is not, in our opinion, desirable that men should be drawn into this profession by the magnitude of the economic rewards which it offers; but it is for this reason the more needful that men of high gifts and character should be drawn into it by the assurance of an honorable and secure position, and of freedom to perform honestly and according to their own consciences the distinctive and important function which the nature of the profession lays upon them.

That function is to deal at first hand, after prolonged and specialized technical training, with the sources of knowledge and to impart the results of their own and of their fellow-specialists' investigation and reflection, both to students and to the general public, without fear or favor. The proper discharge of this function requires (among other things) that the university teacher shall be exempt from any pecuniary motive or inducement to hold, or to express, any conclusion which is not the genuine and uncolored product of his own study or that of fellow-specialists. Indeed, the proper fulfillment of the work of the professorate requires that our universities shall be so free that no fair-minded person shall find any excuse for even a suspicion that the utterances of university teachers are shaped or restricted by the judgment, not of professional scholars, but of inexpert and possibly not wholly disinterested persons outside of their ranks. The lay public is under no compulsion to accept or to act upon the opinions of the scientific experts whom, through the universities, it employs. But it is highly needful, in the interest of society at large, that what purport to be conclusions of men trained for, and dedicated to, the quest for truth, shall in fact be the conclusions of such men, and not echoes of the opinions of the lay public, or of the individuals who endow or manage universities. To the degree that professional scholars, in the formation and promulgation of their opinions, are, or by the character of their tenure appear to be, subject to any motive other than their own scientific conscience and a desire for the respect of their fellow-experts, to that degree the university teaching profession is corrupted; its proper influence upon public opinion is diminished and vitiated; and society at large fails to get from its scholars, in an unadulterated form, the peculiar and necessary service which it is the office of the professional scholar to furnish.

These considerations make still more clear the nature of the relationship between university trustees and members of university faculties. The latter are the appointees, but not in any proper sense the employees, of the former. For, once appointed, the scholar has professional functions to perform in which the appointing authorities have neither competency nor moral right to intervene. The responsibility of the university teacher is primarily to the public itself, and to the judgment of his own profession; and while, with respect to certain external conditions of his vocation, he accepts a responsibility to the authorities of the institution in which he serves, in the essentials of his professional activity his duty is to the wider public to which the institution itself is morally amenable. So far as the university teacher's independence of thought and utterance is concerned—though not in other regards—the relationship of professor to trustees may be compared to that between judges of the Federal courts and the Executive who appoints them. University teachers should be understood to be, with respect to the conclusions reached and expressed by them, no more subject to the control of the trustees than are judges subject to the control of the President with respect to their decisions; while of course, for the same reason, trustees are no more to be held responsible for, or to be presumed to agree with, the opinions or utterances of professors than the President can be assumed to approve of all the legal reasoning of the courts. A university is a great and indispensable organ of the higher life of a civilized community, in the work of which the trustees hold an essential and highly honorable place, but in which the faculties hold an independent place, with quite equal responsibilities—and in relation to purely scientific and educational questions, the primary responsibility. Misconception or obscurity in this matter has undoubtedly been a source of occasional difficulty in the past, and even in several instances during the current year, however much, in the main, a long tradition of kindly and courteous intercourse between trustees and members of university faculties has kept the question in the background.

3. The Function of the Academic Institution

The importance of academic freedom is most clearly perceived in the light of the purposes for which universities exist. These are three in number.

  A. To promote inquiry and advance the sum of human knowledge.
  B. To provide general instruction to the students.
  C. To develop experts for various branches of the public service.

Let us consider each of these. In the earlier stages of a nation's intellectual development, the chief concern of education institutions is to train the growing generation and to diffuse the already accepted knowledge. It is only slowly that there comes to be provided in the highest institutions of learning the opportunity for the gradual wresting from nature of her intimate secrets. The modern university is becoming more and more the home of scientific research. There are three fields of human inquiry in which the race is only at the beginning: natural science, social science, and philosophy and religion, dealing with the relations of man to outer nature, to his fellowmen, and to ultimate realities and values. In natural science all that we have learned but serves to make us realize more deeply how much more remains to be discovered. In social science in its largest sense, which is concerned with the relations of men in society and with the conditions of social order and well-being, we have learned only an adumbration of the laws that govern these vastly complex phenomena. Finally, in the spiritual life, and in the interpretation of the general meaning and ends of human existence and its relation to the universe, we are still far from a comprehension of the final truths, and from a universal agreement among all sincere and earnest men. In all of these domains of knowledge, the first condition of progress is complete and unlimited freedom to pursue inquiry and publish its results. Such freedom is the breath in the nostrils of all scientific activity.

The second function—which for a long time was the only function of the American college or university—is to provide instruction for students. It is scarcely open to question that freedom of utterance is as important to the teacher as it is to the investigator. No man can be a successful teacher unless he enjoys the respect of his students, and their confidence in his intellectual integrity. It is clear, however, that this confidence will be impaired if there is suspicion on the part of the student that the teacher is not expressing himself fully or frankly, or that college and university teachers in general are a repressed and intimidated class who dare not speak with that candor and courage which youth always demands in those whom it is to esteem. The average student is a discerning observer, who soon takes the measure of his instructor. It is not only the character of the instruction but also the character of the instructor that counts; and if the student has reason to believe that the instructor is not true to himself, the virtue of the instruction as an educative force is incalculably diminished. There must be in the mind of the teacher no mental reservation. He must give the student the best of what he has and what he is.

The third function of the modern university is to develop experts for the use of the community. If there is one thing that distinguishes the more recent developments of democracy, it is the recognition by legislators of the inherent complexities of economic, social, and political life, and the difficulty of solving problems of technical adjustment without technical knowledge. The recognition of this fact has led to continually greater demand for the aid of experts in these subjects, to advise both legislators and administrators. The training of such experts has, accordingly, in recent years, become an important part of work of the universities; and in almost every one of our higher institutions of learning the professors of the economic, social, and political sciences have been drafted to an increasing extent into more or less unofficial participation in the public service. It is obvious that here again the scholar must be absolutely free not only to pursue his investigations but to declare the results of his research, no matter where they may lead him or to what extent they may come into conflict with accepted opinion. To be of use to the legislator or the administrator, he must enjoy their complete confidence in the disinterestedness of his conclusions.

It is clear, then, that the university cannot perform its threefold function without accepting and enforcing to the fullest extent the principle of academic freedom. The responsibility of the university as a whole is to the community at large, and any restriction upon the freedom of the instructor is bound to react injuriously upon the efficiency and the *morale* of the institution, and therefore ultimately upon the interests of the community.

The attempted infringements of academic freedom at present are probably not only of less frequency than, but of a different character from, those to be found in former times. In the early period of university development in America the chief menace to academic freedom was ecclesiastical, and the disciplines chiefly affected were philosophy and the natural sciences. In more recent times the danger zone has been shifted to the political and social sciences—though we still have sporadic examples of the former class of cases in some of our smaller institutions. But it is precisely in these provinces of knowledge in which academic freedom is now most likely to be threatened, that the need for it is at the same time most evident. No person of intelligence believes that all of our political problems have been solved, or that the final stage of social evolution has been reached. Grave issues in the adjustment of men's social and economic relations are certain to call for settlement in the years that are to come; and for the right settlement of them mankind will need all the wisdom, all the good will, all the soberness of mind, and all the knowledge drawn from experience, that it can command. Toward this settlement the university has potentially its own very great contribution to make; for if the adjustment reached is to be a wise one, it must take due account of economic science, and be guided by that breadth of historic vision which should be one of the functions of a university to cultivate. But if the universities are to render any such service toward the right solution of the social problems of the future, it is the first essential that the scholars who carry on the work of universities shall not be in a position of dependence upon the favor of any social class or group, that the disinterestedness and impartiality of their inquiries and their conclusions shall be, so far as is humanly possible, beyond the reach of suspicion.

The special dangers to freedom of teaching in the domain of the social sciences are evidently two. The one which is the more likely to affect the privately endowed colleges and universities is the danger of restrictions upon the expression of opinions that point toward extensive social innovations, or call in question the moral legitimacy or social expediency of economic conditions or commercial practices in which large vested interests are involved. In the political, social, and economic field almost every question, no matter how large and general it at first appears, is more or less affected with private or class interests; and, as the governing body of a university is naturally made up of men who through their standing and ability are personally interested in great private enterprises, the points of possible conflict are numberless. When to this is added the consideration that benefactors, as well as most of the parents who send their children to privately endowed institutions, themselves belong to the more prosperous and therefore usually to the more conservative classes, it is apparent that, so long as effectual safeguards for academic freedom are not established, there is a real danger that pressure from vested interests may, sometimes deliberately and sometimes unconsciously, sometimes openly and sometimes subtly and in obscure ways, be brought to bear upon academic authorities.

On the other hand, in our state universities the danger may be the reverse. Where the university is dependent for funds upon legislative favor, it has sometimes happened that the conduct of the institution has been affected by political considerations; and where there is a definite governmental policy or a strong public feeling on economic, social, or political questions, the menace to academic freedom may consist in the repression of opinions that in the particular political situation are deemed ultraconservative rather than ultra-radical. The essential point, however, is not so much that the opinion is one or another shade, as that it differs from the views entertained by the authorities. The question resolves itself into one of departure from accepted standards; whether the departure is in the one direction or the other is immaterial.

This brings us to the most serious difficulty of this problem; namely, the dangers connected with the existence in a democracy of an overwhelming and concentrated public opinion. The tendency of modern democracy is for men to think alike, to feel alike, and to speak alike. Any departure from the conventional standards is apt to be regarded with suspicion. Public opinion is at once the chief safeguard of a democracy, and the chief menace to the real liberty of the individual. It almost seems as if the danger of despotism cannot be wholly averted under any form of government. In a political autocracy there is no effective public opinion, and all are subject to the tyranny of the ruler; in a democracy there is political freedom, but there is likely to be a tyranny of public opinion.

An inviolable refuge from such tyranny should be found in the university. It should be an intellectual experiment station, where new ideas may germinate and where their fruit, though still distasteful to the community as a whole, may be allowed to ripen until finally, perchance, it may become a part of the accepted intellectual food of the nation or of the world. Not less is it a distinctive duty of the university to be the conservator of all genuine elements of value in the past thought and life of mankind which are not in the fashion of the moment. Though it need not be the "home of beaten causes," the university is, indeed, likely always to exercise a certain form of conservative influence. For by its nature it is committed to the principle that knowledge should precede action, to the caution (by no means synonymous with intellectual timidity) which is an essential part of the scientific method, to a sense of the complexity of social problems, to the practice of taking long views into the future, and to a reasonable regard for the teachings of experience. One of its most characteristic functions in a democratic society is to help make public opinion more self-critical and more circumspect, to check the more hasty and unconsidered impulses of popular feeling, to train the democracy to the habit of looking before and after. It is precisely this function of the university that is most injured by any restriction upon academic freedom; and it is precisely those who most value this aspect of the university's work who should most earnestly protect against any such restriction. For the public may respect, and be influenced by, the counsels of prudence and of moderation which are given by men of science if it believes those counsels to be the disinterested expression of the scientific temper and of unbiased inquiry. It is little likely to respect or heed them if it has reason to believe that they are the expression of the interests, or the timidities, of the limited portion of the community which is in a position to endow institutions of learning, or is most likely to be represented upon their boards of trustees. And a plausible reason for this belief is given the public so long as our universities are not organized in such a way as to make impossible any exercise of pressure upon professorial opinions and utterances by governing boards of laymen.

Since there are no rights without corresponding duties, the considerations heretofore set down with respect to the freedom of the academic teacher entail certain correlative obligations. The claim to freedom of teaching is made in the interest of the integrity and of the progress of scientific inquiry; it is, therefore, only those who carry on their work in the temper of the scientific inquirer who may justly assert this claim. The liberty of the scholar within the university to set forth his conclusions, be they what they may, is conditional by their being conclusions gained by a scholar's method and held in a scholar's spirit; that is to say, they must be the fruits of competent and patient and sincere inquiry, and they should be set forth with dignity, courtesy, and temperateness of language. The university teacher, in giving instruction upon controversial matters, while he is under no obligation to hide his own opinion under a mountain of equivocal verbiage, should, if he is fit for his position, be a person of a fair and judicial mind; he should, in dealing with such subjects, set forth justly, without suppression or innuendo, the divergent opinions of other investigators; he should cause his students to become familiar with the best published expressions of the great historic types of doctrine upon the questions at issue; and he should, above all, remember that his business is not to provide his students with ready-made conclusions, but to train them to think for themselves, and to provide them access to those materials which they need if they are to think intelligently.

It is, however, for reasons which have already been made evident, inadmissible that the power of determining when departures from the requirements of the scientific spirit and method have occurred, should be vested in bodies not composed of members of the academic profession. Such bodies necessarily lack full competency to judge of [sic] those requirements; their intervention can never be exempt from the suspicion that it is dictated by other motives than zeal for the integrity of science; and it is, in any case, unsuitable to the dignity of a great profession that the initial responsibility for the maintenance of its professional standards should not be in the hands of its own members. It follows that university teachers must be prepared to assume this responsibility for themselves. They have hitherto seldom had the opportunity, or perhaps the disposition, to do so. The obligation will doubtless, therefore, seem to many an unwelcome and burdensome one; and for its proper discharge members of the profession will perhaps need to acquire, in a greater measure than they at present possess, the capacity for impersonal judgment in such cases, and for judicial severity when the occasion requires. But the responsibility cannot, in this committee's opinion, be rightfully evaded. If this profession should prove itself unwilling to purge its ranks of the incompetent and the unworthy, or to prevent the freedom which it claims in the name of science from being used as a shelter for inefficiency, for superficiality, or for uncritical and intemperate partisanship, it is certain that the task will be performed by others—by others who lack certain essential qualifications for performing it, and whose action is sure to breed suspicions and recurrent controversies deeply injurious to the internal order and the public standing of universities. Your committee has, therefore, in the appended "Practical Proposals" attempted to suggest means by which judicial action by representatives of the profession, with respect to the matters here referred to, may be secured.

There is one case in which the academic teacher is under an obligation to observe certain special restraints—namely, the instruction of immature students. In many of our American colleges, and especially in the first two years of the course, the student's character is not yet fully formed, his mind is still relatively immature. In these circumstances it may reasonably be expected that the instructor will present scientific truth with discretion, that he will introduce the student to new conceptions gradually, with some consideration for the student's preconceptions and traditions, and with due regard to character-building. The teacher ought also to be especially on his guard against taking unfair advantage of the student's immaturity by indoctrinating him with the teacher's own opinions before the student has had an opportunity fairly to examine other opinions upon the matters of question, and before he has sufficient knowledge and ripeness in judgment to be entitled to form any definitive opinion of his own. It is not the least service which a college or university may render to those under its instruction, to habituate them to looking not only patiently but methodically on both sides before adopting any conclusion upon controverted issues. By these suggestions, however, it need scarcely be said that the committee does not intend to imply that it is not the duty of an academic instructor to give to any students old enough to be in college a genuine intellectual awakening and to arouse in them a keen desire to reach personally verified conclusions upon all questions of general concern to mankind, or of special significance for their own time. There is much truth in some remarks recently made in this connection by a college president:

> Certain professors have been refused re-election lately, apparently because they set their students to thinking in ways objectionable to the trustees. It would be well if more teachers were dismissed because they fail to stimulate thinking of any kind. We can afford to forgive a college professor what we regard as the occasional error of his doctrine, especially as we may be wrong,

provided he is a contagious center of intellectual enthusiasm. It is better for students to think about heresies than not to think at all; better for them to climb new trails, and stumble over error if need be, than to ride forever in upholstered ease in the overcrowded highway. It is a primary duty of a teacher to make a student take an honest account of his stock of ideas, throw out the dead matter, place revised price marks on what is left, and try to fill his empty shelves with new goods.

It is, however, possible and necessary that such intellectual awakening be brought about with patience, consideration, and pedagogical wisdom.

There is one further consideration with regard to the classroom utterances of college and university teachers to which the committee thinks it important to call the attention of members of the profession and of administrative authorities. Such utterances ought always to be considered privileged communications. Discussions in the classroom ought not to be supposed to be utterances for the public at large. They are often designed to provoke opposition or arouse debate. It has, unfortunately, sometimes happened in this country that sensational newspapers have quoted and garbled such remarks. As a matter of common law, it is clear that the utterances of an academic instructor are privileged, and may not be published, in whole or part, without his authorization. But our practice, unfortunately, still differs from that of foreign countries, and no effective check has in this country been put upon such unauthorized and often misleading publication. It is much to be desired that test cases should be made of any infractions of the rule.

In their extramural utterances, it is obvious that academic teachers are under a peculiar obligation to avoid hasty or unverified or exaggerated statements, and to refrain from intemperate or sensational modes of expression. But subject to these restraints, it is not, in this committee's opinion, desirable that scholars should be debarred from giving expression to their judgments upon controversial questions, or that their freedom of speech, outside the university, should be limited to questions falling within their own specialties. It is clearly not proper that they should be prohibited from lending their active support to organized movements that they believe to be in the public interest. And, speaking broadly, it may be said in the words of a nonacademic body already once quoted in a publication of the Association, that "it is neither possible nor desirable to deprive a college professor of the political rights vouchsafed to every citizen."

It is, however, a question deserving of consideration by members of this Association, and by university officials, how far academic teachers, at least those dealing with political, economic, and social subjects, should be prominent in the management of our great party organizations, or should be candidates for state or national offices of a distinctly political character. It is manifestly desirable that such teachers have minds untrammeled by party loyalties, unexcited by party enthusiasms, and unbiased by personal political ambitions; and that universities should remain uninvolved in party antagonisms. On the other hand, it is equally manifest that the material available for the service of the State would be restricted in a highly undesirable way, if it were understood that no member of the academic profession should ever be called upon to assume the responsibilities of public office. This question may, in the committee's opinion, suitably be made a topic for special discussion at some future meeting of this Association, in order that a practical policy, which shall do justice to the two partially conflicting considerations that bear upon the matter, may be agreed upon.

It is, it will be seen, in no sense the contention of this committee that academic freedom implies that individual teachers should be exempt from all restraints as to the matter or manner of their utterances, either within or without the university. Such restraints as are necessary should in the main, your committee holds, be self-imposed, or enforced by the public opinion of the profession. But there may, undoubtedly, arise occasional cases in which the aberrations of individuals may require to be checked by definite disciplinary action. What this report chiefly maintains is that such action cannot, with safety, be taken by bodies not composed of members of the academic profession. Lay governing boards are competent to judge concerning charges of habitual neglect of assigned duties, on the part of individual teachers, and concerning charges of grave moral delinquency. But in matters of opinion, and of the utterance of opinion, such boards cannot intervene without destroying, to the extent of their intervention, the essential nature of a university—without converting it from a place dedicated to openness of mind, in which the conclusions expressed are the tested conclusions of trained scholars, into a place barred against the access of new light, and pre-committed to the opinions or prejudices of men who have not been set apart or expressly trained for the scholar's duties. It is, in short, not the absolute freedom of utterance of the individual scholar, but the absolute freedom of thought, of inquiry, of discussion, and of teaching, of the academic profession, that is asserted by this declaration of principles. It is conceivable that our profession may prove unworthy of its high calling, and unfit to exercise the responsibilities that belong to it. But it will scarcely be said as yet to have given evidence of such unfitness. And the existence of this Association, as it seems to your committee, must be construed as a pledge, not only that the profession will earnestly guard those liberties without which it cannot rightly render its distinctive and indispensable service to society, but also that it will with equal earnestness seek to maintain such standards of professional character, and of scientific integrity and competency, as shall make it a fit instrument for that service.

PRACTICAL PROPOSALS

As the foregoing declaration implies, the ends to be accomplished are chiefly three:

1. To safeguard freedom of inquiry and of teaching against both covert and overt attacks by providing suitable judicial bodies composed of members of the academic profession, which may be called into action before university teachers are dismissed or disciplined, and may determine in what cases the question of academic freedom is actually involved.
2. By the same means, to protect college executives and governing boards against unjust charges of infringement of academic freedom, or of arbitrary and dictatorial conduct—charges which, when they gain wide currency and belief, are highly detrimental to the good repute and the influence of universities.
3. To render the profession more attractive to men of high ability and strong personality by insuring the dignity, the independence, and the reasonable security of tenure of the professional office.

The measures which it is believed to be necessary for our universities to adopt to realize these ends—measures which have already been adopted in part by some institutions—are four:

Action by faculty committees on reappointments. Official action relating to reappointments and refusals of reappointment should be taken only with the advice and consent of some board or committee representative of the faculty. Your committee does not desire to make at this time any suggestion as to the manner of selection of such boards.

Definition of tenure of office. In every institution there should be an unequivocal understanding as to the term of each appointment; and the tenure of professorships and associate professorships, and of all positions above the grade of instructor after ten years of service, should be permanent (subject to the provisions hereinafter given for removal upon charges). In those state universities which are legally incapable of making contracts for more than a limited period, the governing boards should announce their policy with respect to the presumption of reappointment in the several classes of position, and such announcements, though not legally enforceable, should be regarded as morally binding. No university teacher of any rank should, except in cases of grave moral delinquency, receive notice of dismissal or of refusal of reappointment, later than three months before the close of any academic year, and in the case of teachers above the grade of instructor, one year's notice should be given.

Formulation of grounds for dismissal. In every institution the grounds which will be regarded as justifying the dismissal of members of the faculty should be formulated with reasonable definiteness; and in the case of institutions which impose upon their faculties doctrinal standards of a sectarian or partisan character, these standards should be clearly defined and the body or individual having authority to interpret them, in case of controversy, should be designated. Your committee does not think it best at this time to attempt to enumerate the legitimate grounds for dismissal, believing it to be preferable that individual institutions should take the initiative in this.

Judicial hearings before dismissal. Every university or college teacher should be entitled, before dismissal or demotion, to have the charges against him stated in writing in specific terms and to have a fair trial on those charges before a special or permanent judicial committee chosen by the faculty senate or council, or by the faculty at large. At such trial the teacher accused should have full opportunity to present evidence, and if the charge is one of professional incompetence, a formal report upon his work should be first made in writing by the teachers of his own department and of cognate departments in the university, and, if the teacher concerned so desires, by a committee of his fellow specialists from other institutions, appointed by some competent authority.

The above declaration of principles and practical proposals are respectfully submitted by your committee to the approval of the Association, with the suggestion that, if approved, they be recommended to the consideration of the faculties, administrative officers, and governing boards of the American universities and colleges.

Edwin R. A. Seligman (Economics), Columbia University, Chairman

Charles E. Bennett (Latin), Cornell University

James Q. Dealey (Political Science), Brown University

Richard T. Ely (Economics), University of Wisconsin

Henry W. Farnam (Political Science), Yale University

Frank A. Fetter (Economics), Princeton University

Franklin H. Giddings (Sociology), Columbia University

Charles A. Kofoid (Zoology), University of California

Arthur O. Lovejoy (Philosophy), The Johns Hopkins University

Frederick W. Padelford (English), University of Washington

Roscoe Pound (Law), Harvard University

Howard C. Warren (Psychology), Princeton University

Ulysses G. Weatherly (Sociology), Indiana University

NOTE

1. The "Editor's Note," here printed with minor omissions, was written for a 1954 reproduction of the "Declaration of Principles" (*AAUP Bulletin*, 40:89–112, Spring, 1954).

APPENDIX

1940 AAUP Statement of Principles on Academic Freedom and Tenure

WITH 1970 INTERPRETIVE COMMENTS

In 1940, following a series of joint conferences begun in 1934, representatives of the American Association of University Professors and of the Association of American Colleges agreed upon a restatement of principles set forth in the 1925 Conference Statement on Academic Freedom and Tenure. This restatement is known to the profession as the 1940 Statement of Principles on Academic Freedom and Tenure.

The 1940 Statement is printed below, followed by Interpretive Comments as developed by representatives of the American Association of University Professors and the Association of American Colleges during 1969. The governing bodies of the associations, meeting respectively in November 1989 and January 1990, adopted several changes in language in order to remove gender-specific references from the original text.

The purpose of this statement is to promote public understanding and support of academic freedom and tenure and agreement upon procedures to assure them in colleges and universities. Institutions of higher education are conducted for the common good and not to further the interest of either the individual teacher[1] or the institution as a whole. The common good depends upon the free search for truth and its free exposition.

Academic freedom is essential to these purposes and applies to both teaching and research. Freedom in research is fundamental to the advancement of truth. Academic freedom in its teaching aspect is fundamental for the protection of the rights of the teacher in teaching and of the student to freedom in learning. It carries with it duties correlative with rights.[1][2]

Tenure is a means to certain ends; specifically: (1) freedom of teaching and research and of extramural activities, and (2) a sufficient degree of economic security to make the profession attractive to men and women of ability. Freedom and economic security, hence, tenure, are indispensable to the success of an institution in fulfilling its obligations to its students and to society.

ACADEMIC FREEDOM

(a) Teachers are entitled to full freedom in research and in the publication of the results, subject to the adequate performance of their other academic duties; but research for pecuniary return should be based upon an understanding with the authorities of the institution.

(b) Teachers are entitled to freedom in the classroom in discussing their subject, but they should be careful not to introduce into their teaching controversial matter which has no relation to their subject.[2] Limitations of academic freedom because of religious or other aims of the institution should be clearly stated in writing at the time of the appointment.[3]

(c) College and university teachers are citizens, members of a learned profession, and officers of an educational institution. When they speak or write as citizens, they should be free from institutional censorship or discipline, but their special position in the community imposes special obligations. As scholars and educational officers, they should remember that the public may judge their profession and their institution by their utterances. Hence they should at all times be accurate, should exercise appropriate restraint, should show respect for the opinions of others, and should make every effort to indicate that they are not speaking for the institution.[4]

ACADEMIC TENURE

After the expiration of a probationary period, teachers or investigators should have permanent or continuous tenure, and their service should be terminated only for adequate cause, except in the case of retirement for age, or under extraordinary circumstances because of financial exigencies.

In the interpretation of this principle it is understood that the following represents acceptable academic practice:

1. The precise terms and conditions of every appointment should be stated in writing and be in the possession of both institution and teacher before the appointment is consummated.

2. Beginning with appointment to the rank of full-time instructor or a higher rank,[5] the probationary period should not exceed seven years, including within this period full-time service in all institutions of higher education; but subject to the proviso that when, after a term of probationary service of more than three years, in one or more institutions, a teacher is called to another institution it may be agreed in writing that the new appointment is for a probationary period not more than four years, even though thereby the person's total probationary period in the academic profession is extended beyond the normal maximum of seven years.[6] Notice should be given at least one year prior to the expiration of the probationary period if the teacher is not to be continued in service after the expiration of that period.[7]

3. During the probationary period a teacher should have the academic freedom that all other members of the faculty have.[8]

4. Termination for cause of a continuous appointment, or the dismissal for cause of a teacher previous to the expiration of a term appointment, should, if possible, be considered by both a faculty committee and the governing board of the institution. In all cases where the facts are in dispute, the accused teacher should be informed before the hearing in writing of the charges and should have the opportunity to be heard in his or her own defense by all bodies that pass judgment upon the case. The teacher should be permitted to be accompanied by an advisor of his or her own choosing who may act as counsel. There should be a full stenographic record of the hearing available to the parties concerned. In the hearing of charges of incompetence the testimony should include that of teachers and other scholars, either from the teacher's own or from other institutions. Teachers on continuous appointment who are dismissed for reasons not involving moral turpitude should receive their salaries for at least a year from the date of notification of dismissal whether or not they are continued in their duties at the institution.[9]

5. Termination of a continuous appointment because of financial exigency should be demonstrably *bona fide*.

1940 INTERPRETATIONS

At the conference of representatives of the American Association of University Professors and of the Association of American Colleges on November 7–8, 1940, the following interpretations of the 1940 *Statement of Principles on Academic Freedom and Tenure* were agreed upon:

1. That its operation should not be retroactive.

2. That all tenure claims of teachers appointed prior to the endorsement should be determined in accordance with the principles set forth in the 1925 Conference Statement on Academic Freedom and Tenure.

3.   If the administration of a college or university feels that a teacher has
     not observed the admonitions of paragraph (c) of the section on Aca-
     demic Freedom and believes that the extramural utterances of the
     teacher have been such as to raise grave doubts concerning the teacher's
     fitness for his or her position, it may proceed to file charges under para-
     graph (a)(4) of the section on Academic Tenure. In pressing such
     charges the administration should remember that teachers are citizens
     and should be accorded the freedom of citizens. In such cases the ad-
     ministration must assume full responsibility, and the American Associ-
     ation of University Professors and the Association of American Col-
     leges are free to make an investigation.

1970 INTERPRETIVE COMMENTS

*Following extensive discussions on the 1940 Statement of Principles on Aca-
demic Freedom and Tenure with leading educational associations and with individual faculty members and administrators, a joint committee of the AAUP and
the Association of American Colleges met during 1969 to reevaluate this key policy statement. On the basis of the comments received, and the discussions that
ensued, the joint committee felt the preferable approach was to formulate interpretations of the Statement in terms of the experience gained in implementing and
applying the Statement for over thirty years and of adapting it to current needs.*

*The committee submitted to the two associations for their consideration the
following "Interpretive Comments." These interpretations were adopted by the
Council of the American Association of University Professors in April 1970 and
endorsed by the Fifty-sixth Annual Meeting as association policy.*

In the thirty years since their promulgation, the principles of the *1940
Statement of Principles on Academic Freedom and Tenure* have undergone a
substantial amount of refinement. This has evolved through a variety of
processes, including customary acceptance, understandings mutually ar-
rived at between institutions and professors or their representatives, investigations and reports by the American Association of University Professors, and formulations of statements by that association either alone or
in conjunction with the Association of American Colleges. These comments represent the attempt of the two associations, as the original sponsors of the *1940 Statement,* to formulate the most important of these re-
finements. Their incorporation here as Interpretive Comments is based
upon the premise that the *1940 Statement* is not a static code but a fundamental document designed to set a framework of norms to guide adapta-
tions to changing times and circumstances.

Also, there have been relevant developments in the law itself reflecting a growing insistence by the courts on due process within the academic community which parallels the essential concepts of the 1940 *Statement*; particularly relevant is the identification by the Supreme Court of academic freedom as a right protected by the First Amendment. As the Supreme Court said in *Keyishian v. Board of Regents*, 385 U.S. 589 (1967), "Our Nation is deeply committed to safeguarding academic freedom, which is of transcendent value to all of us and not merely to the teachers concerned. That freedom is therefore a special concern of the First Amendment, which does not tolerate laws that cast a pall of orthodoxy over the classroom."

The numbers refer to the designated portion of the 1940 *Statement* on which interpretive comment is made.

1. The Association of American Colleges and the American Association of University Professors have long recognized that membership in the academic profession carries with it special responsibilities. Both associations either separately or jointly have consistently affirmed these responsibilities in major policy statements, providing guidance to professors in their utterances as citizens, in the exercise of their responsibilities to the institution and to students, and in their conduct when resigning from their institution or when undertaking government-sponsored research. Of particular relevance is the *Statement on Professional Ethics*, adopted in 1966 as Association policy. (A revision, adopted in 1987, was published in *Academe: Bulletin of the AAUP* 73 (July-August 1987): 49.)

2. The intent of this statement is not to discourage what is "controversial." Controversy is at the heart of the free academic inquiry that the entire statement is designed to foster. The passage serves to underscore the need for teachers to avoid persistently intruding material that has no relation to their subject.

3. Most church-related institutions no longer need or desire the departure from the principle of academic freedom implied in the 1940 *Statement*, and we do not now endorse such a departure.

4. This paragraph is the subject of an interpretation adopted by the sponsors of the 1940 *Statement* immediately following its endorsement that reads as follows:

If the administration of a college or university feels that a teacher has not observed the admonitions of paragraph (c) of the section on Academic Freedom and believes that the extramural utterances of the teacher have been such as to raise grave doubts concerning the teacher's fitness for his or her position, it may proceed to file charges under paragraph (a)(4) of the section on Academic Tenure. In pressing such charges the administration should remember that teachers are citizens and should be accorded the freedom of citizens. In such cases the administration must assume full responsibility, and the American Association of University Professors and the Association of American Colleges are free to make an investigation.

Paragraph (c) of the *1940 Statement* should also be interpreted in keeping with the 1964 "Committee A Statement on Extramural Utterances" (*AAUP Bulletin* 51 (1965): 29), which states *inter alia*: "The controlling principle is that a faculty member's expression of opinion as a citizen cannot constitute grounds for dismissal unless it clearly demonstrates the faculty member's unfitness for his or her position. Extramural utterances rarely bear upon the faculty member's fitness for the position. Moreover, a final decision should take into account the faculty member's entire record as a teacher and scholar."

Paragraph V of the *Statement on Professional Ethics* also deals with the nature of the "special obligations" of the teacher. The paragraph reads as follows:

As members of their community, professors have the rights and obligations of other citizens. Professors measure the urgency of other obligations in the light of their responsibilities to their subject, to their students, to their profession, and to their institution. When they speak or act as private persons they avoid creating the impression of speaking or acting for their college or university. As citizens engaged in a profession that depends upon freedom for its health and integrity, professors have a particular obligation to promote conditions of free inquiry and to further public understanding of academic freedom.

Both the protection of academic freedom and the requirements of academic responsibility apply not only to the full-time probationary as well as to the tenured teacher, but also to all others, such as part-time faculty and teaching assistants, who exercise teaching responsibilities.

5. The concept of "rank of full-time instructor or a higher rank" is intended to include any person who teaches a full-time load regardless of the teacher's specific title.

6. In calling for an agreement "in writing" on the amount of credit for a faculty member's prior service at other institutions, the *Statement* furthers the general policy of full understanding by the professor of the terms and conditions of the appointment. It does not necessarily follow that a professor's tenure rights have been violated because of the absence of a written agreement on this matter. Nonetheless, especially because of the variation in permissible institutional practices, a written understanding concerning these matters at the time of appointment is particularly appropriate and advantageous to both the individual and the institution.

7. The effect of this subparagraph is that a decision on tenure, favorable or unfavorable, must be made at least twelve months prior to the completion of the probationary period. If the decision is negative, the appointment for the following year becomes a terminal one. If the decision is affirmative, the provisions in the *1940 Statement* with respect to the termination of services of teachers or investigators after the expiration of a probationary period should apply from the date when the favorable decision is made.

   The general principle of notice contained in this paragraph is developed with greater specificity in the *Standards for Notice of Nonreappointment*, endorsed by the Fiftieth Annual Meeting of the American Association of University Professors (1964). These standards are:

   Notice of nonreappointment, or of intention not to recommend reappointment to the governing board, should be given in writing in accordance with the following standards:

   (1) *Not later than March 1 of the first academic year of service*, if the appointment expires at the end of that year; or, if a one-year appointment terminates during an academic year, at least three months in advance of its termination.

   (2) *Not later than December 15 of the second academic year of service*, if the appointment expires at the end of that year; or, if an initial two-year appointment terminates during an academic year, at least six months in advance of its termination.

   (3) At least twelve months before the expiration of an appointment after two or more years in the institution.

   Other obligations, both of institutions and of individuals, are described in the *Statement on Recruitment and Resignation of Faculty Members*, as endorsed by the Association of American Colleges and the American Association of University Professors in 1961.

8. The establishment of a regular procedure for the periodic evaluation and assessment of the teacher's academic performance during probationary status enhance the freedom of probationary teachers. Provision should be made for regularized procedures for the consideration of complaints by probationary teachers that their academic freedom has been violated. One suggested procedure to serve these purposes is contained in the *Recommended Institutional Regulations on Academic Freedom and Tenure*, prepared by the American Association of University Professors.

9. A further specification of the academic due process to which the teacher is entitled under this paragraph is contained in the *Statement on Procedural Standards in Faculty Dismissal Proceedings*, jointly approved by the American Association of University Professors and the Association of American Colleges in 1958. This interpretive document deals with the issue of suspension, about which the *1940 Statement* is silent.

The *1958 Statement* provides: "Suspension of the faculty member during the proceedings is justified only if immediate harm to the faculty member or others is threatened by the faculty member's continuance. Unless legal considerations forbid, any such suspension should be with pay." A suspension, which is not followed by either reinstatement or the opportunity for a hearing, is in effect a summary dismissal in violation of academic due process.

The concept of "moral turpitude" identifies the exceptional case in which the professor may be denied a year's teaching or pay in whole or in part. The statement applies to that kind of behavior which goes beyond simply warranting discharge and is so utterly blameworthy as to make it inappropriate to require the offering of a year's teaching or pay. The standard is not that the moral sensibilities of persons in the particular community have been affronted. The standard is behavior that would evoke condemnation by the academic community generally.

ENDORSERS

Association of American Colleges, 1941

American Association of University Professors, 1941

American Library Association (adapted for librarians), 1946

Association of American Law Schools, 1946

American Political Science Association, 1947

American Association of Colleges for Teacher Education, 1950

American Association for Higher Education, 1950

Eastern Psychological Association, 1950

Southern Society for Philosophy and Psychology, 1953

American Psychological Association, 1961

American Historical Association, 1961

Modern Language Association of America, 1962

American Economic Association, 1962

American Agricultural Economics Association, 1962

Midwest Sociological Society, 1963

Organization of American Historians, 1963

American Philological Association, 1963

American Council of Learned Societies, 1963

Speech Communication Association, 1963

American Sociological Association, 1963

Southern Historical Association, 1963

American Studies Association, 1963

Association of American Geographers, 1963

Southern Economic Association, 1963

Classical Association of the Middle West and South, 1964

Southwestern Social Science Association, 1964

Archaeological Institute of America, 1964

Southern Management Association, 1964

American Theatre Association, 1964

South Central Modern Language Association, 1964

Southwestern Philosophical Society, 1964

Council of Independent Colleges, 1965

Mathematical Association of America, 1965

Arizona-Nevada Academy of Science, 1965

American Risk and Insurance Association, 1965

Academy of Management, 1965

American Catholic Historical Association, 1966

American Catholic Philosophical Association, 1966

Association of Education in Journalism, 1966

Western History Association, 1966

Mountain-Plains Philosophical Conference, 1966

Society of American Archivists, 1966

Southeastern Psychological Association, 1966

Southern Speech Communication Association, 1966

American Association for the Advancement of Slavic Studies, 1967

American Mathematical Society, 1967

College Theology Society, 1967

Council on Social Work Education, 1967

American Association of Colleges of Pharmacy, 1967

American Academy of Religion, 1967

Association for the Sociology of Religion, 1967

American Society of Journalism School Administrators, 1967

John Dewey Society, 1967

South Atlantic Modern Language Association, 1967

American Finance Association, 1967

Association for Social Economics, 1967

United Chapters of Phi Beta Kappa, 1968

American Society of Christian Ethics, 1968

American Association of Teachers of French, 1968

Eastern Finance Association, 1968

American Association for Chinese Studies, 1968

American Society of Plant Physiologists, 1968

University Film and Video Association, 1968

American Dialect Society, 1968

American Speech-Language-Hearing Association, 1968

Association of Social and Behavioral Scientists, 1968

College English Association, 1968

National College Physical Education Association for Men, 1969

American Real Estate and Urban Economics Association, 1969

History of Education Society, 1969

Council for Philosophical Studies, 1969

American Musicological Society, 1969

American Association of Teachers of Spanish and Portuguese, 1969

Texas Junior College Teachers Association, 1970

College Art Association of America, 1970

Society of Professors of Education, 1970

American Anthropological Association, 1970

Association of Theological Schools, 1970

American Association of Schools and Departments of Journalism, 1971

American Business Law Association, 1971

American Council for the Arts, 1972

New York State Mathematics Association of Two-Year Colleges, 1972

College Language Association, 1973

Pennsylvania Historical Association, 1973

Massachusetts Regional Community College Faculty Association, 1973

American Philosophical Association, 1974

American Classical League, 1974

American Comparative Literature Association, 1974

Rocky Mountain Modern Language Association, 1974

Society of Architectural Historians, 1975

American Statistical Association, 1975

American Folklore Society, 1975

Association for Asian Studies, 1975

Linguistic Society of America, 1975

African Studies Association, 1975

American Institute of Biological Sciences, 1975

North American Conference on British Studies, 1975

Sixteenth-Century Studies Conference, 1975

Texas Association of College Teachers, 1976

Society for Spanish and Portuguese Historical Studies, 1976

Association for Jewish Studies, 1976

Western Speech Communication Association, 1976

Texas Association of Colleges for Teacher Education, 1977

Metaphysical Society of America, 1977

American Chemical Society, 1977

Texas Library Association, 1977

American Society for Legal History, 1977

Iowa Higher Education Association, 1977

American Physical Therapy Association, 1979

North Central Sociological Association, 1980

Dante Society of America, 1980

Association for Communication Administration, 1981

American Association of Physics Teachers, 1982

Middle East Studies Association, 1982

National Education Association, 1985

American Institute of Chemists, 1985

American Association of Teachers of German, 1985

American Association of Teachers of Italian, 1985

American Association for Applied Linguistics, 1986

American Association of Teachers of Slavic and East European Languages, 1986

American Association for Cancer Education, 1986

American Society of Church History, 1986

Oral History Association, 1987

Society for French Historical Studies, 1987

History of Science Society, 1987

American Association of Pharmaceutical Scientists, 1988

American Association for Clinical Chemistry, 1988

Council for Chemical Research, 1988

Association for the Study of Higher Education, 1988

American Psychological Society, 1989

University and College Labor Education Association, 1989

Society for Neuroscience, 1989

Renaissance Society of America, 1989

Society of Biblical Literature, 1989

National Science Teachers Association, 1989

Medieval Academy of America, 1990

American Society of Agronomy, 1990

Crop Science Society of America, 1990

Soil Science Society of America, 1990

Society of Protozoologists, 1990

Society for Ethnomusicology, 1990

American Association of Physicists in Medicine, 1990

Animal Behavior Society, 1990

Illinois Community College Faculty Association, 1990

American Society for Theatre Research, 1990

National Council of Teachers of English, 1991

Latin American Studies Association, 1992

Society for Cinema Studies, 1992

American Society for Eighteenth-Century Studies, 1992

Council of Colleges of Arts and Sciences, 1992

American Society for Aesthetics, 1992

Association for the Advancement of Baltic Studies, 1994

American Council of Teachers of Russian, 1994

Council of Teachers of Southeast Asian Languages, 1994

American Association of Teachers of Arabic, 1994

Association of Teachers of Japanese, 1994

Academic Senate for California Community Colleges, 1996

Council of Graduate Programs in Communication Sciences and Disorders, 1996

Association for Women in Mathematics, 1997

Philosophy of Time Society, 1998

World Communication Association, 1999

The Historical Society, 1999

Association for Theatre in Higher Education, 1999

National Association for Ethnic Studies, 1999

Association of Ancient Historians, 1999

American Culture Association, 1999

American Conference for Irish Studies, 1999

Society for Philosophy in the Contemporary World, 1999

Eastern Communication Association, 1999

Association for Canadian Studies in the United States, 1999

American Association for the History of Medicine, 2000

Missouri Association of Faculty Senates, 2000

NOTES

1. The word "teacher" as used in this documents is understood to include the investigator who is attached to an academic institution without teaching duties.

2. Boldface numbers in brackets refer to Interpretive Comments which follow.

APPENDIX

1966 AAUP Statement on Professional Ethics

The statement that follows, a revision of a statement originally adopted in 1966, was approved by the Committee on Professional Ethics, adopted by the Association's Council in June 1987, and endorsed by the Seventy-third Annual Meeting.

INTRODUCTION

From its inception, the American Association of University Professors has recognized that membership in the academic profession carries with it special responsibilities. The Association has consistently affirmed these responsibilities in major policy statements, providing guidance to professors in such matters as their utterances as citizens, the exercise of their responsibilities to students and colleagues, and their conduct when resigning from an institution or when undertaking sponsored research. *The Statement on Professional Ethics* that follows sets forth those general standards that serve as a reminder of the variety of responsibilities assumed by all members of the profession.

In the enforcement of ethical standards, the academic profession differs from those of law and medicine, whose associations act to ensure the integrity of members engaged in private practice. In the academic profession the individual institution of higher learning provides this assurance and so should normally handle questions concerning propriety of conduct within its own framework by reference to a faculty group. The Association supports such local action and stands ready, through the general secretary and Committee B, to counsel with members of the academic community concerning questions of professional ethics and to inquire into complaints when local consideration is impossible or inappropriate. If the alleged offense is deemed sufficiently serious to raise the possibility of adverse action, the procedures should be in accordance with the *1940 Statement of Principles on Academic Freedom and Tenure*, the *1958 Statement on Procedural Standards in Faculty Dismissal Proceedings*, or the applicable provisions of the Association's *Recommended Institutional Regulations on Academic Freedom and Tenure*.

THE STATEMENT

1. Professors, guided by a deep conviction of the worth and dignity of the advancement of knowledge, recognize the special responsibilities placed upon them. Their primary responsibility to their subject is to seek and to state the truth as they see it. To this end professors devote their energies to developing and improving their scholarly competence. They accept the obligation to exercise critical self-discipline and judgment in using, extending, and transmitting knowledge. They practice intellectual honesty. Although professors may follow subsidiary interests, these interests must never seriously hamper or compromise their freedom of inquiry.

2. As teachers, professors encourage the free pursuit of learning in their students. They hold before them the best scholarly and ethical standards of their discipline. Professors demonstrate respect for students as individuals and adhere to their proper roles as intellectual guides and counselors. Professors make every reasonable effort to foster honest academic conduct and to ensure that their evaluations of students reflect each student's true merit. They respect the confidential nature of the relationship between professor and student. They avoid any exploitation, harassment, or discriminatory treatment of students. They acknowledge significant academic or scholarly assistance from them. They protect their academic freedom.

3. As colleagues, professors have obligations that derive from common membership in the community of scholars. Professors do not discriminate against or harass colleagues. They respect and defend the free inquiry of associates. In the exchange of criticism and ideas professors show due respect for the opinions of others. Professors acknowledge academic debt and strive to be objective in their professional judgment of colleagues. Professors accept their share of faculty responsibilities for the governance of their institution.

4. As members of an academic institution, professors seek above all to be effective teachers and scholars. Although professors observe the stated regulations of the institution, provided the regulations do not contravene academic freedom, they maintain their right to criticize and seek revision. Professors give due regard to their paramount responsibilities within their institution in determining the amount and character of work done outside it. When considering the interruption or termination of their service, professors recognize the effect of their decision upon the program of the institution and give due notice of their intentions.

5. As members of their community, professors have the rights and obligations of other citizens. Professors measure the urgency of these obligations in the light of their responsibilities to their subject, to their students, to their profession, and to their institution. When they speak or act as private persons they avoid creating the impression of speaking or acting for their college or university. As citizens engaged in a profession that depends upon freedom for its health and integrity, professors have a particular obligation to promote conditions of free inquiry and to further public understanding of academic freedom.

APPENDIX

1966 AAUP Statement on Government of Colleges and Universities

Editorial Note: The statement which follows is directed to governing board members, administrators, faculty members, students, and other persons in the belief that the colleges and universities of the United States have reached a stage calling for appropriately shared responsibility and cooperative action among the components of the academic institution. The statement is intended to foster constructive joint thought and action, both within the institutional structure and in protection of its integrity against improper intrusions.

It is not intended that the statement serve as a blueprint for governance on a specific campus or as a manual for the regulation of controversy among the components of an academic institution, although it is to be hoped that the principles asserted will lead to the correction of existing weaknesses and assist in the establishment of sound structures and procedures. The statement does not attempt to cover relations with those outside agencies which increasingly are controlling the resources and influencing the patterns of education in our institutions of higher learning: for example, the United States government, state legislatures, state commissions, interstate associations or compacts, and other inter-institutional arrangements. However, it is hoped that the statement will be helpful to these agencies in their consideration of educational matters.

Students are referred to in this statement as an institutional component coordinate in importance with trustees, administrators, and faculty. There is, however, no main section on students. The omission has two causes: (1) the changes now occurring in the status of American students have plainly outdistanced the analysis by the educational community, and an attempt to define the situation without thorough study might prove unfair to student interests, and (2) students do not in fact at present have a significant voice in the government of colleges and universities; it would be unseemly to obscure, by superficial equality of length of statement, what may be a serious lag entitled to separate and full confrontation. The concern for student status felt by the organizations issuing this statement is embodied in a note, "On Student Status," intended to stimulate the educational community to turn its attention to an important need.

The American Association of University Professors, the American Council on Education (ACE), and the Association of Governing Boards of Universities and Colleges (AGB) jointly formulated this statement. In October 1966, the board of directors of the ACE took action by which its council "recognizes the statement as a significant step forward in the clarification of the respective roles of governing boards, faculties, and administrations," and "commends it to the institutions that are members of the Council." The Council of the AAUP adopted the statement in October 1966, and the Fifty-third Annual Meeting endorsed it in April 1967. In November 1966, the executive committee of the AGB took action by which that organization also "recognizes the statement as a significant step forward in the clarification of the respective roles of governing boards, faculties, and administrations," and "commends it to the governing boards which are members of the Association." (In April 1990, the Council of the AAUP adopted several changes in language in order to remove gender-specific references from the original text.)

I. INTRODUCTION

This statement is a call to mutual understanding regarding the government of colleges and universities. Understanding, based on community of interest and producing joint effort, is essential for at least three reasons. First, the academic institution, public or private, often has become less autonomous; buildings, research, and student tuition are supported by funds over which the college or university exercises a diminishing control. Legislative and executive governmental authorities, at all levels, play a part in the making of important decisions in academic policy. If these voices and forces are to be successfully heard and integrated, the academic institution must be in a position to meet them with its own generally unified view. Second, regard for the welfare of the institution remains important despite the mobility and interchange of scholars. Third, a college or university in which all the components are aware of their interdependence, of the usefulness of communication among themselves, and of the force of joint action will enjoy increased capacity to solve educational problems.

II. THE ACADEMIC INSTITUTION: JOINT EFFORT

A. Preliminary Considerations

The variety and complexity of the tasks performed by institutions of higher education produce an inescapable interdependence among governing board, administration, faculty, students, and others. The relationship calls for adequate communication among these components, and full opportunity for appropriate joint planning and effort.

Joint effort in an academic institution will take a variety of forms appropriate to the kinds of situations encountered. In some instances, the president will make an initial exploration or recommendation with consideration by the faculty at a later stage; in other instances, the faculty, subject to the endorsement of the president and the governing board will make a first and essentially definitive recommendation. In still others, a substantive contribution can be made when student leaders are responsibly involved in the process. Although the variety of such approaches may be wide, at least two general conclusions regarding joint effort seem clearly warranted: (1) important areas of action involve at one time or another the initiating capacity and decision-making participation of all the institutional components, and (2) differences in the weight of each voice, from one point to the next, should be determined by reference to the responsibility of each component for the particular matter at hand, as developed hereinafter.

B. Determination of General Educational Policy

The general educational policy, i.e., the objectives of an institution and the nature, range, and pace of its efforts, is shaped by the institutional charter or by law, by tradition and historical development, by the present needs of the community of the institution, and by the professional aspirations and standards of those directly involved in its work. Every board will wish to go beyond its formal trustee obligation to conserve the accomplishment of the past and to engage seriously with the future; every faculty will seek to conduct an operation worthy of scholarly standards of learning; every administrative officer will strive to meet his or her charge and to attain the goals of the institution. The interests of all are coordinate and related, and unilateral effort can lead to confusion or conflict. Essential to a solution is a reasonably explicit statement on general educational policy. Operating responsibility and authority, and procedures for continuing review, should be clearly defined in official regulations.

When an educational goal has been established, it becomes the responsibility primarily of the faculty to determine the appropriate curriculum and procedures of student instruction.

Special considerations may require particular accommodations: (1) a publicly supported institution may be regulated by statutory provisions, and (2) a church-controlled institution may be limited by its charter or bylaws. When such external requirements influence course content and the manner of instruction or research, they impair the educational effectiveness of the institution.

Such matters as major changes in the size or composition of the student body and the relative emphasis to be given to the various elements of the educational and research program should involve participation of governing board, administration, and faculty prior to final decision.

C. Internal Operations of the Institution

The framing and execution of long-range plans, one of the most important aspects of institutional responsibility, should be a central and continuing concern in the academic community.

Effective planning demands that the broadest possible exchange of information and opinion should be the rule for communication among the components of a college or university. The channels of communication should be established and maintained by joint endeavor. Distinction should be observed between the institutional system of communication and the system of responsibility for the making of decisions.

A second area calling for joint effort in internal operation is that of decisions regarding existing or prospective physical resources. The board, president, and faculty should all seek agreement on basic decisions regarding buildings and other facilities to be used in the educational work of the institution.

A third area is budgeting. The allocation of resources among competing demands is central in the formal responsibility of the governing board, in the administrative authority of the president, and in the educational function of the faculty. Each component should therefore have a voice in the determination of short- and long-range priorities, and each should receive appropriate analyses of past budgetary experience, reports on current budgets and expenditures, and short- and long-range budgetary projections. The function of each component in budgetary matters should be understood by all; the allocation of authority will determine the flow of information and the scope of participation in decisions.

Joint effort of a most critical kind must be taken when an institution chooses a new president. The selection of a chief administrative officer should follow upon a cooperative search by the governing board and the faculty, taking into consideration the opinions of others who are appropriately interested. The president should be equally qualified to serve both as the executive officer of the governing board and as the chief academic officer of the institution and the faculty. The president's dual role requires an ability to interpret to board and faculty the educational views and concepts of institutional government of the other. The president should have the confidence of the board and the faculty.

The selection of academic deans and other chief academic officers should be the responsibility of the president with the advice of, and in consultation with, the appropriate faculty.

Determinations of faculty status, normally based on the recommendations of the faculty groups involved, are discussed in Part V of this statement; but it should here be noted that the building of a strong faculty requires careful joint effort in such actions as staff selection and promotion and the granting of tenure. Joint action should also govern dismissals; the applicable principles and procedures in these matters are well established.[1]

D. External Relations of the Institution

Anyone—a member of the governing board, the president or other member of the administration, a member of the faculty, or a member of the student body or the alumni—affects the institution when speaking of it in public. An individual who speaks unofficially should so indicate. An individual who speaks officially for the institution, the board, the administration, the faculty, or the student body should be guided by established policy.

It should be noted that only the board speaks legally for the whole institution, although it may delegate responsibility to an agent.

The right of a board member, an administrative officer, a faculty member, or a student to speak on general educational questions or about the administration and operations of the individual's own institution is a part of that person's right as a citizen and should not be abridged by the institution.[2] There exist, of course, legal bounds relating to defamation of character, and there are questions of propriety.

III. THE ACADEMIC INSTITUTION: THE GOVERNING BOARD

The governing board has a special obligation to ensure that the history of the college or university shall serve as a prelude and inspiration to the future. The board helps relate the institution to its chief community: for example, the community college to serve the educational needs of a defined population area or group, the church-controlled college to be cognizant of the announced position of its denomination, and the comprehensive university to discharge the many duties and to accept the appropriate new challenges which are its concern at the several levels of higher education.

The governing board of an institution of higher education in the United States operates, with few exceptions, as the final institutional authority. Private institutions are established by charters; constitutional or statutory provisions establish public institutions. In private institutions the board is frequently self-perpetuating; in public colleges and universities the present membership of a board may be asked to suggest candidates for appointment. As a whole and individually, when the governing board confronts the problem of succession, serious attention should be given to obtaining properly qualified persons. Where public law calls for election of governing board members, means should be found to ensure the nomination of fully suited persons, and the electorate should be informed of the relevant criteria for board membership.

Since the membership of the board may embrace both individual and collective competence of recognized weight, its advice or help may be sought through established channels by other components of the academic community. The governing board of an institution of higher education, while maintaining a general overview, entrusts the conduct of administration to the administrative officers—the president and the deans—and the conduct of teaching and research to the faculty. The board should undertake appropriate self-limitation.

One of the governing board's important tasks is to ensure the publication of codified statements that define the overall policies and procedures of the institution under its jurisdiction.

The board plays a central role in relating the likely needs of the future to predictable resources; it has the responsibility for husbanding the endowment; it is responsible for obtaining needed capital and operating funds; and in the broadest sense of the term it should pay attention to personnel policy. In order to fulfill these duties, the board should be aided by, and may insist upon, the development of long-range planning by the administration and faculty. When ignorance or ill will threatens the institution or any part of it, the governing board must be available for support. In grave crises it will be expected to serve as a champion. Although the action to be taken by it will usually be on behalf of the president, the faculty, or the student body, the board should make clear that the protection it offers to an individual or a group is, in fact, a fundamental defense of the vested interests of society in the educational institution.[3]

IV. THE ACADEMIC INSTITUTION: THE PRESIDENT

The president, as the chief executive officer of an institution of higher education, is measured largely by his or her capacity for institutional leadership. The president shares responsibility for the definition and attainment of goals, for administrative action, and for operating the communications system that links the components of the academic community. The president represents the institution to its many publics. The president's leadership role is supported by delegated authority from the board and faculty.

As the chief planning officer of an institution, the president has a special obligation to innovate and initiate. The degree to which a president can envision new horizons for the institution, and can persuade others to see them and to work toward them, will often constitute the chief measure of the president's administration.

The president must at times, with or without support, infuse new life into a department; relatedly, the president may at times be required, working within the concept of tenure, to solve problems of obsolescence. The president will necessarily utilize the judgments of the faculty but may also, in the interest of academic standards, seek outside evaluations by scholars of acknowledged competence.

It is the duty of the president to see to it that the standards and procedures in operational use within the college or university conform to the policy established by the governing board and to the standards of sound academic practice. It is also incumbent on the president to ensure that faculty views, including dissenting views, are presented to the board in those areas and on those issues where responsibilities are shared. Similarly, the faculty should be informed of the views of the board and the administration on like issues.

The president is largely responsible for the maintenance of existing institutional resources and the creation of new resources; has ultimate managerial responsibility for a large area of nonacademic activities; is responsible for public understanding; and by the nature of the office is the chief person who speaks for the institution. In these and other areas the president's work is to plan, to organize, to direct, and to represent. The presidential function should receive the general support of board and faculty.

V. THE ACADEMIC INSTITUTION: THE FACULTY

The faculty has primary responsibility for such fundamental areas as curriculum, subject matter and methods of instruction, research, faculty status, and those aspects of student life which relate to the educational process. On these matters the power of review or final decision lodged in the governing board or delegated by it to the president should be exercised adversely only in exceptional circumstances, and for reasons communicated to the faculty. It is desirable that the faculty should, following such communication, have opportunity for further consideration and further transmittal of its views to the president or board. Budgets, personnel limitations, the time element, and the policies of other groups, bodies, and agencies having jurisdiction over the institution may set limits to realization of faculty advice.

The faculty sets the requirements for the degrees offered in course, determines when the requirements have been met, and authorizes the president and board to grant the degrees thus achieved.

Faculty status and related matters are primarily a faculty responsibility; this area includes appointments, reappointments, decisions not to reappoint, promotions, the granting of tenure, and dismissal. The primary responsibility of the faculty for such matters is based upon the fact that its judgment is central to general educational policy. Furthermore, scholars in a particular field or activity have the chief competence for judging the work of their colleagues; in such competence it is implicit that responsibility exists for both adverse and favorable judgments. Likewise, there is the more general competence of experienced faculty personnel committees having a broader charge. Determinations in these matters should first be by faculty action through established procedures, reviewed by the chief academic officers with the concurrence of the board. The governing board and president should, on questions of faculty status, as in other matters where the faculty has primary responsibility, concur with the faculty judgment except in rare instances and for compelling reasons which should be stated in detail.

The faculty should actively participate in the determination of policies and procedures governing salary increases.

The chair or head of a department, who serves as the chief representative of the department within an institution, should be selected either by departmental election or by appointment following consultation with members of the department and of related departments; appointments should normally be in conformity with department members' judgment. The chair or department head should not have tenure in office; tenure as a faculty member is a matter of separate right. The chair or head should serve for a stated term but without prejudice to reelection or to reappointment by procedures which involve appropriate faculty consultation. Board, administration, and faculty should all bear in mind that the department chair or head has a special obligation to build a department strong in scholarship and teaching capacity.

Agencies for faculty participation in the government of the college or university should be established at each level where faculty responsibility is present. An agency should exist for the presentation of the views of the whole faculty. The structure and procedures for faculty participation should be designed, approved, and established by joint action of the components of the institution. Faculty representatives should be selected by the faculty according to procedures determined by the faculty.[4]

The agencies may consist of meetings of all faculty members of a department, school, college, division, or university system, or may take the form of faculty-elected executive committees in departments and schools and a faculty-elected senate or council for larger divisions or the institution as a whole.

The means of communication among the faculty, administration, and governing board now in use include: (1) circulation of memoranda and reports by board committees, the administration, and faculty committees, (2) joint ad hoc committees, (3) standing liaison committees, (4) membership of faculty members on administrative bodies, and (5) membership of faculty members on governing boards. Whatever the channels of communication, they should be clearly understood and observed.

VI. ON STUDENT STATUS

When students in American colleges and universities desire to participate responsibly in the government of the institution they attend, their wish should be recognized as a claim to opportunity both for educational experience and for involvement in the affairs of their college or university. Ways should be found to permit significant student participation within the limits of attainable effectiveness. The obstacles to such participation are large and should not be minimized: inexperience, untested capacity, a transitory status which means that present action does not carry with it subsequent responsibility, and the inescapable fact that the other components of the institution are in a position of judgment over the students. It is important to recognize that student needs are strongly related to educational experience, both formal and informal.

Students expect, and have a right to expect, that the educational process will be structured, that they will be stimulated by it to become independent adults, and that they will have effectively transmitted to them the cultural heritage of the larger society. If institutional support is to have its fullest possible meaning, it should incorporate the strength, freshness of view, and idealism of the student body.

The respect of students for their college or university can be enhanced if they are given at least these opportunities: (1) to be listened to in the classroom without fear of institutional reprisal for the substance of their views, (2) freedom to discuss questions of institutional policy and operation, (3) the right to academic due process when charged with serious violations of institutional regulations, and (4) the same right to hear speakers of their own choice as is enjoyed by other components of the institution.

NOTES

1. See the "1940 Statement of Principles on Academic Freedom and Tenure," AAUP, *Policy Documents and Reports*, 9th ed. (Washington, D.C., 2001), 3–10, and the "1958 Statement on Procedural Standards in Faculty Dismissal Proceedings," Ibid., 11–14. The Association of American Colleges (now the Association of American Colleges and Universities) and the American Association of University Professors jointly adopted these statements; numerous learned and scientific societies and educational associations have endorsed the "1940 Statement."

2. With respect to faculty members, the "1940 Statement of Principles on Academic Freedom and Tenure" reads: "College and university teachers are citizens, members of a learned profession, and officers of an educational institution. When they speak or write as citizens, they should be free from institutional censorship or discipline, but their special position in the community imposes special obligations. As scholars and educational officers, they should remember that the public may judge their profession and their institution by their utterances. Hence they should at all times be accurate, should exercise appropriate restraint, should show respect for the opinions of others, and should make every effort to indicate that they are not speaking for the institution" (*Policy Documents and Reports*, 4).

3. Traditionally, governing boards developed within the context of single-campus institutions. In more recent times, governing and coordinating boards have increasingly tended to develop at the multi-campus regional, system-wide, or statewide levels. As influential components of the academic community, these supra-campus bodies bear particular responsibility for protecting the autonomy of individual campuses or institutions under their jurisdiction and for implementing policies of shared responsibility. The American Association of University Professors regards the objectives and practices recommended in the "Statement on Government" as constituting equally appropriate guidelines for such supra-campus bodies, and looks toward continued development of practices that will facilitate application of such guidelines in this new context. [Preceding note adopted by AAUP's Council in June 1978.]

4. The American Association of University Professors regards collective bargaining, properly used, as another means of achieving sound academic government. Where there is faculty collective bargaining, the parties should seek to ensure appropriate institutional governance structures that will protect the right of all faculty to participate in institutional governance in accordance with the "Statement on Government." [Preceding note adopted by the Council in June 1978.]

APPENDIX F

1998 Association of Governing Boards' Statement on Governance

The enormous diversity among American colleges and universities is reflected in their disparate governance structures and functions. Although the culture and process of governance vary widely among institutions, the presence of lay citizen governing boards distinguishes American higher education from most of the rest of the world where universities ultimately are dependencies of the state. The nation's public and private institutions also depend on government, but they historically have been accorded autonomy in carrying out their educational functions through the medium of independent governing boards. These boards usually are gubernatorially appointed (and less frequently elected) in the case of public institutions and are generally self-perpetuating in private institutions.

The Association of Governing Boards of Universities and Colleges (AGB) has concluded that the governing boards responsible for the nation's 3,600 nonprofit colleges and universities should consider a number of principles and standards of good practice. In setting forth these principles and standards of effective governance, AGB respects the distinctive history, culture, missions, structures, and aspirations of our public and private institutions. Thus, this document is not intended to be prescriptive but rather a template of good practices and policy guidelines for boards to consider and adapt to their needs.

Much has changed in the three decades since the American Association of University Professors issued its "Statement on Government of Colleges and Universities." In 1966, AGB "commended" that document to the attention of its members, but it did not "endorse" it. This new statement, which addresses institutional decision making from the governing board perspective, takes into consideration some of the changes in the landscape of American higher education. These changes include but are not limited to the following facts and perceptions.

FACTS

- The proportion of part-time or adjunct faculty has increased rapidly.
- Community colleges now enroll almost one-half of all students in higher education.
- The majority of students attend public institutions that are part of multi-campus systems.
- As a result of various demands on limited state treasuries, state funding for public institutions has not kept pace with enrollment or cost increases. Many institutions, including independent colleges and universities, have had to downsize or significantly reallocate resources.
- The average length of service by institutional chief executives has declined, in part, as a result of conflicting demands from constituents, the politicization of public-sector governing boards, and the frequency of budget crises.

PERCEPTIONS

- The public demands greater accountability—particularly regarding student learning outcomes—and elected officials have intensified their scrutiny of higher education.
- There is a widespread perception that faculty members, especially in research universities, are divided in their loyalties between their academic disciplines and the welfare of their own institutions.
- Higher education officials are increasingly sensitive to changing student interests and the shifting demands of the job market.
- Scholars, think-tanks, and a variety of commissions project a major transformation of higher education as a result of a revolution in information technology, the reorientation of the focus of education from teaching to learning, and the new competition from corporate, for-profit and online enterprises in the higher education market.
- Many governing boards, faculty members, and chief executives believe that internal governance arrangements have become so cumbersome that timely decisions are difficult to make, and small factions often are able to impede the decision-making process.

- Alternatively, in the quest for consensus or efficiency, the governance process sometimes produces a "lowest common denominator" decision, which does not adequately address underlying issues.

- The AGB Board of Directors has concluded that these facts and perceptions are so compelling that a new statement on internal governance is necessary—a new perspective as seen through the lens of governing boards and trustees. Its purpose is to encourage AGB-member boards to examine the clarity, coherence, and appropriateness of their institutions' governance structures, policies, and practices and to revise them as necessary.

PRINCIPLES

1. The ultimate responsibility for the institution rests in its governing board. Boards cannot delegate their fiduciary responsibility for the academic integrity and financial health of the institution. Traditionally, and for practical reasons, boards delegate some kinds of authority to other stakeholders with the implicit and sometimes explicit condition that the board reserves the right to question, challenge, and occasionally override decisions or proposals it judges to be inconsistent with the mission, integrity, or financial position of the institution. For example, the delegation of authority to the administration and faculty in adding, reducing, or discontinuing academic programs is made with the implicit understanding that the board still retains the ultimate responsibility.

2. The governing board should retain ultimate responsibility and full authority to determine the mission of the institution (within the constraints of state policies, in the case of public institutions or multi-campus systems) in consultation with and on the advice of the chief executive. The board is also responsible for establishing the strategic direction of the institution or system through its insistence on and participation in comprehensive planning. As with many other issues, the board should work toward a consensus or an understanding on the part of the stakeholders concerning strategic direction and set forth a realistic view of the resources necessary to compete in the educational marketplace, accomplish these strategic goals, and carry out the mission.

3. Colleges and universities have many of the characteristics of business enterprises. Consequently, boards should ensure that, as corporations, their institutions' fiscal and managerial affairs are administered with appropriate attention to commonly accepted business standards. At the same time, nonprofit colleges and universities differ from businesses in many respects. They do not operate with a profit motive, and the "bottom lines" of col-

leges and universities are far more difficult to measure. They also differ from businesses in the sense that the processes of teaching, learning, and research often are at least as important as "the product," as measured by the conferring of degrees or the publication of research results. And by virtue of their special mission and purpose in a pluralistic society, they have a tradition of participation in institutional governance that is less common in and less appropriate for businesses.

4. The governing board should conduct its affairs in a manner that exemplifies the behavior it expects of other participants in institutional governance. From time to time, boards should examine their membership, structure, and performance and should expect the same of faculty and staff. Boards and their individual members should engage in periodic evaluations of their effectiveness and commitment to their institution or public system. They should strive to understand and respect the unique culture of their organization and its place in the academic landscape. They should comprehend all sides of an issue and—in appropriate instances and in consultation with the chief executive—afford contending parties an opportunity to present their views. The board should be prepared to set forth the reasons for its decisions.

Just as administrators and boards should respect the need for individual faculty members to exercise academic freedom in their classrooms and laboratories, boards should avoid the temptation to micromanage in matters of administration. And just as responsible faculty participation in governance places good institutional citizenship ahead of departmental or personal professional interest, so should individual board members avoid even the perception of any personal or special interests. In the case of public institutions or systems, trustees and governing boards should not be seen as advocates for their appointing authorities or of certain segments of the electorate. Board members as well as faculty members should avoid undermining their administrations.

5. Historically, higher education governance has included three principal internal stakeholders—governing boards, administrators, and the full-time faculty. In fact, other stakeholders exist and in increasing numbers. For example, the nonacademic staff usually substantially outnumbers the faculty, and yet this group rarely has a formal voice in governance. The same is true of the nontenure-eligible, part-time, and adjunct faculty. These latter groups now predominate in community colleges and are an ever-larger component of the faculty in senior institutions, particularly in the public sector. Students have a vital stake in the institution and should be given opportunities to be heard on various issues and in some cases to participate directly in the governance process, preferably as members of board committees rather than as voting members of governing boards.

The involvement of these diverse internal stakeholder groups will vary according to subject matter and the culture of the institution, but the board is responsible for establishing the rules by which their voices are considered. Boards should ensure that no single stakeholder group is given an exclusive franchise in any area of governance, while recognizing that the subject matter in question will determine which groups have predominant or secondary interests.

6. All board members, regardless of how they came to the board, should feel a responsibility to serve the institution or the system as a whole and not any particular constituency or segment of the organization. Faculty, student, and staff involvement in the work of the board most appropriately occurs by membership on standing or ad-hoc committees of the board. While there are many instances of successful involvement to the contrary, it is AGB's view that faculty, staff, and students ordinarily should not serve as voting members of their own institution's governing board because such involvement violates the principle of independence of judgment. Particularly in the case of faculty or staff members, board membership inevitably places them in conflict with their employment status. In any event, boards should be mindful that the presence of one or more students, faculty, or staff members on the board or its committees neither constitutes nor substitutes for full communication and consultation with these stakeholders.

7. Most senior public institutions and many community colleges are parts of multi-campus systems that accord the system or corporate board the legal authority and responsibility for a set of institutions or campuses. The system governing board should clarify the responsibilities of the campus heads, the system head, and any institutional quasi-governing or advisory boards—as, for instance, boards and administrative officers of the professional schools of law, medicine, the health sciences, and business, and of intercollegiate athletics. The system board should clarify the authority, responsibilities, and expectations of such subordinate boards and officers, as well as of single-campus advisory boards. In multi-campus systems, governing boards should lean strongly in the direction of maximum possible autonomy for individual campuses or schools—unless, in particular instances, such autonomy clearly is not being exercised responsibly.

STANDARDS OF GOOD PRACTICE

1. Governing boards should state explicitly who has the authority for what kinds of decisions—that is, to which persons or bodies it has delegated authority and whether that delegation is subject to board review. For example, curricular matters and decisions regarding individual faculty appoint-

ments, promotions, and contract renewal normally would fall within the delegated decision-making authority of appropriate faculty and administrative entities operating within the framework of policies and delegations of the board.

The board should also reserve the right to review and ratify specified academic decisions, as well as proposals to adopt major new academic programs or eliminate others. The board should set budget guidelines concerning resource allocation on the basis of assumptions, usually developed by the administration, that are widely communicated to interested stakeholders and subject to ample opportunity for challenge. But the board should not delegate the determination of the overall resources available for planning and budgetary purposes. Once the board makes these overarching decisions, it should delegate resource-allocation decisions to the chief executive officer who may, in turn, delegate to others.

In all instances in which the board believes resources will need to be reallocated in ways that will lead to reducing or eliminating some programs, the board should ask the administration to create a process for decision making that includes full consultation, clear and explicit criteria, and full communication with stakeholder groups. The board should recognize that institutional consensus is more likely when all parties have agreed on the process and criteria. If, for example, the board decides the institution is in such financial jeopardy that faculty and staff reductions and reallocations are necessary, it first should consult the stakeholders, then share the information and describe the analysis that led them to make such a determination.

2. Boards and chief executives should establish deadlines for the conclusion of various consultative and decision-making processes with the clear understanding that failure to act in accordance with these deadlines will mean that the next highest level in the governance process may choose to act. While respecting the sometimes lengthy processes of academic governance, a single individual or group should not be empowered to impede decisions through inaction.

3. The chief executive is the board's major window on the institution, and the board should expect both candor and sufficient information from the chief executive. In turn, the board should support the chief executive, while ensuring that the voices of other stakeholders are heard.

4. Governing boards have the sole responsibility to appoint and assess the performance of the chief executive. The selection and support of the chief executive is the most important exercise of board responsibility. Boards should assess the chief executive's performance on an annual basis for progress toward attainment of goals and objectives, as well as for com-

pensation review purposes, and more comprehensively every several years in consultation with other stakeholder groups, as the board may deem appropriate. In assessing the chief executive's performance, boards should bear in mind that board and presidential effectiveness are interdependent. Consequently, boards should concurrently assess their own performance and that of the chief executive every several years. Performance reviews assisted by qualified third parties can contribute significantly to the professionalism and objectivity of the process.

5. There should be a conscious effort to minimize the ambiguous or overlapping areas in which more than one stakeholder group has authority. The respective roles of the administration, faculty, and governing board in faculty appointments, promotions, and tenure illustrate the principle of collaboration. For example, although the board may wish to exert its ultimate responsibility by insisting on approving individual tenure decisions, it might choose to delegate other kinds of actions to the administration, which might, in turn, delegate some authority for some decisions to an appropriate faculty body. Clarity does not preclude gray or overlapping areas of authority, but each group should understand whether its purview, and that of others in the governance process, is determinative or consultative. Moreover, the board and the chief executive should ensure the systematic review of all institutional policies over time, including those affecting internal governance.

"Communication," "consultation," and "decision making" should be defined and differentiated in board and institutional policies. Governing boards should communicate their investment and endowment spending policies, for example, but they may choose not to invite consultation on these matters. Student financial-aid policies and broad financial-planning assumptions call for both communication and consultation with stakeholder groups.

6. In institutions with faculty or staff collective-bargaining contracts, internal governance arrangements should be separate from the structure and terms of the contract. If a collective-bargaining contract governs the terms and conditions of faculty and staff employment, the board should consider a formal policy regarding the role of union officials in institutional governance. Specifically, the board should articulate any limitations the existence of a bargaining agreement may place on participation in governance by union officials.

EXTERNAL STAKEHOLDERS

The preceding sections primarily address the internal governance of institutions or multi-campus systems. But public institutions receive large proportions of their financial resources through governors, legislatures, statewide coordinating bodies (in some cases), and increasingly through foundations affiliated with the institution or system—and governing boards are accountable for these funds. The responsibilities of these officials and bodies vary widely among the states, but governing boards should serve as important buffers between the college or university and the political structures, partisan politics, and pressures of state government. Together with the chief executive, they should also serve as a bridge between the institution or system and its affiliated asset-management and fund-raising organization. These board responsibilities require a skillful balancing of effective communication and sensitive advocacy in articulating and defending the mission, priorities, and programs of the institution and in conveying to institutional constituents the concerns of external stakeholders. Boards should also serve as bridges to state government leaders whose views and perspectives concerning the conduct of public higher education, as it relates to state needs and priorities, should be heard and considered.

The relationship between the institution or system and the various external political and regulatory oversight groups should reflect an understanding by which the institution or system is held accountable for results in relation to agreed-upon objectives and, in return, oversight and regulation are minimized. This arrangement preserves the essential autonomy of the institution or system, which differentiates it from other state entities, and makes it clear that it is accountable for results.

Alumni are an especially important stakeholder group in both public and private institutions. Alumni are a vital resource, and their participation in the life of the institution should be actively encouraged. But alumni organizations frequently give rise to a brand of activism that intrudes on the roles of governing boards and chief executives. AGB recommends that alumni organizations be under the direct authority of the chief executive. Further, while the governing board should have appropriate alumni members, the board should always retain full legal, moral, and fiduciary responsibility for the institution.

Other organizations—higher education associations, disciplinary organizations, and accrediting bodies, among others—sometimes attempt to prescribe institutional policies and practices. The board should exercise caution in adopting the policies and procedures promulgated by any of these organizations. With the possible exception of those institutions owned by or closely affiliated with sponsoring organizations that contribute to their finances or otherwise hold title to their property and assets, the board should not feel obligated to adopt the policies and prescriptions of any external bodies.

CONCLUSION

College and university governing board membership is one of the most serious and consequential exercises of voluntary leadership in our society. It calls for balancing and sometimes buffering the often-conflicting claims of multiple internal and external stakeholders. It requires good judgment in avoiding becoming managerial while being sufficiently informed to assess management. It calls for listening and questioning more than pronouncing and demanding. Most of all, it requires a commitment to the institution as a whole rather than to any of its parts. Governing board membership is both challenging and enormously rewarding in the service of the current and future generations of students and, therefore, the nation's ultimate well-being.

QUESTIONS TO CONSIDER

These questions should help boards assess whether policies and practices concerning the participation of trustees, administration, faculty, staff, and students in institutional governance are reasonably clear, coherent and consistent. Answers to these questions will help boards and chief executives determine whether to establish a process to revise the policies or improve how they are used.

1. Do all trustees, administrators, faculty, staff, and students understand that the board has ultimate responsibility for determining, in consultation with appropriate stakeholders, the institution's mission? Do these constituents clearly understand that the board is ultimately responsible for the institution's welfare? Do the trustees understand that such responsibility requires not only monitoring the fiscal and physical assets of the institution but also having sufficient knowledge of the academic programs to ask hard questions concerning program quality, coherence, relevance, attractiveness, and appropriateness?

2. Has the board explicitly defined the major areas of delegated authority? Has it specified to whom the authority is given, the extent of the delegation, and the measure of accountability?

3. If the board governs a multi-campus system, is the authority of the system head, campus heads, and institution-based advisory or quasi-governing boards reasonably clear and demonstrably effective?

4. If a collective-bargaining contract governs the relations of faculty or staff with the institution, has the board considered a formal policy regarding the role of union officials in institutional governance and the limitations a bargaining agreement may place on their participation in governance?

5. Does the board conduct its affairs in a manner that exemplifies the behavior it expects from other campus constituents as they participate in governance? As the board strives to promote quality by means of rigorous review of programs, processes, and people, does it demonstrate a similar commitment to the assessment of its own performance? As the board seeks to encourage more open and effective communication on campus, does it exemplify openness and respect in its interactions with stakeholders? As the board calls for a greater commitment to the institution on the part of campus stakeholders, do trustees eschew advocacy of personal interests and exemplify dedication to the institution?

6. Has the board enhanced communication with the campus stakeholders? Has it clearly distinguished between information gathering, consultation, and decision making in its communication with campus constituents? Do stakeholder groups regularly consult with the chief executive and then, as appropriate, with the board on substantive matters that may affect major institutional policy?

7. Does the board establish clear deadlines for the conclusion of consultative and decision-making processes, and do campus constituents understand and accept the need for timely decision making?

8. Has the board, in concert with the chief executive, established a process and timeline for a periodic, systematic review of the institution's policies and procedures governing institutional decision making?

9. Has the board, in concert with the chief executive and in consultation with appropriate stakeholders, assessed the participation of stakeholders in institutional decision making and their collaboration in policy implementation? What initiatives might be undertaken to clarify and strengthen communication, participation, and collaboration in institutional governance?

APPENDIX

1967 Joint Statement on Rights and Freedoms of Students

In June 1967, a committee composed of representatives from the American Association of University Professors, the United States National Student Association (now the United States Student Association), the Association of American Colleges (now the Association of American Colleges and Universities), the National Association of Student Personnel Administrators, and the National Association of Women Deans and Counselors (now the National Association for Women in Education) formulated the Joint Statement. The document was endorsed by each of its five national sponsors, as well as by a number of other professional bodies. The governing bodies of the Association of American Colleges and the American Association of University Professors acted respectively in January and April 1990 to remove gender-specific references from the original text.

In September 1990, September 1991, and November 1992, an inter-association task force met to study, interpret, update, and affirm (or reaffirm) the Joint Statement. Members of the task force agreed that the document has stood the test of time quite well and continues to provide an excellent set of principles for institutions of higher education. The task force developed a set of interpretive notes to incorporate changes in law and higher education that have occurred since 1967. These interpretive notes are references within the original text. . . .

PREAMBLE

Academic institutions exist for the transmission of knowledge, the pursuit of truth, the development of students, and the general well-being of society. Free inquiry and free expression are indispensable to the attainment of these goals. As members of the academic community, students should be encouraged to develop the capacity for critical judgment and to engage in a sustained and independent search for truth. Institutional procedures for achieving these purposes may vary from campus to campus, but the minimal standards of academic freedom of students outlined below are essential to any community of scholars.

Freedom to teach and freedom to learn are inseparable facets of academic freedom. The freedom to learn depends upon appropriate opportunities and conditions in the classroom, on the campus, and in the larger community.[1]

The responsibility to secure and to respect general conditions conducive to the freedom to learn is shared by all members of the academic community. Each college and university has a duty to develop policies and procedures that provide and safeguard this freedom. Such policies and procedures should be developed at each institution within the framework of general standards and with the broadest possible participation of the members of the academic community. The purpose of this statement is to enumerate the essential provisions for students' freedom to learn.

FREEDOM OF ACCESS TO HIGHER EDUCATION

The admissions policies of each college and university are a matter of institutional choice, provided that each college and university makes clear the characteristics and expectations of students that it considers relevant to success in the institution's program.[2] While church-related institutions may give admission preference to students of their own persuasion, such a preference should be clearly and publicly stated. Under no circumstances should a student be barred from admission to a particular institution on the basis of race.[3] Thus, within the limits of its facilities, each college and university should be open to all students who are qualified according to its admissions standards. The facilities and services of a college or university should be open to all of its enrolled students, and institutions should use their influence to secure equal access for all students to public facilities in the local community.

IN THE CLASSROOM

The professor in the classroom and in conference should encourage free discussion, inquiry, and expression. Student performance should be evaluated solely on an academic basis, not on opinions or conduct in matters unrelated to academic standards.

1. Protection of Freedom of Expression

Students should be free to take reasoned exception to the data or views offered in any course of study and to reserve judgment about matters of opinion, but they are responsible for learning the content of any course of study for which they are enrolled.

2. Protection Against Improper Academic Evaluation

Students should have protection through orderly procedures against prejudiced or capricious academic evaluation.[4] At the same time, they are responsible for maintaining standards of academic performance established for each course in which they are enrolled.

3. Protection Against Improper Disclosure

Information about student views, beliefs, and political associations which professors acquire in the course of their work as instructors, advisers, and counselors should be considered confidential. Protection against improper disclosure is a serious professional obligation. Judgments of ability and character may be provided under appropriate circumstances, normally with the knowledge and consent of the student.

STUDENT AFFAIRS

In student affairs, certain standards must be maintained if the freedom of students is to be preserved.[5]

1. Freedom of Association

Students bring to the campus a variety of interests previously acquired and develop many new interests as members of the academic community. They should be free to organize and join associations to promote their common interests.

(a) The membership, policies, and actions of a student organization usually will be determined by vote of only those persons who hold bona fide membership in the college or university community.

(b) Affiliation with an extramural organization should not of itself disqualify a student organization from institutional recognition.[6]

(c) If campus advisers are required, each organization should be free to choose its own adviser, and institutional recognition should not be withheld or withdrawn solely because of the inability of a student organization to secure an adviser. Campus advisers may advise organizations in the exercise of responsibility, but they should not have the authority to control the policy of such organizations.

(d) Student organizations may be required to submit a statement of purpose, criteria for membership, rules of procedure, and a current list of officers. They should not be required to submit a membership list as a condition of institutional recognition.

(e) Campus organizations, including those affiliated with an extramural organization, should be open to all students without respect to race, creed, or national origin, except for religious qualifications which may be required by organizations whose aims are primarily sectarian.[7]

2. Freedom of Inquiry and Expression

(a) Students and student organizations should be free to examine and discuss all questions of interest to them and to express opinions publicly and privately. They should always be free to support causes by orderly means that do not disrupt the regular and essential operations of the institution. At the same time, it should be made clear to the academic and larger community that in their public expressions or demonstrations students or student organizations speak only for themselves.

(b) Students should be allowed to invite and to hear any person of their own choosing. Those routine procedures required by an institution before a guest speaker is invited to appear on campus should be designed only to ensure that there is orderly scheduling of facilities and adequate preparation for the event, and that the occasion is conducted in a manner appropriate to an academic community. The institutional control of campus facilities should not be used as a device of censorship. It should be made clear to the academic and larger community that sponsorship of guest speakers does not necessarily imply approval or endorsement of the views expressed, either by the sponsoring group or by the institution.[8]

3. Student Participation in Institutional Government

As constituents of the academic community, students should be free, individually and collectively, to express their views on issues of institutional policy and on matters of general interest to the student body. The student body should have clearly defined means to participate in the formulation and application of institutional policy affecting academic and student affairs.[9] The role of student government and both its general and specific responsibilities should be made explicit, and the actions of student government within the areas of its jurisdiction should be reviewed only through orderly and prescribed procedures.

4. Student Publications

Student publications and the student press are valuable aids in establishing and maintaining an atmosphere of free and responsible discussion and of intellectual exploration on the campus. They are a means of bringing student concerns to the attention of the faculty and the institutional authorities and of formulating student opinion on various issues on the campus and in the world at large.

Whenever possible the student newspaper should be an independent corporation financially and legally separate from the college or university. Where financial and legal autonomy is not possible, the institution, as the publisher of student publications, may have to bear the legal responsibility for the contents of the publications. In the delegation of editorial responsibility to students, the institution must provide sufficient editorial freedom and financial autonomy for the student publications to maintain their integrity of purpose as vehicles for free inquiry and free expression in an academic community.

Institutional authorities, in consultation with students and faculty, have a responsibility to provide written clarification of the role of the student publications, the standards to be used in their evaluation, and the limitations on external control of their operation. At the same time, the editorial freedom of student editors and managers entails corollary responsibilities to be governed by the canons of responsible journalism, such as the avoidance of libel, indecency, undocumented allegations, attacks on personal integrity, and the techniques of harassment and innuendo. As safeguards for the editorial freedom of student publications the following provisions are necessary:

(a) The student press should be free of censorship and advance approval of copy, and its editors and managers should be free to develop their own editorial policies and news coverage.

(b) Editors and managers of student publications should be protected from arbitrary suspension and removal because of student, faculty, administration, or public disapproval of editorial policy or content. Only for proper and stated causes should editors and managers be subject to removal and then only by orderly and prescribed procedures. The agency responsible for the appointment of editors and managers should be the agency responsible for their removal.

(c) All institutionally published and financed student publications should explicitly state on the editorial page that the opinions there expressed are not necessarily those of the college, university, or student body.

OFF-CAMPUS FREEDOM OF STUDENTS

1. Exercise of Right of Citizenship

College and university students are both citizens and members of the academic community. As citizens, students should enjoy the same freedom of speech, peaceful assembly, and right of petition that other citizens enjoy and, as members of the academic community, they are subject to the obligations that accrue to them by virtue of this membership. Faculty members and administration officials should ensure that institutional powers are not employed to inhibit such intellectual and personal development of students as is often promoted by their exercise of the rights of citizenship both on and off campus.

2. Institutional Authority and Civil Penalties

Activities of students may upon occasion result in violation of law. In such cases, institutional officials should be prepared to apprise students of sources of legal counsel and may offer other assistance. Students who violate the law may incur penalties prescribed by civil authorities, but institutional authority should never be used merely to duplicate the function of general laws. Only where the institution's interests as an academic community are distinct and clearly involved should the special authority of the institution be asserted. Students who incidentally violate institutional regulations in the course of their off-campus activity, such as those relating to class attendance, should be subject to no greater penalty than would normally be imposed. Institutional action should be independent of community pressure.

NOTES

1. To protect the freedom of students to learn, as well as enhance their participation in the life of the academic community, students should be free from exploitation or harassment.

2. To enable them to make appropriate choices and participate effectively in an institution's programs, students have the right to be informed about the institution, its policies, practices, and characteristics. Institutions preparing such information should take into account applicable federal and state laws.

3. The reference to race must not be taken to limit the nondiscrimination obligations of institutions. In all aspects of education, students have a right to be free from discrimination on the basis of individual attributes not demonstrably related to academic success in the institution's programs, including, but not limited to: race, color, gender, age, disability, national origin, and sexual orientation. Under *Regents of the University of California v. Bakke*, 438 U.S. 265 (1978), when colleges and universities determine that achieving diversity within the student body is relevant to their academic mission, their admissions offices may consider, among several stated criteria, individual attributes that otherwise would be prohibited.

4. The student grievance procedures typically used in these matters are not appropriate for addressing charges of academic dishonesty or other disciplinary matters arising in the classroom. In these instances, students should be afforded the safeguards or orderly procedures consistent with those set forth in "Procedural Standards in Disciplinary Proceedings" below. (In 1977, AAUP's Committee A on Academic Freedom and Tenure approved a statement on "The Assignment of Course Grades and Student Appeals," AAUP, *Policy Documents and Reports*, 9th ed. [Washington, D.C., 2001], 113-14.)

5. As in the case of classroom matters, students shall have protection through orderly procedures to ensure this freedom.

6. "Institutional recognition" should be understood to refer to any formal relationship between the student organization and the institution.

7. The obligation of institutions with respect to nondiscrimination, with the exception noted above for religious qualifications, should be understood in accordance with the expanded statement on nondiscrimination in n.3, above. Exceptions may also be based on gender as authorized by law.

8. The events referred to in this section should be understood to include the full range of student-sponsored activities, such as films, exhibitions, and performances.

9. "Academic and student affairs" should be interpreted broadly to include all administrative and policy matters pertinent to students' educational experiences.

APPENDIX

2000 AAUP Statement on Graduate Students

This statement which follows was approved by the Association's Committee on College and University Teaching, Research, and Publication in October 1999. It was adopted by the AAUP's Council in June 2000 and endorsed by the Eighty-sixth Annual Meeting.

PREAMBLE

Graduate programs in universities exist for the discovery and transmission of knowledge, the education of students, the training of future faculty, and the general well-being of society. Free inquiry and free expression are indispensable to the attainment of these goals.

In 1967 the American Association of University Professors participated with the National Student Association, the Association of American Colleges, and others in the formulation of the *Joint Statement on Rights and Freedoms of Students*. The *Joint Statement* has twice been revised and updated, most recently in November 1992. The AAUP's Committee on College and University Teaching, Research, and Publication, while supporting the Association's continuing commitment to the *Joint Statement*, believes that the distinctive circumstances of graduate students require a supplemental statement.

The statement which follows has been formulated to reflect the educational maturity and the distinguishing academic characteristics and responsibilities of graduate students. These students not only engage in more advanced studies than their undergraduate counterparts, but often they also hold teaching or research assistantships. As graduate assistants, they carry out many of the functions of faculty members and receive compensation for these duties. The statement below sets forth recommended standards that we believe will foster sound academic policies in universities with graduate programs. The responsibility to secure and respect general conditions conducive to a graduate student's freedom to learn and to teach is shared by all members of a university's graduate community. Each university should develop policies and procedures that safeguard this freedom. Such policies and procedures should be developed within the framework of those general standards that enable the university to fulfill its responsibilities to students, faculty, and society.[1]

RECOMMENDED STANDARDS

1. Graduate students have the right to academic freedom. Like other students, they "should be free to take reasoned exception to the data or views offered in any course of study and to reserve judgment about matters of opinion, but they are responsible for learning the content of any course of study for which they are enrolled."[2] Moreover, because of their advanced education, graduate students should be encouraged by their professors to exercise their freedom of "discussion, inquiry and expression."[3] Further, they should be able to express their opinions freely about matters of institutional policy, and they should have the same freedom of action in the public political domain as faculty members should have. Graduate students' freedom of inquiry is necessarily qualified by their still being learners in the profession; nonetheless, their faculty mentors should afford them latitude and respect as they decide how they will engage in teaching and research.

2. Graduate students have the right to be free from illegal or unconstitutional discrimination, or discrimination on a basis not demonstrably related to job function, including, but not limited to, age, sex, disability, race, religion, national origin, marital status, or sexual orientation, in admissions and throughout their education, employment, and placement.[4]

Graduate students should be informed of the requirements of their degree programs. When feasible, they should be told about acceptance, application, and attrition rates in their fields, but it is also their responsibility to keep themselves informed of these matters. If degree requirements are altered, students admitted under previous rules should be able to continue under those rules. Graduate students should be assisted in making timely progress toward their degrees of being provided with diligent advisers, relevant course offerings, adequate dissertation or thesis supervision, and periodic assessment of and clear communication on their progress. Students should understand that dissertation or thesis work may be constrained by the areas of interest and specialization of available faculty supervisors.

If a graduate student's dissertation or thesis adviser departs from the institution once the student's work is under way, the responsible academic officers should endeavor to provide the student with alternative supervision, external to the institution if necessary. If a degree program is to be discontinued, provisions must be made for students already in the program to complete their course of study.

3. Graduate students are entitled to the protection of their intellectual property rights, including recognition of their participation in supervised research and their research with faculty, consistent with generally accepted standards of attribution and acknowledgment in collaborative settings. Written standards should be publicly available.

4. Graduate students should have a voice in institutional governance at the program, department, college, graduate school, and university levels.

5. Under the Association's *Recommended Institutional Regulations on Academic Freedom and Tenure*, graduate student assistants are to be informed in writing of the terms and conditions of their appointment and, in the event of proposed dismissal, are to be afforded access to a duly constituted hearing committee.[5] They should be informed of all academic or other institutional regulations affecting their roles as employees. Graduate student employees with grievances, as individuals or as a group, should submit them in a timely fashion and should have access to an impartial faculty committee or, if provided under institutional policy, arbitration. Clear guidelines and timelines for grievance procedures should be distributed to all interested parties. Individual grievants or participants in a group grievance should not be subjected to reprisals. Graduate student employees may choose a representative to speak for them or with them at all stages of a grievance.

6. Good practice should include appropriate training and supervision in teaching, adequate office space, and a safe working environment. Departments should endeavor to acquaint students with the norms and traditions of their academic discipline and to inform them of professional opportunities. Graduate students should be encouraged to seek departmental assistance in obtaining future academic and nonacademic employment. Departments are encouraged to provide support for the professional development of graduate students by such means as funding research expenses and conference travel.

7. Graduate students should have access to their files and placement dossiers. If access is denied, graduate students should be able to have a faculty member of their choice examine their files and, at the professor's discretion, provide the student with a redacted account. Graduate students should have the right to direct that items be added to or removed from their placement dossiers.

NOTES

1. We recognize that the responsibilities of graduate students vary widely among individuals, courses of study, and institutions. Some provisions of this statement may not apply to students in professional schools who may have different types of responsibilities from students in other disciplines.

2. "Joint Statement on Rights and Freedoms of Students," AAUP, *Policy Documents and Reports*, 9th ed. (Washington, D.C., 2001), 262.

3. Ibid.

4. "On Discrimination," *Policy Documents and Reports*, 185.

5. "Recommended Institutional Regulations on Academic Freedom and Tenure," Regulation 13, ibid., 29.

Selected Bibliography

American Association for the Advancement of Science and U.S. Office of Research Integrity. *The Role and Activities of Scientific Societies in Promoting Research Integrity*. Washington, DC, Sept. 2000.

American Association of University Professors. "Record of the Council, Nov. 13–14, 1999." *Academe* 86 (January–February 2000): 52–53.

American Association of University Professors. *AAUP, Policy Documents and Reports*. 9th ed. Washington, DC: The Association, 2000.

American Association of University Professors. *AAUP, Policy Documents and Reports*. 8th ed. Washington, DC: The Association, 1995.

American Association of University Professors. "The Standard of 'Compelling Reasons' in the Joint Statement on Government of Colleges and Universities." *Academe* 79 (September–October 1993): 54.

American Association of University Professors. "'Academic Responsibility': Comments by Members of Committee A Incident to Consideration of the Koch Case." *AAUP Bulletin* 49 (1963): 40.

American Association of University Professors. "Advisory Letters from the Washington Office." *AAUP Bulletin* 49 (1963): 393.

American Association of University Professors. "1946 Report of Committee A." *AAUP Bulletin* 31 (1946): 60–61.

American Association of University Professors Committee B. "On The Duty of Faculty Members to Speak Out on Misconduct." *Academe* 84 (November–December 1998): 58.

American Council on Education. *Corporate Lessons for American Higher Education*. Washington, DC: American Council on Education, 1994.

Anderson, Melissa. "Misconduct and Departmental Context." *Journal of Information Ethics* 5 (1996): 15–33.

Ashby, Eric. "A Hippocratic Oath for the Academic Profession." *Minerva* 7 (Autumn–Winter 1968): 64–66.

Association of Governing Boards. *Renewing the Academic Presidency: Stronger Leadership for Tougher Times.* Washington, DC: AGB Publications Department, 1996.

Association of Governing Boards of Universities and Colleges, "AGB Statement on Institutional Governance." November 8, 1998. <http://www.agb.org/governance.cfm>.

Barker, Stephen F. "What Is a Profession?" *Professional Ethics* 1 (1992): 73–99.

Benjamin, Ernst, and Donald Wagner, eds. *Academic Freedom: An Everyday Concern.* San Francisco: Jossey-Bass Publishers, 1994.

Bennett, John B. *Collegial Professionalism: The Academy, Individualism, and the Common Good.* Phoenix: Oryx Press, 1998.

Bok, Derek. "Universities: Their Temptations and Tensions." *Journal of College and University Law* 18 (1991): 1–19.

Boyer, Earnest. *Scholarship Reconsidered: Priorities of the Professoriate.* Princeton, NJ: The Carnegie Foundation for the Advancement of Teaching, 1990.

Braxton, John, and Alan Bayer, *Faculty Misconduct in Collegiate Teaching.* Baltimore, MD: Johns Hopkins University Press, 1999.

Cahn, Steven. *Saints and Scamps: Ethics in Academia* Washington, DC: Rowman and Littlefield, 1986.

Clark, Burton. *The Higher Education System: Academic Organization in Cross-National Perspective.* Berkeley: University of California Press (1983).

Commission on Academic Tenure in Higher Education. *Faculty Tenure.* San Francisco: Jossey-Bass Publishers, 1973.

Committee on Science, Engineering and Public Policy, National Academy of Sciences. *On Being a Scientist: Responsible Conduct in Research,* 2d ed. Washington, DC: National Academy Press, 1984.

De George, Richard. *Academic Freedom and Tenure: Ethical Issues.* Lanham, MD: Rowman and Littlefield, 1997.

Elliot, Deni and Judy Stern, eds., *Research Ethics: A Reader.* Hanover, NH: University Press of New England, 1997.

Finkin, Matthew W. "'A Higher Order of Liberty in the Workplace': Academic Freedom and Tenure in the Vortex of Employment Practices and Law." *Law and Contemporary Problems* 53 (1990): 357–379.

Finkin, Matthew W. "Intramural Speech, Academic Freedom and the First Amendment." *Texas Law Review* 66 (1988): 1323–1349.

Frankel, Mark S. "Washington Update." *Chronicle of Higher Education,* April 21, 2000, sec. A, p. 38.

Glassick, Charles, Mary Taylor Huber, and Gene I. Maeroff. *Scholarship Assessed: Evaluation of the Professoriate.* San Francisco: Jossey-Bass Publishers, 1997.

Golde, C.M., and T.M. Dore. *At Cross Purposes: What the Experiences of Doctoral Students Reveal about Doctoral Education (www.phd-survey.org)*. Philadelphia, PA: A report prepared for the Pew Charitable Trusts, 2001.

Gordon, Robert. "The Ethical Worlds of Large-Firm Litigators: Preliminary Observations." *Fordham Law Review* 67 (1998): 709–738.

Hamilton, Neil. "The Academic Profession's Leadership Role in Shared Governance." *Liberal Education* (Summer 2000): 12–19.

Hamilton, Neil. "Academic Tradition and the Principles of Professional Conduct," *Journal of College and University Law* 27 (Winter 2001): 609–668.

Hamilton, Neil. "Are We Speaking the Same Language? Comparing AAUP & AGB." *Liberal Education* (Fall 1999): 24–31.

Hamilton, Neil. "The Ethics of Peer Review in the Academic and Legal Professions." *South Texas Law Review* 42 (2001): 227–300.

Hamilton, Neil. "Buttressing the Neglected Traditions of Academic Freedom." *William Mitchell Law Review* 22 (1996): 549–572.

Hamilton, Neil. "Peer Review: The Linchpin of Academic Freedom and Tenure." *Academe* (May–June 1997): 14–19.

Hamilton, Neil. *Zealotry and Academic Freedom: A Legal and Historical Perspective*. New Brunswick, NJ: Transaction Publishers, 1995.

Handlin, Oscar. "A Career at Harvard." *American Scholar* 65 (Winter 1996): 47–58.

Holton, Gerald, and Robert Morison, eds. *Limits of Scientific Inquiry*. New York: Norton, 1979.

Joughin, Louis, ed. *Academic Freedom and Tenure*. Madison: University of Wisconsin Press, 1969.

Kaplin, William A. and Barbara Lee. *The Law of Higher Education*, 3rd ed. San Francisco: Jossey-Bass, 1995.

Kass, Amy, and Leon Kass, eds., *Wing to Wing; Oar to Oar*. Notre Dame, IN: Notre Dame University Press, 2000.

Kennedy, Donald. *Academic Duty*. Boston: Harvard University Press, 1997.

Kerr, Clark. *Higher Education Cannot Escape History: Issues for the Twenty-first Century*. Albany: State University of New York Press, 1999.

Kerr, Clark. "Knowledge Ethics and the New Academic Culture." *Change* 26 (January/February 1994): 8–15.

Krause, Elliott. *Death of the Guilds: Professions, States, and the Advance of Capitalism, 1930 to the Present*. New Haven, CT: Yale University Press, 1996.

LeClercq, Terri. "Failure to Teach: Due Process and Law School Plagiarism." *Journal of Legal Education* 49 (1999): 236–255.

Licata, Christine. "Post-Tenure Review: National Trends, Questions and Concerns." *Innovative Higher Education* 24 (1999): 5–15.

Licata, Christine. "Precepts for Post-Tenure Reviews." *Trusteeship* 7 (December 1999): 8–13.

Macrina, Francis, ed. *Scientific Integrity: An Introductory Text with Cases*, Washington, DC: ASM Press, 2000.

Metzger, Walter P. "The 1940 Statement of Principles on Academic Freedom and Tenure." *Law and Contemporary Problems* 53 (1990): 3–77.

Oakley, Francis. "The Elusive Academic Profession: Complexity and Change." *Daedalus* 126 (Fall 1997): 43–67.

Olivas, Michael. *The Law and Higher Education*, 2d ed. Durham, NC: Carolina Academic Press, 1997.

Pincoffs, Edmund, ed. *The Concept of Academic Freedom*. Austin: University of Texas Press at Austin, 1972.

Poskanzer, Steven. *Higher Education Law: The Faculty*. Baltimore: Johns Hopkins, 2002.

Rabban, David. "Academic Freedom, Professionalism and Intramural Speech." *New Directions for Higher Education* 88 (Winter 1994): 77–88.

Ramo, Keetjie. *Assessing the Faculty's Role in Shared Governance*. Washington, DC: American Association of University Professors, 1998.

Rauch, Jonathan. *Kindly Inquisitors*. Chicago: University of Chicago Press, 1993.

Swazey, Judith, et al. "The Ethical Training of Graduate Students Requires Serious Continuing Attention." *Chronicle of Higher Education*, March 9, 1994, sec. B, p. 1.

Swazey, Judith et al., "Ethical Problems in Academic Research." *American Scientist* 81 (November–December 1993): 542–553.

Tierney, William., "Academic Community and Post-Tenure Review." *Academe* 83 (May–June 1997): 23–25.

Tierney, William, ed. *The Responsive University*. Baltimore, MD: Johns Hopkins University Press, 1998.

Tierney, William, and Robert Rhoads. *Faculty Socialization as Cultural Process: A Mirror of Institutional Commitment* (ASHE-ERIC Higher Education Report No. 6). Washington, DC: School of Education and Human Development, George Washington University, 1993.

Trower, Cathy, ed. *Policies on Faculty Appointment*. Bolton, MA: Anchor Publishers, 2000.

Walter, Paul H.L. "The Professor as Specialist and Generalist." *Academe* 74 (May–June 1988): 25–28.

Yudof, Mark. "Intramural Musings on Academic Freedom: A Reply to Professor Finkin." *Texas Law Review* 66 (1988): 1351–1357.

Index

Note: Page numbers in *italics* refer to ethical problems for peer-group discussion.

About the Author

NEIL W. HAMILTON is Professor at William Mitchell School of Law.